Beyond Knowledge Management

Brian Lehaney
Coventry University, UK

Steve Clarke
University of Hull, UK

Elayne Coakes
University of Westminster, UK

Gillian Jack
University of Glamorgan, UK

IDEA GROUP PUBLISHING

Hershey • London • Melbourne • Singapore

Acquisitions Editor:	Mehdi Khosrow-Pour
Senior Managing Editor:	Jan Travers
Managing Editor:	Amanda Appicello
Development Editor:	Michele Rossi
Copy Editor:	Maria Boyer
Typesetter:	Amanda Appicello
Cover Design:	Michelle Waters
Printed at:	Integrated Book Technology

Published in the United States of America by
  Idea Group Publishing (an imprint of Idea Group Inc.)
  701 E. Chocolate Avenue, Suite 200
  Hershey PA 17033
  Tel: 717-533-8845
  Fax: 717-533-8661
  E-mail: cust@idea-group.com
  Web site: http://www.idea-group.com

and in the United Kingdom by
  Idea Group Publishing (an imprint of Idea Group Inc.)
  3 Henrietta Street
  Covent Garden
  London WC2E 8LU
  Tel: 44 20 7240 0856
  Fax: 44 20 7379 3313
  Web site: http://www.eurospan.co.uk

Coventry University

Library of Congress Cataloging-in-Publication Data

Beyond knowledge management / Brian Lehaney ... [et al.].
    p. cm.
Includes bibliographical references and index.
  ISBN 1-59140-180-1 -- ISBN 1-59140-223-9 (pbk.) -- ISBN 1-59140-181-X
(ebook)
 1. Knowledge management. 2. Intellectual capital--Management. 3.
Creative ability in business. I. Lehaney, Brian, 1953-
  HD30.2.B477 2003
  658.4'038--dc22
                          2003021678

British Cataloguing in Publication Data
A Cataloguing in Publication record for this book is available from the British Library.

All work contributed to this book is new, previously-unpublished material. The views expressed in this book are those of the authors, but not necessarily of the publisher.

Beyond Knowledge Management

Table of Contents

Preface

The Issues

Over the past decade the term knowledge management (KM) has been one of the buzz phrases, yet it is still unclear in many ways what is meant by knowledge management, and it has yet to have the exciting impact that was predicted by many. This book examines knowledge management in a practical sense, and also considers underlying theories, concepts, and principles that may be applied to knowledge management to make it more useful and workable.

Organisations have seen huge changes to their own domestic economies and to world trade. E-commerce is now a commonly used term. Services have become major in most western economies, whilst manufacturing has declined. The increase in services has put the value of knowledge at a premium. Firms could choose to let that value be treated in an ad hoc fashion or manage the asset 'knowledge' in a way that would lever the best value from it and treat it as a prime resource.

However, KM does not provide a magic remedy for a firm's ills. It requires some thought and a view of the firm as a system. Within that system are other systems, and within those there are other systems still. Each of these systems interacts with the others to produce the firm's good or services. These interactions require communication, and if communication is not managed, it may not be effective and valuable knowledge may be left unshared.

To compete effectively in the twenty-first century, organisations must generate, store, retrieve, retain, and use knowledge. As organizations interact with their environments, they obtain information, turn it into knowledge, and take action based on it in combination with their experiences, values, and internal rules. In western economies, organisations have experienced enormous change in recent times. The greater the change, the greater the importance of communication, and the greater the importance of knowledge.

Knowledge management is critically important in regard to organisational adaptation, survival, and competence, especially when the environment is changing at a rapid pace. KM works at the interface of people, processes, and technology, and it is about the creative capacity of human beings, the exchange of ideas, and much more. Any design of a knowledge management framework or system should ensure that adaptation and innovation of business performance take place in line with the changing dynamics of the business environment.

For many reasons knowledge management has become closely associated with technology. Yet discussion, focus groups, interviews, meetings, and workshops do not require a computer. It would be difficult to deny these as means to create and exchange knowledge. Technology may play an enabling part in these activities and in the storage and retrieval of information, but not to the extent suggested by much of the KM literature.

There is a danger that knowledge management is being perceived as being so entwined with technology that its critical aspects and success factors will be lost. Vendors have relabelled document management software, databases, and so forth as knowledge management solutions, and this gives rise to the myth that KM is IT. It is not. Information systems are about providing the right information to the right person at the right time, but knowledge management goes far beyond that.

In the last two decades of the twentieth century, a resource-based theory of the firm became more widely accepted as an alternative to the traditional product-based or competitive advantage view. This resource-based view is linked to strategy and knowledge-based services. The term strategy is usually associated with long-term perspectives about an organisation and its environment. The resource-based approach tends to place more emphasis on the organisation's capabilities or core competencies than do the competitive-based and product-based approaches. Thus KM is strongly linked to the concept of a learning organisation, which again links to communication and change.

A knowledge-based strategy formulation should start with intangible resources, which are the people. Physical products and assets result from human actions, and depend on people for their continued existence. Organisations work on informal structures and dynamic relationships created by people. People can use their abilities to create value by creating and transferring knowledge externally or internally to their organisation.

Organisation of the Book

This book is organised into seven chapters. A brief discussion of each chapter follows. Chapter 1 considers the rise of knowledge management and the main issues surrounding it. The nature of knowledge management is identified, different classifications are discussed, and the reasons why it has come to the fore in recent years are outlined.

Chapter 2 considers KM in more detail. It looks at some basic starting points, then considers the rise of knowledge management. A deeper discussion of what is meant by knowledge management is then held, following which some major concepts are outlined. These are knowledge sharing and communication, knowledge management and learning organisations, and intellectual capital. The conclusions draw together the major ideas from the chapter.

Chapter 3 looks at sociotechnical systems and knowledge management. The chapter includes discussions of knowledge, understanding, and decision-making; knowledge and sociotechnology; a history of the sociotechnical movement; a sociotechnical view of communities of practice and teams; a sociotechnical case—the Abbey National; a charitable case; knowledge management and sociotechnical thinking; knowledge and sociotechnical systems; and a Xerox case study.

Chapter 4 discusses systems thinking and knowledge management. It considers organisations and their management, systems thinking, the philosophy and theory of social systems, social theory, a critical systems framework for knowledge management, and it provides a discussion and critique and suggestions for a future for knowledge management.

Chapter 5 provides a comprehensive review of knowledge management frameworks. A generic review grid for knowledge management frameworks is developed, and this is used to assess forty different published KM frameworks. Chapter 6 outlines a new a framework for knowledge management that is based on the principles discussed in the preceding chapters. Chapter 7 concludes the book.

Acknowledgments

The authors would like to acknowledge the help of all involved in the production of this book.

We would especially like to thank the staff at Idea Group Inc. whose contributions have been invaluable. In particular, Amanda Appicello, Jan Travers and Mehdi Khosrow-Pour provided excellent ongoing professional support.

Brian Lehaney, Steve Clarke, Elayne Coakes and Gillian Jack

September 2003

Chapter I

Introduction

1.1 What Is this Book About?

If you want quick-fix solutions, this book is not for you. If you want to "dare to know" how to look at an organisation differently, harness the power of its knowledge, and create innovative and effective systems, then please read on!

Knowledge management has been one of the most hyped phrases over the first years of the twenty-first century, and it has been mooted as the way forward for organisations to be dynamic, flexible, competitive, and successful. Despite the hype, and despite some individual successes, western economies and organisations may not have been greatly affected by this 'all singing, all dancing' solution to organisations' problems. Has the impact of knowledge management been less than expected? If so, why? In order to address these questions, there are a number of others that must also be considered, such as: What is knowledge management? Why did it arise in the first place? Can it be simplified or categorised? Is it a fad? Is it theoretical? Is it practical? Why should I care about it? What can it do for my organisation? Does it provide a quick and easy solution?

In order to help address these questions, and many others, and to suggest ways forward, this book examines knowledge management in concept and in practice. Knowledge management is considered in conjunction with other major approaches to organisational activities and analyses, especially systems thinking. The consideration of overall systems (not just computer systems) plays a major role in the planning, running, and development, of organisations. This may be evidenced by a wealth of professional and learned publications and through organisations' own strategic plans, mission statements, and publicly available documents. Thus, if knowledge management is to succeed, it must either work with these other important areas, or it must supersede them entirely.

This introductory chapter outlines the nature of knowledge management, how and why it has arisen in recent years, some ways in which it may be classified, its potential benefits, and its potential pitfalls. The following chapters consider knowledge management in more depth, and in relation to the areas outlined above. Each chapter has a list of suggested further reading, and this includes websites as well as printed material. The penultimate chapter discusses a framework for knowledge management, and the final chapter provides a summary of the similarities and differences in theory and practice between the different areas linked with knowledge management.

1.2 What Is Knowledge Management?

Very simply, knowledge management (KM), in an organisational sense, is the management of all, or some part, of the knowledge process. Of course, this statement is about as helpful as the old reply to the question, "What do economists do?...They do economics!" It may therefore be helpful if some definition of KM is given early on in this book, but a dilemma arises in the order that work is presented. As the book is about knowledge management, as may be expected, there are substantial chapters that deal with KM. One of these is about the meaning of the term, how KM may be categorised, how it may be used, why it is important. If this chapter were presented first, before any overall introduction to the book, it would present a level of detail that would be inappropriate as a starting point, and it would be difficult for that detail to be placed in any context by the reader. However, without some brief explanation as to what is meant by knowledge management, this Introduction would refer to something that is key to the book, but which has been given no meaning so far. The dilemma has been resolved by the provision here of the following working definition of KM that has been derived from the discussions in other chapters. Thus, this Introduction may be read with this definition used for KM, but it is not presented without foundation. (As an aside, this uses the root definition approach of soft systems methodology (see Checkland, 1981), but it is unnecessary to discuss that at this juncture.)

> *Knowledge management refers to the systematic organisation, planning, scheduling, monitoring, and deployment of people, processes, technology, and environment, with appropriate targets and feedback mechanisms, under the control of a public or private sector concern, and undertaken by such a concern, to facilitate explicitly and specifically the creation, retention, sharing, identification, acquisition, utilisation, and measurement of information and new ideas, in order to achieve strategic aims, such as improved competitiveness or improved performance, subject to financial, legal, resource, political, technical, cultural, and societal constraints.*

This is quite a daunting and possibly hard to penetrate definition, using a sentence of seventy-four words! All will become clear, and it is sufficient at this stage to grasp the gist of the statement: "to facilitate explicitly and specifically the creation, retention, sharing, identification, acquisition, utilisation, and measurement of information and new ideas, in order to achieve strategic aims, such as improved competitiveness."

1.3 Why has Knowledge Management Arisen?

In order to begin to understand KM further, some historical background to its development may be helpful, so that it can be considered in context. The decline of manufacturing in western economies in the last quarter of the twentieth century is well documented, as is the concomitant rise in services. With this switch in the economic base came an important change in what was being bought by consumers, and by businesses from other businesses. Whilst a range of tangible products (goods) were still being purchased, such as cars, household goods, and foodstuffs, many consumers and businesses began to purchase substantially more intangible products (services). These included areas such as tourism, financial services, IT services, and consultancy. The common element amongst these services is that there is not always a tangible product, or, where there is one, it is only a part of the purchase.

Consider someone purchasing a package holiday. For a particular sum of money (let's say $2,000), they receive a ticket. The latter is no more than a piece of paper, but that piece of paper provides entry to the airline check-in, it opens the door of the hotel bedroom, and it facilitates all the other aspects of a package holiday. What has the consumer bought in this case? Well, undoubtedly there are tangible aspects to the purchase, but a key component is the knowledge of the company supplying the package. Whilst many consumers choose to put together their own holiday package, this involves searching for information about the possible holiday location, the surrounding region, the currency, the visa arrangements, flights, connecting transport, accommodation, leisure facilities, restaurants, and all the other components that make up a holiday. With a package holiday, a great deal of this has been done by the company, which will have a portfolio available from which the consumer may choose. Whilst some work is still needed by the consumer to decide between the various options, it is nothing like the effort required for an individual to put the package together. Thus the consumer is paying, in part, for avoiding that effort, and for not having to gain (through pain?) the knowledge that they seek. In other words, they are paying for the travel company's knowledge.

Consider a different case in which Mr. Jones has purchased a computer. He unpacks the boxes carefully, sets the computer up, switches it on, and installs the software. He gets an error message on the screen. Something really helpful, such as "error 220TG, access denied to FG456. Please contact your network administrator." Of course, this is a completely fictitious story and a completely fictitious message, but does it ring any bells?

What happens next? Well, Mr. Jones looks for the helpline number, which is conveniently printed in his welcome pack. He rings, and a friendly adviser warns him that he is ringing a premium rate telephone line. Does Mr. Jones care? No! At this point, all he wants is his computer to be up and running. Now, why is Mr. Jones paying this premium rate and for what is he paying? Quite clearly, he is paying the rate because he wants his computer to work and because he does not have the necessary knowledge to get it working, but the adviser on the helpline does (or so he believes). In other words, he is paying for the knowledge that the adviser holds. In fact, in this instance, he is paying for perceived knowledge, since, at the beginning of the call, he does not know if the adviser can fix the problem.

Mr. Jones starts his exciting adventure with his new computer.

Of course, all works out well, and Mr. Jones follows the instructions the adviser gives him. Why is this simple (and familiar?) story important and how does it relate to knowledge management? Well, just think back a few years and ask yourself how much the home and business computer markets have grown. Now ask yourself how many times over you think the helpline story might be multiplied in the USA. Now how many times will that be multiplied if you think of the worldwide impact of personal computers?

Mr. Jones is very pleased with his computer and the helpline advice.

Very clearly, if the uptake of computers and their associated services is considered to have been major, then, on that basis alone, the western world may now be considered as a mix of knowledge economies. That is, economies that have large bases in services, where knowledge is at a premium. This change from manufacturing to services has impacted on all organisations within such economies.

1.4 Organisations and Knowledge Management

In a knowledge economy, the efficient and effective management of knowledge may help organisations gain and retain competitive edge, but what exactly is it that is to be managed? Surely knowledge resides inside peoples' heads and cannot be managed? There are a number of ways in which these questions may be addressed, and this section begins by looking at the issues facing organisations in regard to knowledge and the management of the knowledge process.

Consider an organisation that has key staff—that is almost any organisation that you could name. Let us imagine that this is a service organisation, where knowledge is the key ingredient. Let us also imagine that the key members of staff do not return to work tomorrow, for whatever reason. In fact they never return again. How will the organisation fare? Well, if it has encouraged and facilitated knowledge sharing, if it has created contingencies, and if it has engaged in succession planning, the impact, although not trivial, will be far less than if it had done none of those things. These are examples of knowledge management, and are related to one of the major concerns of service organisations today, *knowledge retention*. Knowledge retention could be left to chance, or it could be managed.

Suppose that some staff have left, and suppose that the firm faces stiff competition in its markets. What can change its fortunes? The answer is ideas. The creation of new ideas, new ways to market existing products, new versions of old products, and brand new products are all based on ideas. In other words, they are based on *knowledge creation*, and knowledge creation is a key factor in competitiveness in a service economy. How does one firm create knowledge rather than another? Well, it is not easy to force people to create knowledge, but firms can create the conditions under which staff may want to create knowledge, may feel empowered to create knowledge, and feel rewarded for creating knowledge. Such conditions may include incentive schemes, a good working environment, appropriate technology, a feeling of being listened to by the bosses, and a myriad other factors. These things may be seen purely as costs, or they may be seen as investments. Knowledge creation is the reason that many large organisations have a research and development (R&D) department. If a purely short-term, bottom-line financial perspective were to be taken, such work would be unsupportable. However, firms see the benefits in the medium to long term, and they recognise their investment as just that. Thus, knowledge creation could be left to chance, or it could be managed.

However, investments cost money, and that is one of the reasons that knowledge retention is so important. It would be a severe blow to have someone in R&D leave to go to another firm, before they reveal the results of a project on which they have been working for the last five years. How do firms guard against this?

Knowledge sharing is one important way in which organisations may help reduce knowledge loss through staff leaving. The more people who are involved in a project, and who are familiar with it and understand it, the less of an impact on that project if one person leaves. Such sharing is often considered as a technical exercise. That is, if an organisation obtains more hi-tech machines and a greater networking capability, it is seen as a knowledge-sharing solution. This is far from the truth, and a number of things must be recognised about knowledge sharing. Firstly, to share knowledge, by definition, communications must be open. Improving the quality of communications will help improve knowledge sharing. However, many organisations appear to measure quality in terms of quantity. If you ask how they have improved the quality of communications, they reply along the lines that they have spent thousands of dollars on computers and networks, and they have far more of them than they used to have. Whether or not communications have improved appears to be irrelevant as long as there are more of them, and a further answer given would be something like, "There are more people networked and on email than there used to be." All of this misses the point. Technology may help facilitate communication between people, but it is people who decide whether to communicate and what they will or will not communicate. 'Rubbish in, rubbish out' is the old adage. In addition, people are impinged upon by the structures of an organisation (i.e., its business processes). They also help to create such processes, and the structure may help or hinder knowledge sharing. Thus knowledge sharing depends upon staff, structures, and technology, and these three are intertwined.

These three elements are also intertwined when it comes to *knowledge identification*. Staff may be willing to share knowledge, but how do other staff know that knowledge is there and how do they identify it as being relevant to their needs? Having identified knowledge, it is important also to examine *knowledge acquisition*. That is, in what ways is it possible for people to gain knowledge from inside or outside the organisation? Finally, all of the rest is of no use whatsoever, unless that knowledge is used. Thus *knowledge utilisation* must be considered. How is knowledge used, why is it used, and in what ways? Could it be used to better effect? Finally, unless there are some *knowledge targets* and a knowledge *feedback loop*, we will not know if we are succeeding and if we can do better.

The question of "how do we know?" is key to knowledge management, and it is linked to the really difficult question: "How do we know what we know?" This, in turn, is linked to the question: "What do we mean by the word 'know'?"

"Know-how" may be used in the sense that we know how to do a particular task or activity, and the way we use the phrase in everyday terms, such as, "He has a lot of know-how when it comes to cars." This is concerned with the knowledge of how to get things done, and sometimes such knowledge is explicit in organisational policies and procedures, but it is very often tacit, within peoples' heads. You may even have experienced this in regard to car repairs. You can buy the manual, follow the instructions, and it is straightforward—except that it often isn't. You become frustrated because the picture in the manual is slightly different to how your car is on the ground. The instruction to release the micro-adjuster bolt on the distributor is meaningless because there is no bolt. You take the car to the garage, and the guy fixes it—without even looking at a manual. Hey, guess what? You've just paid for his knowledge.

"Know-who" may be used to mean knowing who can help, knowing who won't help, knowing who will hinder, knowing who will laugh, knowing who will cry. This is very much about people and people skills. It relies to some extent on judgement, sensitivity, and the ability to understand others' strengths and weaknesses. One of the most important abilities a manager can have is the judgement of people. This starts at recruitment, when the manager is faced with a stack of applications to shortlist. After that it may be a fifteen-minute interview with each candidate which decides who gets the job. How does the manger know which person to select? If we could distil that knowledge from good managers, and pass it around, we would all be much wiser. How many mangers can say that they have never made a mistake in recruitment?

"Know-when" may be used in the standard everyday sense, and it is about timing your words or actions. For example, skilled stock market operators seem to have the knack of buying when everyone else is selling. Some companies have made a virtue of their timing of takeovers and market entry strategies.

Know-where can mean knowing where knowledge may be obtained, and it can mean knowing where things are best carried out. Levers of change are often reinforced or reach critical mass in specific localities where people with specific skills congregate—places like the Silicon Valley for high technology, or the City of London or New York for international finance.

Know-why refers to the wider context and the vision. This context knowledge allows individuals to go about unstructured tasks in the most appropriate ways. An example is doing what is right by a customer rather than slavishly following a procedure.

Know-that is the basic sense of knowing. It represents accepted 'facts', but also experience and access to learning. A skilled repairman, for example, instinctively knows that the cause of a problem is likely to be found in a particular component.

1.5 Summary

The foregoing discussion may be summarised in the form of a diagram as shown in Figure 1.1, which shows that three areas interact in knowledge management: staff, structures, and technology. Knowledge processes are about the creation, retention, sharing, identification, acquisition, utilisation, and measurement of information and new ideas, in order to achieve strategic aims, such as improved competitiveness or improved performance. Knowledge types are about the ability to know-that, know-who, know-how, know-where, know-why, know-when. Organisational systems are about an organisation's staff, structures, and technology.

In order to engage in successful knowledge management, it is important that all of these areas and the relationships between them are considered holistically. This is why a systems approach to knowledge management offers a new way forward in this challenging area and why this book is entitled, *Beyond Knowledge Management*. In the next few chapters, knowledge management will be considered in greater depth, systems thinking will be considered, and existing knowledge management frameworks will be reviewed. A new framework for the implementation of knowledge management will be advocated and explained.

We stated at the beginning of the chapter that if you want quick-fix solutions, this book is not for you. If you want to "dare to know" how to look at an organisation differently, harness the power of its knowledge, and create innovative and effective systems, then please read on!

Figure 1.1: The Knowledge Management Mix

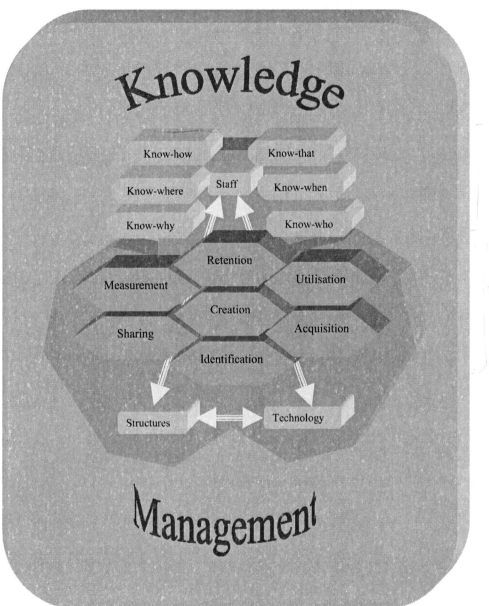

Chapter II

Knowledge Management in More Detail

2.1 Some Starting Points

The previous chapter provided a broad introduction to knowledge management. As you might imagine, this is a complex area. This chapter begins to peel away the layers bit by bit to examine knowledge management in greater depth.

Knowledge management has various approaches and definitions according to the perspective and discipline of the individual or organisation that engages with the concept. These include management, individual and organisational learning, communications, information systems and technology, artificial intelligence, intellectual assets, and so on. Each discipline approaches KM with a different perception, for example, computer science focuses heavily on technology, human resources takes an individual and organisational approach emphasising learning and reward factors, and intellectual assets focus on the explicit capture and registration of knowledge.

There is no single unifying definition or approach, but there are principles and content that may encompass the whole. Knowledge management involves people, processes, activities, technology, and the broader environment that enable the identification, creation, communication or sharing, and use of organisational and individual knowledge. It is about the processes that govern the creation, dissemination, and utilisation of knowledge to attain organisational objectives. It requires a mix of business awareness, creative attitudes and practices, systems, tools, policies, and procedures, designed to release the power of information and ideas.

"Knowledge management is about:

- supporting innovation, the generation of new ideas. and the exploitation of the organisation's thinking power;
- capturing insight and experience to make them available and usable when, where, and by whom required;
- making it easy to find and re-use sources of know-how and expertise, whether they are recorded in physical form or held in someone's mind;
- fostering collaboration, knowledge sharing, continual learning and improvement;
- improving the quality of decision-making and other intelligent tasks;
- understanding the value and contribution of intellectual assets and increasing their worth, effectiveness, and exploitation" (KPMG, 1999, p. 2).

KM must focus an organisation on improving its actions to exploit the power of knowledge. Knowledge management is concerned with the creation, generation, codification, and transfer of information and ideas. The power of knowledge management is in allowing organisations to enable and support explicitly these activities to leverage their value for the group and organisation as well as for the individual.

Given all of the above, why is it that KM has only recently emerged as a major organisational challenge? The next section discusses this.

2.2 The Rise of Knowledge Management

In the last decade business success and survival have become increasingly difficult to ensure, due to the emergence of a new era of organisational forms that embrace change. The emphasis is now on adaptability to the business environment and on addressing market and customer needs proactively. Organisations are evolving from traditional, "permanently" structured entities, to more fluid businesses, across a wide range of sectors. These include manufacturing, healthcare, entertainment, and education. Whatever the sector, there is a growing view that knowledge creation and retention is the key to gaining and retaining competitive edge.

Knowledge management is of major importance to all kinds of organisations, and this importance is growing. A trawl of the Web will result in literally thousands of entries regarding this area. Table 2.1 shows a range of knowledge management application areas (Sveiby, 1999).

There is little doubt that knowledge management has grown quickly and is set to continue to grow. There has been a wider recognition that the nature of western economies has shifted permanently from manufacturing to services, where knowledge, rather than physical assets, is at a premium. It may be argued that knowledge is the most valuable resource today and that the traditional economic factors of production (land, labour, capital, technology) have become secondary, and these can only be obtained and utilised through knowledge. Thus, knowledge is the prime resource, as without it, the other resources are effectively unavailable and it is knowledge that is key to success. Organisations must now recognise that technology-based competitive advantages are transient and the only sustainable advantages are employees, and that the locus of success in the new economy is not in the technology, but in the human mind and organisational memory.

Stewart (1997, p. 6) supports the above by stating, "Knowledge management for an organisation is critical, for knowledge is emerging as the pre-eminent economic resource above raw materials, and often money...fundamental sources of wealth are knowledge and communication rather than natural resources and physical labour." He adds that there is a need to couple knowledge with communication, and this emphasises that it is not just knowledge, but the sharing of knowledge that is of importance.

Table 2.1: Knowledge Management Initiatives (Sveiby, 1999)

Knowledge Management Initiatives		
External Structure Initiatives	**Internal Structure Initiatives**	**Competence Initiatives**
Gain Knowledge from Customers	Build Knowledge Sharing Culture	Create Careers Based on Knowledge Management
Offer Customers Additional Knowledge	Create New Revenues from Existing Knowledge	Create Micro Environments for Tacit Knowledge Transfer
	Capture Individuals' Tacit Knowledge, Store it, Spread it, and Re-Use it	Learn from Simulations and Pilot Installations
	Measure Knowledge Creating Processes and Intangible Assets	
Companies		
Benetton, General Electric, National Bicycle, Netscape, Ritz-Carlton, Agro Corp, Frito-Lay, Dow Chemical, Outokumppu, Skandia Switzerland, Steelcase	3M, Analog Devices, Boeing, BucKnowledge Management Labs, Chaparral Steel, Ford Motor Co., Hewlett Packard, Oticon, WM-Data, McKinsey, Bain & Co., Chevron, British Petroleum, PSL Consult, Skandia ASF, Celemi, Skandia	BucKnowledge Management Labs, IBM, Pfizer, WM-Data, Affaersvaerlden, Hewlett-Packard, Honda, PLS-Consult, Xerox, National Technological University, Matsushita

This growing importance is not just acknowledged by management writers, and in business this realisation is making its way into the boardroom. A survey by Breu, Grimshaw, and Myers (2000) had 576 responses from senior UK business decision-makers, with 50.4% stating that exploiting knowledge was on their board agenda. In the same survey, 28.5% of companies had responded as having an organisation-wide knowledge exploitation strategy. In addition a survey by Murray and Myers (1997) found that over 89% of 100 European business leaders said that knowledge was the key to business power.

It is clear that knowledge management has experienced a speedy and recent rise in importance, but what exactly is KM? The next section addresses this question.

2.3 What Is Knowledge Management?

Although the time is right for knowledge management initiatives, to achieve sustained competitive advantage, KM must be considered beyond just the automation of manual tasks, if it is to avoid the fate of expert systems. These were used mainly in routine decision support roles, and are not seen as particularly useful by many organisations. However, expert systems still appear to dominate the field of knowledge management as can be demonstrated by reviewing the Europe 2001 Knowledge Management Conference and Exhibition. A total of 76 exhibitors attended this conference, of which 67 focussed on IT including technical consultancy, software manufacturing, and knowledge software and associated IT systems. Nine exhibitors offered management consultancy and included the human side of knowledge management. With such emphasis on IT systems, there is a danger that knowledge management will only be seen as a technological process, so it is important to establish what is meant by the term "knowledge management," both in concept and practice.

Knowledge management may be considered in a variety of ways. One typology is to classify knowledge management by distinguishing between tacit and explicit. Pure data would have little effect, for a typical manager and structured data—as information—is useful to analyse and solve problems. Knowledge, however, is obtained from experts and is based on expert experience, as it requires a higher understanding than information alone. Explicit information comprises facts or data that is organised in a structured way, whereas knowledge incorporates values, beliefs, perspectives, judgements, and know-how.

Knowledge only becomes meaningful when it is seen in the larger context of culture, which evolves out of beliefs and philosophy. It is important to recognise context-dependent information as this distinguishes information and knowledge. For example, creating and reproducing conditional statements when exchanging and sharing knowledge presents problems for the codification of knowledge into information, and certain tacit knowledge cannot be reproduced anyway.

An alternative typology is by emphasis on technology or emphasis on people, but it is important that both aspects of knowledge management are addressed, and that the available or developing technology is related to user requirements and is user driven. Within the technical domain, researchers and practitioners are likely to have a computing or information technology background, and will be involved in putting together the information technology needed for management of information systems, artificial intelligence, reengineering, groupware, etc. In this sense, knowledge may be seen as objects that can be identified, monitored, and controlled. If knowledge management is considered this way, it is a relatively new discipline.

Within the people domain, researchers and practitioners are likely to have a background in business, organisational behaviour and management, or social science, and they will be involved in assessing, changing, and improving skills or behaviour of individuals, or the examination and adjustment of the social systems which make up organisations. In this sense, knowledge may be seen as processes that comprise a range of experience and skills that are continually changing. They are traditionally involved in learning and in managing these competencies individually (like psychologists) or at an organisational level (like philosophers, sociologists, or organisational theorists). If knowledge management is considered this way, it may be seen as a discipline that stretches back for thousands of years.

Whilst the concepts of knowledge and management are old, only quite recently have they been put together in this way. This is probably because management has been seen to be principally about clearly definable objects and processes such as finances, project management, corporate strategy, etc. Those elements that did not appear on the financial returns often escaped specific attention. Even the task of managing people (human resource management) has experienced difficulties in gaining recognition. Thus, despite its obvious importance for many industries, the roles of the various types of knowledge have seldom been specifically addressed in management theory and practice. Accountants normally cover it under terms such as intangibles and goodwill.

Failure to consider concerns, which were not accounted for in traditional financial analysis, such as the feelings of communities and the social costs of a company's actions, could result in strategic weaknesses. For example, David Snowden, presenting at the Knowledge Management Annual Conference 2000, discusses the codification of tacit and explicit knowledge in IBM. Snowden points out that whilst gathering and processing knowledge is expensive, e.g., IBM invests 5% of its total revenue into gathering and processing knowledge, he adds that "a company which did not embrace the concept might well be more concerned with survival" (Cummings, 2000, pp. 12-13) and in today's competitive environment simply surviving is not enough. Similar weaknesses may arise if firms ignore the acceptability of strategic options to key stakeholders. Stakeholders may seem relatively passive and even disinterested, but stakeholder groups tend to emerge and influence strategy as a result of specific events, such as the formulation and evaluation of potential new strategies. It is vitally important that the likely reactions of such groups, whether internal or external, are given appropriate consideration. Damaging situations may arise if their interest levels are underestimated. This is of particular concern if such groups act to thwart the implementation of a strategy that has involved time and cost to develop, and, even worse, if no sensible and acceptable alternative strategy has been formulated.

It should be clear from the previous paragraphs that these issues are not raised here because of ethical considerations, but because, in the twenty-first century, they may help determine the long-term success of an organisation. Managers will typically try to reduce ambiguity by looking for that which is familiar. It is the abilities of managers to relate to their external environment, their internal culture, and the people around them, that will determine such success. Knowledge management can help adaptability by enabling the sharing of knowledge more easily, more effectively, more efficiently, and more systematically.

The foregoing discussions are especially important in a post-industrial society and for service organisations within such a society. For both internal and external purposes, knowledge management is important to success and competitive edge. If knowledge sharing is to occur, and if it is to be managed, it is self-evident that for the former communication is vital, and for the latter, policies, procedures, and strategies will play a key role if anything other than ad hoc communications are to be achieved. Good communications are key to knowledge management and knowledge creation, and Nonaka and Takeuchi (1995, p. 3) describe organisational knowledge creation as "the capability of a company as a whole to create new knowledge, disseminate it throughout the organisation, and embody it in products, services, and systems." The importance of communication and knowledge sharing is discussed next.

2.4 Knowledge Sharing and Communication

Whilst communication is regarded as key to knowledge management, it is also an essential ingredient in many management theories, from an operational and strategic perspective. For example, it would be difficult to deny the importance of corporate communications, the role and function of communication executives, and the impact of corporate communications upon the formulation of corporate strategy. It would also be difficult to deny the importance of informal communications in excellent companies and the advantages in relation to action and progress, rather than formal bureaucratic paper-based communication, often found in large organisations.

Accepting that communication is central to the success of knowledge management, this is both from an information theory perspective in relation to the technical domain, and constructivist perspective in relation to the people domain. Organisations often experience difficulties achieving effective communication in both domains. This may be a common difficulty more often in traditional bureaucratic organisations and specifically in relation to tacit knowledge.

When thinking about classical management approaches and organisation hierarchies, communication problems could be as a result of the environment and organisational structure, but may also be because the concept of communication is not fully recognised and often reflects a one-way process rather than an exchange or dialogue. Nonaka and Takeuchi (1995) argue that western society is too focussed on explicit knowledge, which involves formal and systematic communication, whereas Japanese companies recognise and value the concept of tacit knowledge. However, they state "tacit knowledge is highly personal and hard to formalise, making it difficult to communicate or share with others. Subjective insights, intuitions, and hunches fall into this category of knowledge" (Nonaka & Takeuchi, 1995, p. 8).

Formal and explicit knowledge can easily be processed by a computer, transmitted electronically, or stored in databases. Explicit knowledge tends to be about hard facts, quantifiable information, policies, and procedures, whereas tacit knowledge is the experience and wisdom developed as a result of using and applying hard information, whilst absorbing the internal and external environment and culture of the organisation and its industry. Whilst converting tacit knowledge into explicit knowledge is important, this could simply mean the systemisation of people's thought processes and wisdom, rather than valuing the workforce's collective knowledge as well as individuality and the contribution they make to the organisation. The process of converting tacit to explicit for purposes of communication and providing value to an organisation, therefore, appears to be an idealistic concept.

It could be argued that formal organisational systems are limited in scope and cannot capture the culture of the organisation. Alternatively there may be methods that could provide means of translating tacit knowledge to an understandable language with aspects of knowledge converting to explicit. However, only aspects of tacit knowledge will successfully convert, as much of tacit knowledge is built on a foundation of social conditioning, values, and beliefs, which form individual perspectives of the world. Alternatively, perhaps there is no need to convert the tacit to the explicit, but to manage tacit knowledge in a way that complements and implicitly contributes to the organisation, managers create and access their own networks of informal communication.

Whilst a communication process may incorporate a variety of techniques ranging from reports, visual identity, correspondence, and electronic communications, there is no guarantee that the intended message has been received and understood. In the technical domain, often the information is more quantifiable so the same problems are less likely to arise. However, tacit and explicit knowledge are not entirely separable forms of knowledge, because all explicit knowledge has a tacit dimension. This is further highlighted when considering that communication is a broader concept than just exchanging information, but incorporating behaviour as well. Thus, communication addresses issues such as the interpretation of the intended message, intention of those delivering the information, relationship influences, and the context in which the message is set, all of which clarify meaning, but still only to a certain extent. Social conditioning, cultural differences, and other external influences will always impact to convert the message into a meaningful translation and context for the individual receiving, or not at all as the case may be.

Table 2.2 demonstrates a continuum of communication. The continuum is intended to demonstrate different levels of communication with polarised concepts of hard technical information at one end of the scale and purely tacit at the other. This is not, however, intended to detract from the tacit elements of communication and thought that are implicit in all elements of communication, but to highlight the differences.

Table 2.2: Continuum of Communication

Explicit   Tacit

Hard data (IT-based) organisation non-personal	Procedures, manuals IT-based or paper-based organisational	Policies Written correspondence Email Organisational/ departmental	Meetings messages email interpersonal workgroups individual	Social semi-formal smaller groups, individuals	Social informal Smaller groups, individual	Rumour, speculation story telling, legends history

In this continuum, hard data refers to facts with limited scope for interpretation. As the continuum moves towards the tacit, there is more room for personal or contextual interpretation, and the exchange of information and dialogue becomes more loose and intangible but not unimportant. Story telling (narrative) is emerging as an important informal method of communication in modern organisations and is regarded as important to convey experiences of work whilst communicating shared knowledge, and learning and maintaining organisational memory. Individual knowledge, organisational memory, intellectual content, and knowledge through teamwork and learning are all important.

A critical discursive process is what distinguishes knowledge sharing, because the emphasis shifts from non-action or simple problem solving to "learning and solution questioning" (Ulrich, 2003, p. 326). Ulrich continues by pointing out that the questions asked should not be pre-defined by the problem or those who may ask the question, implying the importance of open and cross-organisational interaction incorporating diverse perspectives and complex relationships.

Significant areas that relate to knowledge management generally therefore are communication and learning, and the role of people as possessors of knowledge. The whole concept of learning involves sharing and acquiring knowledge, and from a sociological perspective, the interpersonal relationships that construct and convey meaning. Putting this in context, organisations consist of individuals and groups, which require management of complex relationships and processes that constitute or contribute to managing knowledge. Referring back to the idea of constructivist communication, to fully understand a message requires that the sender and receiver possess mutual mental models, and any prior knowledge individuals possess will influence the process. Teams, however, can eventually develop a common understanding and shared knowledge, but communicating the team knowledge to those outside the team can be difficult.

This raises two issues. First, operational management processes in relation to individuals in a social context, and it is a truism that knowledge sharing will only be successful if the facilities and systems are easily accessible and easy to use. Second, the concept of knowledge management and complexity of communication appears to relate comfortably to the concept of systems and contingency strategic management. Knowledge management could be dependent on cross-organisational influences and interactions internally and externally, which set the context in which knowledge is shared.

The relationship between managing knowledge and people can be difficult and contentious, because knowledge is still regarded as a personal rather than organisational commodity and is still associated with power, money, and organisational politics. Indeed, the status, incomes, and power of professionals depend to a large extent on their expertise. The less able people are to understand this expertise, the greater the difference between the supply and demand for professional services.

The idea that organisations have knowledge is appropriate, assuming that individuals remain with the organisation. However, when a member of staff leaves, they take with them tacit knowledge and in some cases explicit knowledge if it has not been codified effectively. Tacit knowledge is difficult if not impossible to replace, because the individual's contribution to the success of the organisation could have been unique to that person. Furthermore attempts to measure tacit knowledge require the organisation to understand the concept of what the knowledge is that they are looking for in the first place; for example, Snowden (2000) states that about 90% of knowledge resides in the informal communities of an organisation and presents three associated heuristics:

- knowledge cannot be conscripted but volunteered;
- we can always know more than we tell, after we have told it and after we have written it down;
- people only recognise what they know when they need to know it.

The foregoing puts to question the view that no one is indispensable; for example, levels of dispensability may be different according to the amount of expertise and knowledge an individual has. If it is organisationally desirable for knowledge to be shared and transparent, then why would an individual volunteer that knowledge? Further, to what extent do managers truly know what knowledge resides in their organisation and how this could be communicated effectively? If an organisation does not have appropriate codification and communication of explicit knowledge, again, problems emerge if the member of staff responsible for a particular area leaves and has not shared that knowledge. One approach that could be considered to address this could be found by considering knowledge management in the context of learning organisations.

2.5 Knowledge Management and Learning Organisations

Learning in an organisation may be described as a process by which an organisation gathers and uses new knowledge, with appropriate consideration for the tools, behaviours, and values at all levels. Newly learned knowledge is translated into new goals, procedures, roles, and performance measures. Learning organisations, however, can mean different things to different people; for example, one view refers to the organisation as a whole. An alternative view makes reference to all of the individual systems and subsystems of learning throughout the organisation. Learning is an issue in organisations that operate in fast-changing environments, and the role of learning, conceptualisation of training and development, and maximisation of learning becomes of greater importance as the pace of change increases.

Senge (1992) introduces the concept of the learning organisation as a collective capacity to learn at all levels of the organisation rather than a top-down directive for individuals to act on specific orders. Such collective learning requires trust and interdependency among teams with individual strengths compensating for individual weaknesses. Senge (1992) explains the difference between learning organisations and traditional organisations through five main principles:

- *Systems thinking,* which is events and actions that influence each other beyond individual learning horizons and the awareness that decisions can impact right across the organisation, both present and future. In addition there is understanding about individual ability to change working patterns to improve the organisation.

- *Personal mastery,* which relates to the level of proficiency, and in this case individuals are usually committed to lifelong learning to clarify and deepen personal vision, developing patience and seeing reality objectively.

- *Mental models,* which are "deeply engrained assumptions, generalisations…pictures or images that influence how we understand the world and how we take action" (Senge, 1992, p. 8). To work effectively with mental models requires increased self-awareness of our internal pictures of the world and to carry on "learningful conversations that balance inquiry and advocacy, where people expose their own thinking effectively and make that thinking open to the influence of others" (Senge, 1992, p. 9).

- *Building a shared vision,* which requires leadership in an organisation that binds people together and establishes a common identity and sense of purpose. This involves revealing or converting shared pictures of the future to cultivate positive commitment rather than reluctant compliance.

- *Team learning,* which requires effective communication, i.e., dialogue and collective thinking because collective intelligence exceeds the intelligence of individuals in the team. The skills to achieve such team working include recognition, respect, trust, and confidence.

Comparing Senge's five principles to Quinn, Anderson, and Finkelstein (1996, p. 72), synergy can be seen in relation to knowledge types:

- *Cognitive knowledge,* which is the basic mastery of a discipline and relates to personal mastery.
- *Advanced skills,* which are beyond book learning into practical execution and could be connected with mental models.
- *Systems understanding,* which is a deep knowledge of cause and effect, the ultimate expression of which is intuition. Again this could be linked to mental models and that which is beyond the 'learning horizon'.
- *Self-motivated creativity,* which is the will and motivation to succeed.

Quinn's typology of knowledge, however, does not include building a shared vision and teamwork, both of which influence knowledge sharing.

Management in learning organisations differs from management in traditional organisations; for example, common management practice in traditional organisations looks outward and relates to practical skills. Management in learning organisations focuses more on how individuals think, what they truly want, and how they interact and learn with one another. Learning provides the opportunity to create and recreate, change one's external perception of the world and relationship with it, and extends individual ability to be creative. Senge (1992) states that there are two aspects to this: "adaptive learning," which is about survival; and "generative learning," which enhances one's ability to create. The ability of the learning organisation to draw out and retain knowledge is determined by the organisational structure and culture, and the ability of its people to recognise what they know and the way(s) in which they know.

Cohen and Levinthal (1990) discuss "absorptive capacity," which is the individual recognition, sharing, and assimilation of knowledge. The ability of individuals to absorb knowledge collectively impacts at an organisation level; however, decision-making processes and communication will determine how effective this is likely to be at an organisational level. Cohen and Levinthal (1990) state that organisations with a low absorptive capacity will have difficulties in managing their internal and external communications and knowledge flows.

Tobin (1996) discusses the knowledge network in relation to transformational learning, focussing on artefacts such as inventories of knowledge assets, i.e., databases which provide the organisation with information about internal and external knowledge bases, learning resources and tools database, and individual and group learning facilitation. With regard to group learning facilitation, Owen (1997, p. 16) states: "If the issue is the future of the corporation, and the people are willing to admit that they just do not know the answer, collaboratively they have a shot at creating a viable solution." Brown and Duguid (1991) indicate that doing to learn, informal learning, and sharing can contribute to the successful functioning of organisations, and may help maintain organisational memory and continuity.

The foregoing and previous sections highlight that organisations have various resources and capabilities, based around the individual and collective human resources and learning, with internal and external influences. Key issues to emerge include cross-organisational working in people and service-based organisations. The concept of the learning organisation can provide individual and collective contribution to improve performance, engendering the trust and interdependency among teams to achieve higher outputs. This involves knowledge sharing from, and influences on, the workforce at all levels and experiences within the organisation, and management recognition of the intellectual capital therein.

2.6 Intellectual Capital

The concept of intangible assets has become important as organisations increasingly become knowledge driven. Research, development, and innovation policies, as well as education and training policies, should include actions aimed to stimulate innovation, creativity, and the competitive development of organisations through investment in intangibles.

Whilst traditionally, strategic management viewed organisations as a compilation of physical and human resources and systems, the main objective related to profit maximisation; however, with the increase in service organisations and focus on human resources, human assets are now considered as a key resource. Since 1994, the European Commission (EC) has launched a series of studies, actions, and projects that aim to better understand the knowledge economy and the importance of intangibles as competitiveness factors. One example of this was a workshop that took place in November 1999 in Helsinki, entitled

"Intellectual Capital/Intangible Investments: How Much Is Your Business Worth?" The main issues to arise were:

- Industry is aware that knowledge management is a key factor for business value, but at present there is a need for indicators to measure the performance of a company.

- This problem transcends all aspects of business management (accounting, corporate investment strategy, disclosure of information and aspects of economic management, etc.) and needs to be tackled on an inter-disciplinary basis.

- It is very urgent to recognise at a policy level the need to invest more in intangibles (research and development, innovation, training, and marketing) in all sectors (Liikanen, 1999).

The ability to manage the intellect of human resources, including creativity and sharing of knowledge, has a direct impact on the maximisation of the organisation overall, not necessarily to be realised in the tangibles of the profit margin, but the overall market value of the organisation.

Quinn, Anderson, and Finkelstein (2000) highlight the importance of managing intellect to convert it into useful outputs. They define intellect as including:

- cognitive knowledge;

- advanced skills;

- system understanding and trained intuition;

- self-motivated creativity.

Intellectual capital includes organisational and individually accumulated knowledge, ability, skill, and expertise. Individuals, however, do not necessarily possess the skills that incorporate everything, therefore the manager's challenge is to "fully understand how their actions affect other elements of the organisation or how to improve the total entity's effectiveness" (Quinn et al., 2000, p. 507).

Allee (1997) describes intellectual capital as including people, processes, structure, and the customer:

- The customer represents external capital, i.e., "relationships with customers, strategic partners, suppliers, investors, and communities."

- Human capital comprises the "individual capabilities, knowledge skills, experience, and problem-solving abilities that reside in people in the organisation."
- Structural capital includes the "systems and work processes that leverage competitiveness, including IT, communication technologies, images, concepts, and models of how the business operates, databases, documents, patents, copyrights, and other codified knowledge" (Allee, 2000, pp. 18-19).

From this perspective, managing knowledge should be on the strategic management agenda to achieve exceptional performance and sustainable competitive advantage, and to use knowledge efficiently and rapidly rather than rely on particular products or technologies, which, although tangible, can be easily imitated.

Intellectual capital is difficult to measure. Whereas physical assets are stable and consistent and can be accurately valued and depreciated, intellectual capital cannot be accurately valuated and can appreciate as well as depreciate; therefore physical assets provide a less complex system of valuation. It has long been recognised that the value of a company depends on a range of assets whose replacement costs cannot be easily calculated, for example the workforce. Traditional accountancy procedures differentiate between tangible and intangible assets, and intellectual capital represents all the assets of a company not represented on a balance sheet. Renewed emphasis on information or knowledge assets, intangible assets, and intellectual capital has resulted in virtual companies achieving valuation many times over of their physical base.

Traditional accounting procedures are less able to account for production that includes knowledge capital, intellectual capital, and intangible assets. This view is supported by Allee (2000, p. 29): "Our financial accounting systems do not illuminate diversity but drive toward conformity. Intangibles offer us the chance to profile, analyse, understand, and appreciate the difference of one company from another." To succeed, this requires organisations to consider the value-added elements of organisations within the social domain, and such consideration is progressing. Harrison and Sullivan (2000) provide an update on current best practice and the evolution of intellectual capital management, reporting on the values, roles, and optimisation of intellectual capital. Liebowitz and Suen (2000, pp. 54-67) introduce knowledge management metrics for measuring intellectual capital, recommending that organisations should undertake intellectual capital audits to "consolidate the knowledge management field and give the discipline further credibility."

2.7   Conclusions

This chapter explored various aspects of knowledge management; establishing that business success, the new era of organisational forms, and the continual changing environment require new approaches to management. The emphasis is now on adaptability, addressing market and customer needs proactively, and a shift away from traditional, "permanently" structured organisations, to more fluid businesses. Knowledge management is seen as essential to the survival of organisations, to capture the creativity, sharing, and utilisation of knowledge and expertise that provides an organisation with competitive edge.

Communication is key to knowledge management. It is also an essential ingredient in many management theories, from an operational and strategic perspective. Improving technologies provide opportunities for increasing information exchange, but much organisational knowledge is tacit and cannot so easily be transferred electronically. Communication should not be regarded as just electronic information exchange, but a dialectic and critical process.

The relationship between managing knowledge and people can be difficult and contentious, because knowledge is still regarded as a personal rather than organisational commodity and is still associated with power, money, and organisational politics. There are approaches, however, that may reduce some of the obstructions to sharing knowledge, which include the concept of intellectual capital or intangible asset management. The concept of intangible assets has become an important issue as organisations increasingly become knowledge driven. Research, development, and innovation policies, as well as education and training policies, should include actions aimed to stimulate innovation, creativity, and the competitive development of organisations through investment in intangibles. Intellectual capital includes organisational and individually accumulated knowledge, ability, skill, and expertise. Individuals do not necessarily possess the skills that incorporate everything, or have the opportunity to express themselves. Management challenges, therefore, are changing in relation to teamwork, organisational structure, communication and collaboration, and ability of the organisation to learn.

The next chapter considers these issues from a sociotechnical perspective.

Chapter III

Sociotechnical Systems and Knowledge Management

3.1 Introduction

Sociotechnical thinking is a subset of social theory and philosophy. This way of thinking is particularly relevant in domains such as information management which are closely related to knowledge management. The wider social context is addressed in the following chapter. In this chapter we are going to look at the concepts underpinning sociotechnical thinking and how we can apply these ideas to knowledge management.

As discussed previously, knowledge management is not about managing technology alone, but is about managing how humans can share their knowledge effectively, using technical tools where appropriate. In this sense we use the phrase 'information system' to include technology and people, and also non-technical means of sharing information such as story telling, newsletters, and notice boards. A lecture is one of the most obvious means of sharing knowledge through the means of an information system, with the lecturer explicating understanding of the topic. Lecturers share knowledge with students, and this knowledge may be both tacit and explicit in form; but what they receive is information that is interpreted for them in the context of the lecturer's understanding. What the students gain from it is, of course, dependent on their understanding and world view. In order to share knowledge, lecturers use technology as appropriate: sometimes when in a large theatre, a microphone and possibly a computer to project slides that contain the main points of the talk. Often lectures are supported outside the lecture theatre by websites or Virtual Learning Environments, with further information or links to this information for students to follow; often of course, lecturers just stand in front of students and narrate, or tell stories.

Telling stories is one of the best forms of knowledge sharing. It is culturally dependent and unique to the situation being discussed. So here we take as our context that the 'real' information system is built upon organisational culture and interpersonal communication. This system contains the rich and dynamic tacit knowledge, which, if it is harnessed and managed effectively, may give organisations leverage to gain competitive advantage.

When considering both the social system and the technical systems that we use in our working life, we need to think about the way humans use technology for their own purposes. We should consider the statement:

> *"The very nature of information technology shifts and changes, historically and contextually, conceptually and empirically. Organisational work, too, is a multi-valenced concept as well as a multi-dimensional practice. It has included and continues to cover much territory: clerical, artistic, managerial, craft, supervisory, production, professional, routine, knowledge, symbolic, emotional, informal, technical, individual, and collaborative. Animating both technology and work is the human capacity to act in the world, to construct and use information technology, to define, control, and modify work. Human agency is routine and innovative, mindless and reflective, planned and improvisational. It has both intended and unintended consequences. Most importantly, the assumptions, interests, concepts, approaches, and theories that we use, shape and refine our views of the world and of ourselves"* (Orlikowki, Walsham, & Jones, 1996, p. 9).

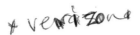

In this chapter we use sociotechnical theory to discuss the issues relating to knowledge and the organisation, and it is this theory that shapes our view on the world. Before exploring the relationship between knowledge and sociotechnology, this chapter looks at the linkages between knowledge, understanding, and decision-making. The chapter then offers a definition for the word 'sociotechnology', which is then implied in the remainder of the chapter. We also look at the history of the sociotechnical movement, explaining its origins and early applications of theory to organisational change. A sociotechnical organisation can be considered equivalent to a post-Fordist organisation, with participation key. It will be flat in structure, flexible, decentralised with few work boundaries and encouraging of initiative. A key tenet of sociotechnical theory is the value of (semi-) autonomous groups and the development of their expertise, in the organisation, so we next explore these ideas and apply them to the new autonomous groups that have sprung up for managing knowledge as Communities of Practice (CoPs).

The chapter then looks into the linkages that have been made in theory and the literature between knowledge management and sociotechnical thinking. Following this section, we continue by discussing sociotechnical systems and knowledge. We show how such systems can be designed by using the principles for organisational design laid down by sociotechnical theorists. Having discussed the theoretical grounding of the linkages, the chapter then details a case study of an organisation using these principles in practical knowledge management. Finally, we demonstrate how the sociotechnical principles can be adapted and enhanced for the purposes of knowledge management.

3.2 Knowledge, Understanding, and Decision-Making

In this section the relationship between knowledge, understanding, and decision-making is addressed in relation to sociotechnical ideas. There is no attempt here to set this relationship into a wider social context, as this is undertaken in the following chapter.

There are many definitions in the literature as to what knowledge exists, the ways in which it can be codified, and how it can be distinguished from data and information. The use of knowledge, however, is, as Ackoff (1991) points out, only as good as the user's understanding of what that knowledge means. From experience comes knowledge, which leads to memory, which gives us thought and then action. But knowledge without understanding is not very useful. Understanding comes from a number of attributes, both of the knowledge itself and the format in which it is used, and the previous experience of the user. This is the social context. But knowledge is always limited by this past experience and cannot be complete, but can only be fragmented.

When accumulating knowledge there is a conscious choice to learn or discard the knowledge of others. Very often you choose that with which you already agree and that does not challenge your own assumptions. This is a form of self-prejudice. In fact the mind always follows a certain pattern—knowledge can therefore gradually become formulaic. Experiences give us memories and values that guide and discipline us and therefore condition our minds. We use 'dead' memories and values to understand new experience.

It is essential for organisations that some suggestions are promoted and developed that lead to organisational knowledge being used for timely decisions that lead (among other things) to true competitive advantage for the organisation. (See the comments from Xerox.) The emerging focus in management and system literature on the importance of organisational knowledge is, according to Prusak (1997), due to six specifics for organisations:

- the pace of change itself (fast);

- the nature of goods and services (an increasing emphasis on intangible goods);

- the scope of the typical firm and its market (ever increasing with the increasing use of the World Wide Web);

- the size and attrition rate of employee bases (shrinking or growing according to the market forces);

- the structure of organisations (under change as circumstances change and thus increasingly fluid); and

- the capabilities and costs of information technology (increasing capabilities for decreasing costs).

These specifics affect most of the organisations operating in the developed economies and often many in the developing economies too. The issue here is that a problem is always new (otherwise it would not be a problem!), so if we approach the problem with existing knowledge and actions, formed into patterns by memory, our responses will be conditioned by our past. Therefore we cannot solve the 'new' in the problem—we cannot understand through the barriers of past thought. Thus to understand the new we need wisdom, we need to be free of the past conditioning, and we need creativity.

Taylor (1998) suggests that the real problem is not in acquiring knowledge, but that "organisations will need the skills to interpret this material to make effective decisions," and "people will be the biggest factor in determining the success of failure of knowledge management by the quality of their decisions" (Taylor, 1998, p. 26).

3.3 Knowledge and Sociotechnology

In traditional philosophy, knowledge is seen as abstract, universal, impartial, and rational—a stand-alone artefact that we can capture in technology and one that will be truthful in its essence. This is evident in the works of the ancient Greek philosophers where, if we look at epistemology (the theory of knowledge, its possibilities, scope, and general basis), we find that it originates with these philosophers. Plato and Aristotle, for instance, were very concerned about the nature of knowledge and what distinguishes knowledge from belief. Plato put forward in the *Meno* the idea that correct belief can be turned into knowledge by fixing it through the means of reason or a cause. Aristotle thought that knowledge of a thing involved understanding it in terms of the reasons for it. For Aristotle, the object of the knowledge required a context of explanatory and reason-giving propositions. In modern terms 'to understand' is to be fully aware of not only the meaning of something, but also its implications.

In comparison, writers such as Gilligan (1982) see people in a web of relationships that imply that knowledge is interconnected and contextual (and possibly biased). Boje, Gephart, and Thatchenkerry (1996, p. 2) put this in context when they define organisations as:

> *"...rather than conceiving of organisations substantively as concrete facilities embedded in artefacts such as policies and buildings, we regard organisations relationally as a concept of social*

actors that is produced in contextually embedded social discourse and used to interpret the social world. The meaning of organisation thus resides in the contexts and occasions where it is created and used by members rather than in a special fixed substantive form. "

A third view, one which takes elements of both the rational and the contextual, is however more predominant in most of the current writings on the topic of knowledge management. This view can perhaps be traced back to the work of Locke in the late seventeenth century. To Locke, knowledge was the perception of a connection between ideas that can be perceived by the use of reason. When the connection is direct, then this is intuitive knowledge. When the connection is indirect and is determined through the utilisation of other ideas and known connections, then the knowledge is demonstrative. We can consider this perhaps to be equivalent to tacit and explicit knowledge, as explicit knowledge is made evident and can be explained. Demonstrative knowledge, as Locke describes it, requires understanding and contextual application. Locke argues that observation and experimentation (experience) will lead to belief and opinion. It is also evident therefore that demonstrative knowledge will be based on past learning and activities, and will be bounded by one's own ideas and world view. All of this is echoed in philosophical positions adopted toward the concept of knowledge.

As discussed above, what we find is that our minds follow a certain pattern of thought—we develop knowledge according to our own pre-set formulae or methods. Our experiences give us memories and values that guide and discipline us, and therefore set up the conditions within which our minds operate. In fact, it could be said that we use 'dead' memories and values to understand new experience. When we accumulate knowledge, there is a conscious choice or discard of the knowledge of others.

Knowledge is therefore socially constructed. It is not a stand-alone artefact or universal truth. If knowledge is a social construct, not simply a tool or resource, it will be discovered in a social context. It will be developed in our interactions with people. The term 'socio' of sociotechnology is derived from the Latin "socius" and had the original meaning of associate or companion; it now relates to the social world or society. Technology, on the other hand, is derived from the Greek word "technologia," whose meaning was related to that of systematic treatment. The word sociotechnology therefore is made up of these two root paradigms and is intended to imply a broad and inclusive viewpoint of the way technology is implemented in the social environment.

Here we would argue that consideration of one set of conceptual theories, whether the social or the technological, is insufficient to fully consider the technology and the social environment in which knowledge is acted upon.

3.4 A History of the Sociotechnical Movement

The historical origins of the sociotechnical movement and its historical usages in organisational change management give us the foundations for understanding how this theory can help us in developing knowledge management theory.

Mumford (1996a) gives a history of the sociotechnical design approach. She identifies that the sociotechnical approach was aimed at combining the effective use of technology with the effective and humanistic use of people. She begins by looking at the work of Eric Trist, one of the founder members of the Tavistock Institute. She traces his work back to the 1930s and the Scottish jute industry where the introduction of changes in technology caused unemployment, deskilling, and alienation. The inter-play between social and technical systems became the foundation of his new designs for work organisation.

The Tavistock Institute began work after the Second World War to look at both the psychology of work and work groups, and the concepts of open systems (Von Bertalanffy, 1950). In an open system, the boundaries between the entity (say an organisation) and the external environment are permeable. Matter can pass between the two. Organisations will react to their environment and change their behaviour appropriately. This would relate to the concepts of systems thinking where one would need to understand the whole in the context of its parts. New systems thinking (as it has been called) takes a view of reality that it is an inseparable network of relationships, so scientific observations cannot be objective. The boundaries by which we isolate objects in order to study them can only be arbitrary.

The Trist and Bamforth (1951) study looked at a technological system that was expressive of the mass-production era and a social structure that consisted of the occupational roles that had been institutionalised in its use. The interactive technological and sociological patterns were assumed to have psychological effects in the life-space of the worker. The worker's contribution to the field of determinants (factors involved in the study) arose from the nature and quality of the attitudes and relationships that he developed when performing tasks and taking roles.

In the coal-mining industry of the time, the coal was obtained by small groups of two or three people that contracted their work directly to the management. Leadership and the supervision of tasks were internal to the group, which thus had responsible autonomy. Each worker in the group was multi-skilled and group members were self-selected. The groups were able to vary their work pace in response to changing conditions. Many of these groups were related by kinship to each other, and a united collective through community and class connectedness was evident. Nonetheless there was an amount of rivalry and competition amongst the groups that channelled aggression but also reinforced loyalty. Groups tended to be fiercely loyal to each other but not necessarily to the workforce at large.

The existing social structure was disturbed by the mechanisation of the long faces of coal, which meant a more economical working of the entire coal mine. A coalface is where the coal is cut underground. Long faces had been recently opened up, which meant that, unlike the previous shorter faces, machines could be used efficiently to cut the coal out of the face. This mechanisation required a more factory-like unit and structure, with larger groups and overall supervisory management. The constant movement of the cutting equipment along the faces, and the large scale of the operations meant that maintaining the existing group relationships became problematical. Single workgroups were no longer able to contract their work to the management; enlarged or multiple groups were required to work alongside each other now that the working face had been enlarged. Each group within this extended group was now wholly dependent on the other groups' correct performance of their tasks and appointed roles.

Under the long face mining method, multi-skilling became unnecessary. Tasks were divided up in sequence and a production line effectively came into being. In addition, shift work was now required so that each task could be completed for the entire coalface before the next task began. This further disturbed the social structure of the groups who no longer worked at the same time, in the same place, in the pit. Groups were thus fragmented and social relationships broken. Ties of kinship and mutual dependence were no longer necessary to form and hold the workgroups together. Instead, shifts of workers became dependent on each other.

Coalmining, however, is not 'normal' factory work, as the conditions are not predictable. Often unforeseen faults in the seams or other environmental conditions meant that some workers were disadvantaged in their working conditions and thus earned less pay than others. The close interdependence of the roles meant that incomplete or badly completed work in the previous working role or task rebounded onto the next shift of workforce. Local disturbances became magnified (vicious and virtuous circles were created). Workers operated in a state of uncertainty and expectation that problems might occur that would impact on their own productivity and thus ultimately their pay. The supervisors complained that workers were not concerned with the overall activity, only that which impacted their own. The workers considered the supervisors to be outside their kinship circle and not responsible to the workers but to the management. Thus disagreements between management and workers were common.

The workers attempted to defend their social relationships and to create new groups for mutual support. However, as there was no kinship element per se or necessity to work together, and the system did not support these groups, some worked well, whilst others did not. In particular personality issues or physical attributes (such as age or stamina) mediated against some individuals who were therefore not able to join mutual support groups. Some workers therefore developed a reactive individualism and personal secrecy. Intrigue became a way of working to enable the 'better' working situations to be appropriated. Supervisors were considered capable of victimisation or even bribery in relation to the allocation of working positions. Thus a collective community was destroyed. Due to the fragmented and shift nature of the new working conditions, it became easy to blame others for problems discovered on subsequent shifts. As no one person could be blamed specifically (due to the production line environment), the issue permitted a group mentality whilst retaining anonymity and lack of specificity for the blame and the blaming. Some workers also began absenting themselves from work due to the conditions and the ability to blame others for the poor working conditions, which meant that they had to work extra hard at times.

The researchers concluded that the immediate problem was to once again develop small-group organisation. The management of the coal pits should work out a way around the authority issues by restoring responsible autonomy to primary groups. They should ensure that each group was responsible for a complete (sub) task within a permitted flexibility in working practices. Multi-skilling would again be necessary for these teams and shift work should be organised in such a way that groups only worked either the day or the night shifts, but not rotating around both.

The rationale behind the team-working, multi-skilling, and empowerment approach suggested by the Tavistock Institute was not to increase production (the fact that it did was an unanticipated bonus), but to reduce stress and provide a better working environment—a moral stance. Work should be made for satisfying the individual and the work-group. Later sociotechnical writers also emphasised that the group and work-task design should also enable them to contribute to a high level of technical efficiency. In addition, sociotechnical theorists expected that the task and group design would provide a work system that could adapt and adjust (learn) within a constantly changing environment. In the words of Rice (1958, p. 4):

> *"The concept of a socio-technical system arose from the consider-ation that any production system requires both a technological organisation—equipment and process layout—and a work organisation relating to each other those who carry out the necessary tasks. The technological demands place limits on the type of work organisation possible, but a work organisation has social and psychological properties of its own that are independent of technology."*

The ideas of the Tavistock relating to the organisation of work spread during the 1950s across first to Scandinavia, then more generally across Europe, India, and the United States. The accepted philosophy of the movement was that both technology and the use of people within work situations should be optimised. Work should be structured so as to provide motivation, job satisfaction, good working conditions, and ultimately, increased efficiency.

During the 1960s, sociotechnical ideas began to be more theoretically devel-oped with an increasing system theory involvement. Hill (1971) expounded on the concept of a sociotechnical system. His idea was that the organisation was an open system, that there should be a principle of organisational choice to match social and technical systems. In addition, he put forward the recognition of the importance of autonomous work groups and the importance of understanding workplace alienation. The philosophy of sociotechnical organisational design was therefore to promote working environments and systems that use expertise, knowledge, and technology to achieve an efficient and motivated workforce. Everyone in an organisation should be trained to optimise the whole. Work should be exciting, challenging, and enjoyable.

Parallel to this theoretical development was the work being carried out in Scandinavia on industrial democracy. During the 1960s, '70s, and '80s, experiments and legislation in quality of work, job redesign, and the 'humanisation of work' were undertaken across Europe.

Whilst much of the early work of the Tavistock and the sociotechnical pioneers related to the shop floor and factory automation, more recent work by academics and consultants began to look at the impact of computers on office work. The concepts of sociotechnical design were found to be equally compatible with redesigning work for the introduction of ICT into white-collar work as they had been with factory automation, etc. We see this also in job design for knowledge work. As Mumford (1997) says, Cole in his seminal 1985 paper argued that there was a belief that the small and restricted jobs that had emerged from the Tayloristic view of organisations, had led to employees not only being demotivated, but also prevented them from realising their full intellectual potential.

The values and objectives of the Tavistock, and of sociotechnical design by change agents, have always been directed at helping companies to manage change successfully. This is done by creating work (and process) systems that enable individuals, groups, and organisations to work together productively and harmoniously (Mumford, 1996a).

Mumford (1996b) grounds her arguments in the work of Mary Parker Follett who wrote and lectured in the early 1900s. Follett was a management consultant who espoused group networks with self-government instead of bureaucratic organisations. This was deeply unfashionable at the time she was working and continued to be regarded as subversive by the U.S. business world for a number of years after her death in 1933. However, the Japanese and to some extent the UK organisational theory writers continued to consider her work important.

Mumford explains that Follett believed in a broad attitude towards organisations. They should be coordinated and closely knit, linking and so making a working unit not many separate pieces. Leaders were considered to be a barrier to integration, and individuals should have the freedom to join with others to form group power. Follett emphasised that group freedom meant no domination or compromise, but integration and functional capacity. Rational thinking was required to achieve a full understanding, effective planning, and a way of working through discussion and consensus in the organisation. The freedom of Mary Parker Follett was that of knowledge, discussion, and integration requiring continuous and close communication. A recognition of common interests and a willingness to participate in solving problems should take place. In other words CoPs (communities of practice) will be formed. (See also the work by Habermas on communicative action and forming a rational consensus, and that of early philosophers on the role of groups within the larger community. Each group should have the maximum autonomy feasible, consistent with its function and its relationship to the other groups within its larger community.)

According to Mumford (1996b) there are a number of principles that can be derived from the work of Follett. These would include:

- *participation*—in work and process design;
- *representation*—all users should be represented in the design group;
- *joint problem solving*—all are equal in decision-making and all should agree on the route to change and problem-solving;
- *freedom of speech*—there should be face-to-face communication and honest exchanges of views, solutions will be obtained through integration and not compromise;
- *gaining power*—groups should recognise that joint work increases their power in relation to other organisational groups;
- *integration of all factors*—all relevant factors must be considered in the situation;
- *staying together*—groups should maintain their cohesiveness over long periods.

Land (2000) argues that it seems that the sociotechnical philosophy rests on two—perhaps contradictory—premises. The first is the Humanistic Welfare Paradigm. In this view the design of work systems is performed to improve the welfare of employees. Autonomy is encouraged with the development of self-actualisation, empowerment, and the reduction of workplace stress. Many would argue (Land, Detjearuwat, & Smith, 1983; Mumford & Henshall, 1979; Mumford & MacDonald, 1989) that there is an evident link between these principles and organisational bottom-line improvements.

The second view is the Managerial Paradigm. Here, change is intended to improve the organisational performance that is defined as:

- added shareholder value;
- improved competitiveness;
- bottom-line improvements; and
- responsiveness to change (we see here links to what knowledge management theorists argue will be the outcome of initiating KMS).

In this paradigm sociotechnical change methods will lead to a more 'contented' workforce and thus improved performance that can be measured against these targets. It should be noted here, as it is of relevance to the design of knowledge management systems, that the sociotechnical approach to system design recognises the importance of different interest groups and a multivariate set of objectives. These include social, technical, economic, and organisational objectives. Thus the sociotechnical approach includes social requirements analysis when attempting to understand an organisation and its system needs. Additionally, it requires user community participation and full involvement in any system design—of prime importance in the design of a KMS.

Beekun (1989) discussed the idea that when the social and technical systems of an organisation achieve consonance, the organisation can expect to experience higher productivity. Job satisfaction, together with lower absenteeism amongst the workforce and lower job turnover, can also be expected. He was concerned, however, that the literature up to the date of his paper had tended to concentrate on the positive episodes of sociotechnical intervention. It seemed that no contingency model had been developed against which the effects could be tested. He therefore decided to carry out a meta-analysis to look at the impact of moderator variables that may have had unintended effects on the outcomes of the change processes being reviewed.

The emphasis on workgroup autonomy comes from the principle of minimum critical specification. This is the idea that the workgroup will operate better if it requires no external supervision or control of how to function and also little or no internal control. This type of autonomy requires the workers to be multi-skilled, to be able to choose their own co-workers, to set their own schedules and pace of work (Wall et al., 1986). Most groups, given sufficient opportunity, motivation, and authority, will make improvements to their working methods, processes, and general situation without the need for external intervention. They develop their own knowledge and skills out of interest and in so doing, develop those of the group, thus enhancing its capabilities and potential.

Beekun looked at 17 sociotechnical interventions reported in the literature and discovered that increases in productivity were obtained if certain factors were involved. These factors—the formation of autonomous (rather than semi-autonomous) groups, increasing monetary incentives, and the fact that the intervention occurred outside of the United States—increased the success of the interventions. However, changes in technology, whether there was a sociotechnical intervention or not, resulted in drops in productivity. Sociotechnical interventions that gave workers as much autonomy as possible but did not change the technical system were in fact the most productive. Productivity increases were not limited to blue-collar workers but were also to be found in white-collar workers. However, the increase in productivity was greatest where smaller numbers of workers were impacted by the change. So it seemed that small changes produce less resistance and increase the effectiveness of the intervention.

The results, according to Beekun's analysis relating to pay increases, would seem to be moderated by the intention—where pay increases were intended to equalise pay rates or encourage cooperation, they may have had more impact on the workers concerned and their productivity.

In Beekun's view, the fad for process reengineering tended to underestimate the actions required to transform the way employees behave and work with one another. Changing work structures does not automatically change working practices. The lack of semi-autonomous teams and multi-skilling seems to impact more on productivity than on process-review. With reengineering interventions there seems to be a failure to implant collective responsibility into the organisational culture. Values and behaviours that indicate mutual respect and loyalty are important, he says. Additionally, physical proximity also seems to be important in strengthening the ties that bind groups together. It would also seem that knowledge-sharing initiatives and places are important for process improvement (Marjchrak & Wang, 1996). The group needs to be enabled and thus responsible for designing their own work, to experiment with ideas without fear of failure, and to care enough to undertake these processes. The role of managers thus changes from supervisors to facilitators and to coaches or mentors.

However, work by psychologists also found that there are significant issues with the management of interdisciplinary teams. In particular there is the issue of inter-professional conflict and differential power bases (Teram, 1991). How to recognise and reconcile power attributes of the various professions is problematical. There is a preoccupation in these interdisciplinary teams on how to enhance individual role clarification, which detracts from the fundamental question as to whether the interdisciplinary team should have been established in the first place. Boundary clarifications are important for these teams, and are related to the task requirements and the amount of control that the team needs to exert on its outcomes. We will take up these points relating to group work in the later discussions on communities of practice.

Beekun (1989) also discovered that the effects of the sociotechnical intervention persisted in the organisation. The productivity increases levelled off or were slightly decreased some 8-12 months after the intervention, but then started to increase again after 30 months.

The inside U.S. versus outside U.S. findings were interesting and may relate to underlying political, cultural, and social characteristics. Where workers believed in the sociotechnical ideals (and perhaps also participation and union solidarity), perhaps one might expect such interventions to have a greater effect. Thus interventions outside the U.S. ended up to be more successful, in Beekun's terms, than those inside the U.S. He attributed this to the socialistic movements and ideals that were more common in Europe, for instance.

An important tenet of the sociotechnical movement is that employees should have the right to personal development and learning opportunities. In addition, it advocates organisational systems that reward self-management. Organisations that do not reward such ways of managing have found that the introduction of new technology has not brought them the improvements in speed of production or process completion that they desired. Shenandoah Life Insurance, for instance, found that the introduction of new technology to process claims produced an increase of 50% in the number claims being processed only when they combined the technology with semiautonomous teams that cut across three functions (Hoerr, Pollock, & Whiteside, 1986). Hoerr et al. claim that plants (factories) in the U.S. (and they quote a number of blue chip companies such as Xerox, Honeywell, Gaines Food, Proctor and Gamble)—designed using sociotechnical methods, and run with semiautonomous teams—produce 30-

50% more than their conventional counterparts. These teams have no first-line supervisor, determine their own pace within management-set parameters, schedule their own vacations, are involved in the hiring and firing of team members and decide when they qualify for pay increases.

Currently, the Tavistock Institute in the UK still supports the efforts to develop the sociotechnical approach to work design along with the British Computer Society's Sociotechnical Specialist Group. In the U.S., too, there is an active group of change consultants (the Sociotechnical Round Table) that operates using the well-tested methods of participation and democratic involvement in change initiatives.

3.5   Communities of Practice and Teams—The Sociotechnical View

The sociotechnical view of work organisation has long put forward, as discussed above, the concept of team working across functions as the better way of organisational design. With knowledge work on the increase, it has become apparent that, at the very least, communities of practice (as they have become known) are ways to share knowledge across functions and thus improve processes and outcomes.

CoPs define a particular type of social relationship, and as such may be understood through concepts drawn from social theory, as discussed in more detail in the next chapter. They can be defined as a group of individuals who may be co-located or distributed, motivated by a common set of interests, and willing to develop and share both tacit and explicit knowledge.

CoPs only exist and operate successfully when they trust the other members of that CoP. Knowledge is connected and is a bond between the social and professional links of practitioners in particular areas that enable them to share experience and understanding. These bonds are not fostered by organisations, but exist despite them, although organisations can support them. They are easy to destroy but difficult to construct. Membership, and choice, of a community needs to be voluntary, otherwise members may not participate in the knowledge sharing that is their raison-d'etre.

Each CoP can be a focus of learning and competence for the organisation. Much of an organisation's work can be facilitated and (conversely) frustrated through these CoPs. Some authors have called CoPs "the shop floor of human capital," and thus they are strongly related to the notion of intellectual capital (IC). Many theorists consider IC as a combination of customer capital, organisational capital, and human capital. Here, human capital serves as a collective term for an organisation's core competences, the skills and knowledge that the enterprise draws on to create and innovate in order to remain competitive. This development of human capital can thus take place in a CoP. But CoPs are not yet common in all organisations and are often not fully supported either through technology or through the organisational structure. Yet they are one way that (semi) autonomous team working has infiltrated into organisations that might otherwise be inimical to that idea.

Teamwork, whether semiautonomous or not, has major issues to overcome. The management style of operating and decision-making needs to change to become participative, which can be difficult for some managers to cope with. Within the team too there can be tensions and conflict. Not all teams work well together, personality clashes do occur and need to be dealt with. Wesley Vestal (2003) discusses what he considers are the 10 traits required for a successful CoP. Drawing from previous work by the APQC (McDermott, 2001), he claims that CoPs are typically held together by common interest in a body of knowledge and are "driven by a desire and need to share problems, experiences, insights, templates, tools, and best practices." These traits combine both social and technological elements. For instance, he argues that there should be an easy-to-follow knowledge-sharing process; a recognition plan for participants (for personal development and evaluation); an appropriate technology environment for knowledge exchange, retrieval, and collaboration; and the relevant tools for communication.

Self-managing teams became more common in organisations in the 1990s as a way to improve productivity, quality, and morale, and to reduce costs. The characteristics of self-managing teams include the responsibility for making a product, or providing a service, and self-discretion over work assignment, methods, and scheduling. Whilst not all CoPs are teams (for process work or product development), teams should have CoP attributes in order to perform knowledge sharing and work design. This is illustrated in the case examples discussed later in this chapter.

Theoretical writings from a number of authors have put forward the idea that there are a number of attributes that that improve the task design for groups. These attributes are that there should be:

1.   *variety*—multi-skilling prevents boredom and monotony, and builds flexibility;

2.   *identity*—building an identity encourages a sense of collective responsibility and self-regulation of variances;

3.   *significance*—motivation to care about the outcome of the work process increases cooperation when the outcome is imbued with a sense of significance;

4.   *autonomy*—increases the ownership and responsibility of members to the process and also enables the group to make decisions under changing environmental conditions; the multi-skilling also enables them to flex attributes and change working practices to fit with the environmental changes;

5.   *feedback*—understanding and knowing the results of work processes enables groups to monitor their progress against targets and improve their performance (Cohen, 1996).

It is inherent in the concept of self-regulating groups that there is no external leadership, so an external supervisor can only encourage and mentor groups so that they develop the necessary characteristics, these characteristics being that of self-evaluation, self-goal setting, self-reinforcement, self-criticism, self-expectation, and rehearsal of activities before practical implementation. This would, of course, align closely with the concepts behind the Learning Organisation—for these self-regulating groups must be groups that learn and thus the organisation will ultimately learn.

Groups consist of a balance between homogeneity and heterogeneity in their terms of skills, expertise, and stability. The right mix of expertise is clearly important and is related to the size of the group—the smallest possible number that includes all the relevant skills is easiest to coordinate. Such a group also needs to be relatively stable so that time is not lost orientating new members to culture, values, and beliefs.

Group norms are thus an important part of self-regulating groups. An effective self-regulating group will have a high degree of agreement about what is acceptable behaviour within the group. They will also have the belief that the group is (and can continue to be) effective in the way that they perform, coordinate their activities, and innovate as required.

Self-regulating groups will clearly work best in an organisation with devolved decision-making structures and a significant amount of employee participation. These teams need power to make decisions. They also require information about processes, customers, competitors, organisational changes, etc., as they feel that they need them. They should be offered rewards that are related not just to performance, but also the development of capability. They will need training to develop the required expertise and skills and resources as required. Self-regulating teams then should be highly motivated and continuously learning and sharing knowledge within the team.

According to a paper by Sapsed and colleagues (2002), the teamwork and knowledge management fields are increasingly converging. Team-working has risen to prominence in an attempt to alleviate the issues that past knowledge management approaches that are considered excessively 'hard' or 'IT domi-nated' have discovered. In addition, knowledge sharing in teams is emphasised as the means for the transfer of tacit or sticky knowledge. In teams, it has been argued (see also Nonaka & Takeuchi, 1995), the ideas of individuals can be articulated, challenged, refined, and converted into organisational knowledge, and thus eventually, new products, processes, or services.

CoPs differ from traditional team-working approaches in that they are most likely to be cross-functional and multi-skilled. They therefore align themselves closely to the sociotechnical ideals of inclusivity and fluid boundaries. CoP members will be drawn from those who wish to involve themselves and who desire to share knowledge and learn from others about a specific topic, wherever in an organisation (and in some cases, outside the organisation too) they may be located. Functional position is irrelevant; topic knowledge or interest is all that is necessary to join a CoP. The diversity of a CoP's population may encourage creativity and problem solving, and linkages to external communities will also enhance their activities. CoPs are the legitimate place for learning through participation. They additionally provide an identity for the participator in terms of social position, knowledge attributes, and ownership. CoPs will have a shared domain and domain language, and some members may become apprentices as they are acculturated into this domain and knowledge development. It also important when establishing CoPs to think about the embedded habits, assumptions, and work practices or cultural norms that exist in the organisation.

Shared understanding and shared culture allow the use of such linguistic idiosyncrasies as anaphora, deitic utterances and ellipses. These linguistic devices are used in 'everyday' speech; but note that these linguistic usages are broken by the intervention of a computer. Communication—and how and where, as well when people communicate—are extremely important in relation to information sharing. Anaphora are rhetorical devices used at the beginning of successive sentences such that each sentence begins with the same word or phrase, or the use of a word such as 'it' or 'do' to avoid repetition of a preceding word or phrase. Deitic utterances relate a word to the time or place of utterance and are personal pronouns, demonstrative adverbs, etc.; examples would include 'in front of', 'behind', 'now then', 'once', 'this', 'that', etc. Ellipses are phrases or sentences where words are missed and implied, and therefore require shared knowledge and understanding to be filled in.

Communities are also the places that provide us with different perspectives and lenses through which to view the world. CoPs have become increasingly important as a means of information sharing within professions and of collaboration with like-minded people. CoPs may also be increasingly important due to organisational complexities, including subsidiaries, mergers, and acquisitions. But communities may not yet be possible in every workplace environment. The evidence from the workplace is that ICT-supported strategies for CoP development are better than ICT-led strategies (Kling & Courtright, 2003) and that the sociotechnical approach is valid for CoP development. ICT has different roles to play as knowledge management systems are established and evolve in organisations—it moves from being the underlying infrastructure to the linking mechanism, to the support mechanism (Pan & Leidner, 2003). Yet without an understanding of the underlying work practices and organisational social and cultural aspects, the ICT support will not match the specific elements that make this organisational culture unique and thus will be ineffective.

Many organisational cultures are still not yet ready for this process. Scarbrough (2003) argues that there are four key behaviours that drive collaboration—the knowledge web, the knowledge ladder, the knowledge torch, and the knowledge fortress. It is important to remember, he argues, that one organisation may contain one or more of these behaviours within its different units and functional areas or subsidiaries. This would mean that one knowledge management strategy will not fit all organisational areas.

In Scarbrough's terms the knowledge web connects people with others through social networks. Knowledge is thus valued because it connects people to others. Social networks are the key factor in knowledge sharing and will determine how knowledge is shared through the ICT networks. The use of the ICT mirrors the social networks—who connects to whom, who is the hub of the network, etc.—that exist outside of the technology. Successful CoPs will mirror these social networks and thus strengthen existing behaviours rather than undermine them.

The knowledge ladder is where knowledge is shared in the pursuit of status. In ladder situations, Scarbrough states, there is a risk that knowledge becomes a personal possession and so sharing does not take place (knowledge is power). To prevent knowledge hoarding, the behaviour patterns of the organisational members need to be re-adjusted through rewards (and punishments by a lack of rewards) for knowledge sharing. Some organisations make end-of-project bonuses dependent on an end-of-project review of best (and worst) practices, for instance. This can also be done perhaps by forming social networks and a revaluation of knowledge perceptions in the organisation.

A knowledge torch allows people to follow the light of a leader. Individuals gain a role model and the organisation needs to reinforce the new behavioural patterns in appropriate means. Again suitable rewards and sanctions may be applied that will encourage the formation of relevant communities and leaders. The final behaviour pattern that Scarbrough considers is that of the knowledge fortress, where knowledge is considered a source of protection against external threats. Here there is a negative motivation—the desire to maintain the status quo. Groups will refuse to share knowledge in order to maintain their territory—they will repel new ideas and maintain their silo walls. The only way to break these types of behaviours is to encourage cross-functional teams and collaborative working—to build trust through communities operating together, to share common problems using sociotechnical principles to support these activities.

The next section tells the story of how two organisations have developed communities and the role of the ICT in their support and work.

3.6   A Sociotechnical CoP—
The Abbey National

The story below is taken from two articles written by Bradburn and colleagues (2002a, 2002b). It is the story of how the Abbey National introduced knowledge management in 1999 in order to achieve its vision of becoming the UK's principal financial services organisation.

The corporate values of the Abbey ensured that their considered way forward into knowledge management was through openness and approachability. They therefore saw communities, and partnerships in teams within these communities, as a major and underpinning necessity for the programme. To the Abbey and its Group Knowledge Manager, Phillip Ramsell, tacit knowledge is the hidden company asset and knowledge management is the mechanism to tap into this hidden asset. Knowledge management to Ramsell applies to the processes, people, and systems implemented to promote collaborative work and knowledge sharing—a sociotechnical viewpoint. The challenge is to create a culture in which knowledge sharing is encouraged and rewarded. The organisation needs to develop the view that the collective knowledge of a group is more powerful than that of an individual.

The means by which this vision was to be achieved in the Abbey was through the use of communities. These communities could:

- Create a working environment for people needing to collaborate across business areas or geographical locations. At the same time they eliminate the current constraints of data sharing associated with working in multiple locations.

- Address the issue of who needs to know or who may have an interest in knowing, by making everything available to those who needed it and to those who might seek it.

- Provide an insight into the experiences and interests of people to assist in searching for specific experiences or for selecting appropriate community members.

- Provide a foundation of experience and learning, from both successes and failures, on which to base future communities.

- Simplify the communication structure across a group of people working towards a common goal.

- Encourage the exchange of ideas and thus provide a breeding ground for new ideas.

In selecting their support technology, the Abbey has used a system called *oneTeam* (their internal name for a system known as iTeam from Documentum™). This system provides a Web-browser environment for creating and managing communities to support and promote knowledge sharing. These communities can be either formal (task focused) or informal (general interest focused), and membership can be granted from across the whole oneTeam population of users. Membership of communities are held in each member's personal details, thereby providing an overview of their experiences and interests.

If people are to truly change the way that they currently work, then there has to be a tangible benefit for them on a personal level. The Abbey has found that the creation and maintenance of both formal and informal communities of practice acts as a way to encourage people to alter their behaviours.

One example of a formal community that was developed is where a cross-functional group was created with representatives from across the group and its subsidiaries. Internal consultants were invited to participate in the community and share their experiences. As a result, a formal approach has now been documented regarding the procurement of external consultants and shared throughout the Abbey Group via the business specialists represented in this community. Cost savings for this activity are being tracked through the use of internal consultants and in-house expertise, and tracking logs document the work being undertaken. The Abbey has also developed best-practice guidelines from this activity. The consultancy community now supports any business area with a need for a consultant by providing a standard group-wide agreement and feedback in the firm being used.

Community members are encouraged, in the Abbey, to meet on a face-to-face basis once a month and have been allocated time to do this by their respective managers. Using the collaborative *oneTeam* software, members can conduct both synchronous and asynchronous dialogue threads. This enables them to get the answers they need, when they need them, even though they are based in different parts of the organisation. By employing these techniques, members feel more inclined to contribute their knowledge as well as consume it from others—*you only get out what you put in*. Members who in the past had never met or spoken, now have access to a wealth of knowledge and information from across all business areas in the group. The result of this is that the consultancy community has increased in size from a core group of eight, to developing specialised sub-teams that recognise a need for their involvement. Through the advocacy of these and other community members, the creation of cross-functional communities is now coming to the forefront of the Abbey National way of working.

A contrasting case story of communities at work and the role of ICT is now told.

3.7   A Charitable CoP

This voluntary sector organisation was established more than 60 years ago and has its headquarters in the UK. It also has a significant international presence, focussing on the relief of poverty and suffering in six major world regions. The organisation devotes around £100 million a year to its relief, development, and lobbying campaigns. This story is based on Coakes, Bradburn, and Sugden (2003).

Knowledge management was introduced into this organisation about five years ago when a strategic intent document was produced, which prioritised four main areas. One of these prioritised areas was KM. What the charity means by KM is making use of the knowledge and experiences of staff. In practice what this means is that one person's knowledge becomes information for the next person to assimilate and add to his or her own library of experiential learning.

Experiential learning relates to the sticky knowledge residing in peoples' heads. Managing this knowledge means surfacing it (making it explicit in some way) and using it to build further organisational knowledge by motivating people to share their experiences and learning. Experiential knowledge, especially in terms of projects, can be converted into fluid knowledge so that others can share an understanding of what went right. It can also be used to discover what went wrong, and why things went wrong, thereby enabling the organisation to ensure it does it better next time. Thus fluid knowledge can be determined in such a way that it enables organisational learning to occur.

Knowledge management was written into the organisation's strategic plan and was allocated funds of £200,000 for a planned three-year development project. A number of initiatives were launched in mid-2000 and focussed on three areas. One of these initiatives involved lunch time discussion groups on key areas of focus for the charity's overseas work programme. This is an informal CoP that operates without technology assistance.

A second knowledge management initiative centres on developing an Intranet site concerned with land rights. This has information and articles drawn from white and grey literature, and provides links to other resources on land rights issues around the world. The aim is to encourage international dialogue. There is a hyperlink to this site from the organisation's main website.

This initiative has become by default a community of interest and research. Academic institutions are accessing it for research purposes. Unfortunately there is a downside to this initiative—the lack of ICT connectivity in developing countries. Consequently, many of the target communities for this initiative do not yet have access to the Internet. However, connectivity seems to be sector dependent to some extent, and in the health care sector, communities of practice involved with HIV/AIDS are successfully using the Internet to get experiences from different AIDS work initiatives around the world. This mode of knowledge distribution is enabling different health workers in different countries to communicate and share ideas and experiences.

With IC being developed and built upon through knowledge management activities, and enabled by ICT, the charity is evolving as a stronger international lobbying and advocacy force. The focus here is on not only trying to ameliorate the humanitarian situation at the grassroots, but also on trying to promote change at the world political level and make countries, or multilateral organisations, accept the need for new policies—the aim being to work from the top down and from the bottom up. The organisational advantage in this context is that the charity's advocacy work is increasingly informed and based on its grassroots work with overseas projects.

The charity has a lobbying office in Washington, DC, where its various overseas divisions feed their fluid knowledge to a resident team responsible for lobbying organisations like the World Bank, the International Monetary Fund, and the United Nations. Drawing on its human capital from around the world, through these knowledge management activities, results in much more contact and collaboration with other voluntary sector organisations such as Christian Aid, Action Aid, and other like-minded charities.

Knowledge management has now transformed the organisation's model of communication so that its UK headquarters no longer functions as the hub for a number of channels. Communication is now direct and offers more opportunity for collaboration and interaction between different countries. They can now share sticky knowledge by means of virtual communication. Communities have thus become a mode of operation throughout this organisation that has transformed its way of working and knowledge transfer.

We now look explicitly at the academic and practical linkages between sociotechnology and knowledge management.

3.8 Knowledge Management and Sociotechnical Thinking

There has been very little written in the theoretical literature that explicitly links these two concepts (this is also true of social theory, which is addressed in the next chapter). Searching through the databases, one encounters only a few conference papers and the occasional journal article. The two authors that do seem to have considered this relationship in most depth are Pan and Scarbrough in their work on Buckman Laboratories. Accordingly it seemed appropriate to review briefly their ideas here, without looking at their case study in any depth, as their work (1998, 1999) covers this in detail.

In their 1998 article, Pan and Scarbrough develop a sociotechnical model to highlight the interplay between the organisational context and knowledge management tools. They base their arguments on two previous articles by Spender (1992) and Starbuck (1992) that provide for a broad view that relates to the interplay between social and technical factors. Applying the sociotechnical perspectives as discussed earlier in this chapter, and using the three layers of knowledge management systems according to Bressand and Distler (1995), they summarise the model as follows:

Layer 1—Infrastructure: This provides the physical components for communication between the network members.

Layer 2—Infostructure: This provides the formal rules that govern the communicational exchanges within the actor-network. It provides the cognitive resources such as metaphors and common language that are used to make sense of the communicational exchanges.

Layer 3—Infoculture: This provides the background knowledge that is taken for granted and embedded in the social relations and work processes. This infoculture provides constraints on knowledge and information sharing.

Thus we see that management has a role in providing the necessary elements for these knowledge management systems to operate. In addition, the existing organisational processes and operations, as well as social relations, will impact on the interaction that takes place. Managers, as Majchrzak and Wang (1996) say, need also to change their own positions. They need to see that collective responsibility is "an attitude, a value, a concern. It means taking an interest in one's colleagues and in improving the outcome of mutual (as opposed to individual) efforts" (p. 65). They argue against the functional mindset of many organisations and urge managers not to look to best practice, but rather to consult with employees as to what is required in order to work well together. Managers, they say, should consider not only the possibilities but also the constraints provided by technology, work processes, existing organisational culture, and the organisation's strategic mission. The culture should be developed to encourage compromise, experimentation, and improvement. Knowledge sharing would obviously be the first step towards such improvements.

In their 1999 article, Pan and Scarbrough make the argument for a sociotechnical view more strongly. They cite firstly Kogut and Zander (1992), who look at the explicit and tacit recipes of employee interactions to find a firm's know-how; and secondly Grant (1991) who declares that the key to meeting customers' needs and enhancing a firm's competitive position lies in the compatibility between the social and technical subsystems. Pan and Scarbrough emphasise that a redefinition of the relationship between the environmental and technical subsystems is required whenever new information technologies are introduced. Organisational change is required whether these new systems are for knowledge management or for other purposes. Of course, sociotechnical thinking has long been discussing how to undertake organisational change under these circumstances.

In this 1999 article, Pan and Scarbrough extend the sociotechnical perspective using Scarbrough (1995). They build on the existing precepts of the open systems approach, the 'best match' idea, and redundancy principles to concern themselves with:

> *"The subtle and diffuse structuring of behaviour and perceptions arising from information flows and communication systems"* (p. 361).

They also comment that the socio of sociotechnology needs to encompass the socially constructed aspects of knowledge within an organisation, saying also that the systems perspective needs to place more emphasis on the processual and emergent aspects of the interplay between technology and the organisation. Thus they argue that a critical function of the sociotechnical account of knowledge management in an organisation is to understand the social relationships within which the tacit knowledge, in particular, is embedded. This would emphasise the need to explore the CoPs within an organisation and their internal and social networks. They conclude their article with the statement:

> *"An equal emphasis on technology, structures, and cultural factors might help...management to identify the facilitating and inhibiting factors which influence the success of management"* (p. 374).

Other authors who have considered the linkage of STS thinking and knowledge management include Coakes (2002), Meriluoto (2003), Okunoye (2002, 2003), and Stebbins and Shani (1998).

Coakes (2002) argues that the goal of sociotechnical design is to produce a system capable of self-modification, of adapting to change, and of making the most of the creative capacities of the individual for the benefit of the organisation. In the sociotechnical classification of information systems, as discussed by Nurminen (1987), the IT system interfaces between the social and technical systems for the users by using user-friendly means of communication and action in information tasks. Knowledge is considered to be objective but instrumental. The social system in sociotechnical terms is here usually considered to be the attributes of people (attitudes, skills, values, etc.), the relationship amongst them, the reward systems, and the authority structures. It is these attributes that provide the motivation. The technical systems in Nurminen's terms include the processes, tasks, and technology needed to perform the organisation's operations. So technology provides the capability. Managers are required to nurture a learning environment. They need to have a vision of how ICT systems can be used to support the aspirations of capturing knowledge in order for successful knowledge management to take place.

Managing knowledge, with a sociotechnical perspective, has a wide ranging necessity to manage the organisation through continuous change and a process of continuous learning supported, where appropriate, by technology. Allee (1997) would also tell us that in a quantum worldview, with new thinking, motivation comes from intrinsic creativity where knowledge is collective; life thrives on cooperation with workers being multi-faceted, always learning; and being managed through insight and participation. In other words, through using the sociotechnical principles to design organisational ways of working.

Meriluoto (2003) reported to the ROCKET workshop at ICE about finding a Sociotechnical Golden Mean at Nokia. The main points of his presentation relate to the idea that the cutting edge of knowledge is always changing so the real task is to connect people to people and to ensure that this connection reaches the knowledge level. There is a need to mix the tacit (which in his terms involves holding meetings, having discussions, and rotating jobs) with explicit knowledge. Sharing of explicit knowledge is to be performed through documentation, but in the right proportion and with the right scheduling. Meriluoto argues that using communication technology alone only brings you to the information level. He argues that the sociotechnical approach to knowledge management combines the best approaches of system theory and the humanistic approaches to knowledge management, to find this golden mean.

Okunoye (2002) refers to the Leavitt (1965) diamond that identified four variables in the organisational system—the task, structure, technology, and human elements that interact and need to be considered to undertake organisational change. These four variables are what underpin the work of Pan and Scarbrough discussed above. The diamond would indicate that the knowledge processes should also be coordinated and balanced along the IT infrastructure, with people being the connecting link. Okunoye argues that most recent frameworks proposed for KM include sociotechnical components, giving as examples Alavi (1997), the APQC (1996), and Sena and Shani (1999) in relation to their work on intellectual capital and KM.

Shani, writing with Stebbins (1998), discusses the origins of sociotechnical systems theory and the application of these theories to non-routine work situations. In this article they concern themselves with the organisational design process and the necessity to link the three organisational sub-systems to provide organisational support for non-routine work. The three sub-systems they discuss are the:

- *social*—the people with knowledge, skills, and attitudes (humans);
- *technical*—inputs, and the technology that converts these inputs into outputs; and
- *environment*—the customers, competitors, and other outside forces.

They stress the importance of participation in the design process, especially of the typically autonomous knowledge workers (rather than the executives). It is necessary, they say, to discover these workers' values, as high involvement leads to high commitment in the design process. McKinlay (2002) would agree. He argues that one of the critical weaknesses of the knowledge management projects he investigated was that passive resistance was sufficient to limit the impact of the systems in practice. He also found that there was an over-reliance on technological development without a corresponding development of social processes.

Few organisations expect knowledge management to lead to new ways of working; instead they are looking for increased market share and additional business opportunities. Xerox, who we look at below where we discuss one of its knowledge sharing initiatives, says that knowledge sharing tools and practices form the core of businesses. For Xerox, knowledge management builds on the best ideas of workers in the pursuit of new business value. This means that there is likely to be increased profits and reduced costs, but not increased share prices, as a direct result of knowledge management practices, although there may be some indirect effects. Such an internal focus means that long-term benefits such as increases in intellectual capital are not realised or understood (intellectual capital being rooted in the people element of KM). Knowledge management returns are often seen in terms of ROI (return on investment) rather than human issues (KPMG, 1999). Note that there is an ongoing debate relating to how to measure and value intellectual capital that is outside the scope of this book. It is claimed in the KPMG report that 'failures' in knowledge management initiatives are often caused by:

- a lack of user uptake due to lack of communication;
- a failure to integrate knowledge management into everyday working practices;
- a lack of time to learn how to use systems or that the systems are too complicated;
- a lack of training;
- little benefit is felt by the individual user;
- senior management apparently does not champion the initiative;
- numerous technical problems.

In addition, 'successful' programmes also suffered from:

- the lack of time to share knowledge;
- a failure to use knowledge effectively;
- the difficulty of capturing tacit knowledge.

Thus we see that KMSs have largely, to date, had a significant failure rate and that this has been attributed by consultants (KPMG, 1999, 2000) to their lack of people optimisation and their technological bias. It would seem therefore that many firms have not taken the sociotechnical approach and that this has inhibited their success.

Having identified above the implications of the word 'sociotechnical' as being a way of implementing technology in the social environment, we can now go on to look at sociotechnical systems (STSs) and knowledge in the organisation.

3.9 Knowledge and Sociotechnical Systems

STSs are the systems that operate in our organisations and our working life that link our human bodies to technical bodies of various types.

A simple example of a sociotechnical system at work in our everyday life is that act of joining a bus queue outside any university. Let's take a university in Central London as an example and let one of our authors tell the story.

Bus stops in Central London are now high-tech, that is to say, most bus stops have an electronic notice board that notifies the people in the queue of which buses are coming, their destination and when they will arrive (in 2 minutes time), and where they are in the queue of buses (second). In theory, the electronic tracking of buses should mean that buses are spread out across their routes as they can be contacted by radio to slow down, speed up, etc., and should therefore no longer travel in convoys. In theory also, the electronic notice board is updated in real time and thus should be accurate. The practice however, as one might expect, is somewhat different. A couple of weeks ago, I was standing at a bus stop waiting for a bus, the number 27 (these are fictional numbers for the point of the story). They are supposed to come every 10 minutes. As I stood there, the notice board showed many buses arriving within the 10 minutes but no 27. It identified that the next bus was a number 24 due in 2 minutes, and the third bus was also a 24 due in 7 minutes. Sure enough a 24 came in 2 minutes and was promptly passed by the next 24, which did not stop at our bus-stop but went straight past, and came before the number 2, which was due second. So the third bus came before the second and well before the 7 minutes! Then 9 (yes I counted them) number 28 buses arrived, first one bus, then two in tandem, then another single one, and then five behind each other! All within a space of 30 minutes, and yes, I was still waiting for my number 27. True, it had not yet appeared on the electronic notice board. Finally my bus was announced, 7 minutes away.

The other buses on the notice board got closer, the time to arrival grew shorter, but my bus got farther away—now it was 9 minutes to arrival. Then 4 minutes and then 5 minutes—was my bus moving backwards? I checked my watch and compared it to the notice board. Sure enough, after 10 minutes my bus arrived. When discussing this with my fellow travellers also waiting for the 27, I found this not to be an unusual situation. It seems that electronic tagging of buses did not work and regular bus travellers (of which I am not one) ignored the notice boards in their entirety and relied on past experience and stoicism to catch their bus. It was well known amongst these regular bus users that due to predictable traffic congestion across the various routes, at known times of day, certain buses would either catch up to each other or be delayed. Think about how long it takes to process some 60 or more people boarding a bus at Victoria Station which can be the situation after a train has just arrived, as opposed to one or two people at other stops. What happens when a second bus arrives at that same bus stop? Everyone has already boarded the first bus, which will be travelling slowly as there are many people getting on and off at many stops; inexorably therefore, the second bus will catch it up and maybe overtake.

We see sociotechnical systems operating everywhere that humans need to interact with technology. Sometimes, as at the bus stop, we ignore the technology. Other times, we have to use it. How many coffee machines in the workplace do you know of that are not regularly thumped or kicked when tomato soup is dispensed from the hot chocolate nozzle, and your coffee comes black and unsugared when you wanted milk and sugar (or vice versa!)?

Often, as in this case, the technology frustrates and angers us in its failure to perform a simple task. So much so that we learn that if we circumvent the approved manner of use and thump the machine 'just there', it produces free coffee for all. This misuse of technology is rampant across our societies and organisations. It extends to the use of many of the information systems that we work with in companies to officially do our jobs. Take our use of email. How many of us, hands on hearts, can truthfully say that we have never emailed friends or family using the firm's email system, during work time?

So what can we learn from these examples of sociotechnical systems? Why is it important to consider information systems in their context? Well, from the bus stop example, we can learn that technology does not solve contextual problems. It was initiated to keep passengers informed and to permit better scheduling of buses. It fails in both these aspects (though not in its entirety). What has become important (in fact it was always so) is contextual knowledge about the route buses travel.

Knowledge of the regular occurrences (such as when and where the schools on the route disgorge pupils who take the bus and thus slow down progress and mean that there will be no seats available); knowledge about special hazards of the day (a protest march that has meant a route diversion); knowledge that permits the regular, but not the occasional, bus user to know within a reasonable degree of certainty how long they can expect to wait, irrespective of what the technology might imply—much of this knowledge will be passed on informally, in conversations at the bus-stop: "Oh it's reached St Mary's now and it's 3:45pm—it'll take a while there, there are a lot of pupils getting on coming this way, and the cars picking the others up always slow it down." So although, the information system says the bus is 4 minutes away, the reality is that it will be 9 or 10 minutes before it will arrive.

What do we learn from the coffee machine example? We learn that technology fails or at least that it does not necessarily provide us with the expected outcome. After all, if we had wanted tomato soup, we wouldn't have pressed the hot chocolate button (however, if this is a regular as opposed to an occasional occurrence, we will learn to modify our behaviour to fit that of the technology's). We learn that technology that does not provide us with the expected outcome builds frustration and anger, and that we learn to circumvent the system—the thump that provides us with free coffee, or the kettle hidden in the desk drawer.

We learn from the use of email systems that organisations can either tolerate our misdemeanours or attempt to control them (which will not endear them to us). Thus we see that, except in the cases where computers run the factory from design to production, technical systems in firms interact with social systems. We also see that humans acting in these social systems interact with more or less enjoyment with the technology according to its ability to fulfil their needs.

Sociotechnical design has become, for some practitioners, a philosophy of organisational change with sociotechnical principles having become an underlying backbone of the paradigm. These principles are enshrined in the work of Cherns (1976, 1987). Initially, Cherns conceived of nine principles that underpinned the sociotechnical design of organisational change, but in his later work he added a tenth principle. Below are these later 10 principles with explanations:

1. *Compatibility:* Design has to satisfy an array of objectives which may conflict, and therefore decisions must be reached by consensus through participation and not by power plays.

2. *Minimal Critical Specification:* Success has been measured less by design quality than by the quantity of our own ideas and preferences that are incorporated. Assumptions should be challenged and minimal bound-

aries enforced on design work. The less that is pre-specified as a 'must-have', the more likely that new design will be innovative.

3. *Variance Control:* "The social system is more than an effective system for the control of technical and raw materials variances" (p. 156). Rules are not required outside of what the work-team enforces.

4. *Boundary Location:* "Its essential feature is that boundaries should *not* be drawn so as to impede the sharing of knowledge and learning" (p. 156). Thus one would expect multi-functional teams working across department boundaries to follow the process and to permit teams to complete a process within their own boundaries.

5. *Information Flow:* "The principle of boundary location counsels against, if it cannot absolutely prohibit, the interruption of information or the insertion of loops by misplaced organisational boundaries" (p. 157). Cherns comments here on the information associated with power games that are rife in organisations. If a work-team completes a process within its own boundaries, all the information it requires will be available to it and sticky knowledge can be shared. There will not be the opportunity for information to be with-held or manipulated in favour of other organisational members.

6. *Power and Authority:* People require the power and authority to command the necessary resources for their work and should take the concomitant responsibility for them. Thus work-teams will be able to ask for and receive all the necessary resources to perform their work. They will have devolved decision-making power.

7. *The Multifunction Principle:* "Organisations need to adapt to their environments; elements of organisations need to adapt to their environments of which the most important are usually other organisational elements" (p. 158). There is both an internal and an external environment within which all organisational work is carried out. Processes and organisational work needs to take account of both these environments and to adapt to any changes that are taking place in either.

8. *Support Congruence:* Pay people for what they know, not what they do. "Their value is what is in their heads" (p. 159). This is difficult but relates to differential pay and rewards for learning, and also perhaps knowledge sharing and knowledge creation. Thus organisations may reward people for undertaking courses and training.

9.   *Transitional Organisation:* Organisations are likely to be transforming themselves continuously in reaction to their changing environments. The transitional organisation is both different and also more complex than either the old organisation was, or the new organisation will be, in either situation. The manner of the treatment of staff in selection, for either incorporation into the new organisation or in separation from the old, demonstrates very clearly the adherence to the sociotechnical principles.

10.   *Incompletion:* Cherns also calls this the Forth Bridge principle. He emphasises that all periods of stability are in effect only temporary periods of transition between one state and another. Redesign should be a continuous process and is the function of the self-regulating teams through review, evaluation, and negotiation. This would, of course, contribute to the transitional organisation.

It should be evident that implementing any new or amended system into an organisation is to undertake the process of organisational change.

This is valid whether or not the system contains computers or other technology. Thus the process of involving oneself in the introduction of systems to manage organisational knowledge means also involving oneself in organisational change. As such, one must consider how to implement this change in such a way as to enhance the organisation's capability to retrieve its knowledge. At the same time it is necessary to ensure that organisational members are content to share their knowledge, that they trust each other, and the organisation, sufficiently to do so. Sociotechnical design has the goal of producing a system that is capable of being adaptable to change and that can make the best use of the individual's creative abilities.

Knowledge can also be seen as the capacity of an organisation and its employees to act effectively, thus designing an organisation for effective knowledge management is also designing an organisation sociotechnically. Organisations that have been successful, according to Bhatt (1998), in obtaining benefits from their knowledge management have also been found to coordinate their social relations and their technologies. To manage the knowledge, organisations need to construct a culture and environment of participation and coordination in knowledge sharing. In fact recent surveys by management consultants (see the discussions above) show that changing behaviour is the key implementation problem in knowledge management, not implementing the technology. Knowledge management redefines the power, politics, and information sharing infrastructure that exists in any organisation. It therefore involves changes in work procedures, formal and informal hierarchies, as well as management philosophy and management style. The introduction of knowledge management also means that there is a new set of social relationships that has been forged. These will amend the old relationships and create new along perhaps functional lines and cutting across departmental silos, or even organisational boundaries, through the formation of communities. This must be a challenge to both the change management process and also the existing formal management and reporting ethos.

An example of an organisation that has reformed itself for knowledge management is Xerox.

3.10 Xerox Case Study

This case study was compiled from reports, press releases, articles on the company's website (www.xerox.com), and as supplied by Xerox UK, plus information taken from Brown and Duguid (2000), Storck and Hill (2000), McKenna (1999), and Silverman, Ellul, Yarus, and Zamora (2000).

A number of companies have been cited in the journals and by knowledge management consultancies as being 'excellent' in the field of knowledge management. These companies include Xerox, both in terms of what it has done for its own internal knowledge management and also for what it can offer in knowledge management systems to other companies.

Xerox has stopped being the photocopier company we knew and has become a document management company. Through managing documents and the information therein, companies have been able to improve processes to increase productivity and legal compliance. But is this knowledge management, I hear you ask?

Xerox now has a number of major research centres around the world, including one in Switzerland which works in the knowledge management field, one in the UK, and of course Palo Alto in California, their famous Xerox Parc centre. A major feature of the company's research has been that of human-technology interaction, and so Xerox employs anthropologists to investigate the social and cultural issues relating to technology introduction. This is because, for Xerox, knowledge management is the process of "transforming individual knowledge experiences into knowledge and experience that can be used by the collective organisation. Effective knowledge management has both a social and technical dimension" (Xerox Fact Book, 2002-2003, p. 46).

So in Xerox the management saw the need to start knowledge management with organisational change and communicated this need to the entire organisation. Every Xerox employee participates in a training programme called "Leadership through Quality." This programme looks at and develops sensitivity to group dynamics issues that may limit productivity. A common vocabulary is taught that reinforces the organisational culture and the programme results in a climate of social activism.

Xerox values both individual and collective learning, many employees learning from practising colleagues. Strategic communities have been formed that 'pull' individuals into a learning and knowledge sharing environment. Participation and engagement are dominant modes of activity in these communities. Knowledge sharing practices are embedded into group-work processes. Communities that meet (such as the Alliance, a community of IT management professionals responsible for workstations, servers, and networking hardware) build their agenda by polling members about what they want to learn. They ask members at the end of meetings what they have learnt, and record, post-meeting, the key messages for the larger community. Knowledge sharing thus becomes part of the community processes, and cultural norms operate that may be outside the formal organisational structure. Xerox gives these communities sufficient autonomy to operate outside formal roles and structures. As an example a community's facilitator's prime commitment is to the group rather than the organisation, and a zone of 'safety' may be established where frank, candid (and possibly controversial) discussions can take place without fear of reprisal.

Supporting such communities through technology is not always necessary beyond the use of word processing and email, but sometimes these communities self-organise around particular work-related problems and need assistance to publicise their solutions. Such was the case of the photocopier service representatives. Using an anthropologist, Xerox wanted to discover what the community of service representatives were doing about sharing their knowledge and if technology could be supplied to assist. An anthropologist therefore followed representatives around in their daily working life to discover what they did, how, when, and where. This is what they discovered.

As is to be expected in any large, well-managed organisation, there is a process to be followed when a customer reports a faulty machine. In Xerox, the customer will phone in a fault report which will be documented, and a service representative will be sent to the customer site. Xerox estimates that their technicians make approximately a million service calls a month to maintain printers, copiers, networks, and other aspects of their customer operations. The machine will report an error code, and the service rep had a manual documenting what these codes meant and how to fix the reported problem. The repair processes were hindered by the fact that service manuals were out of date almost as soon as they were printed. These manuals also were created 'in the lab' and not 'in the field', and thus were missing the creative problem-solving solutions that had been improvised (such as the coffee-machine thump…!). So often the documented 'fix' doesn't work. According to service representatives, machines are not so predictable. Each machine has its own idiosyncrasies related to its location and immediate environment, its pattern of use, past (repaired) faults, etc. The process map therefore fails. With no assistance from the manual and no previous experience of this particular fault, a technician is forced to escalate the problem to a technical hotline, thus delaying the repair time and tying up more man-power. However, investigations by the Xerox Parc anthropologists discovered that reps had a unique way of fixing worn or missing routes on their process maps—they went to breakfast. At breakfast together they formed a learning and knowledge sharing community where problems and fixes were discussed constructively and knowledge disseminated. Much of the knowledge sharing came in the form of 'war stories'—stories about problems and solutions, or disasters and triumphs.

The outcome of studying these service representatives in their native environment was the Eureka project. Eureka is a database of hints and tips from the representatives, initially created in France and then rolled out worldwide. However, there are a large number of databases in existence, full of hints and tips of handy knowledge (or maybe not so full, as one issue of such databases is how to persuade people to input their handy hints for others to use, as discussed by Dixon, 2000). What was different about Eureka is the process that tips have to go through before being stored in the database. It took the Xerox researchers a year to discover the right social setting to encourage and facilitate knowledge sharing. At first they tried the normal route of financial incentives. But what Xerox's researchers discovered was that what motivated people was recognition of their expertise. Thus each tip went through a process of peer review before it could be input. Tips are reviewed first locally, and then centrally, before being disseminated worldwide. As in the academic world, peer-reviewed contributions increase an individual's reputation and standing in their community, thus all tips are identified as to their contributor. Thus reinforcement towards further contributions is increased. Recognition and increased community standing appeared to be a greater incentive than monetary or other rewards. Frahman (1999) and Brelade and Harman (2001) comment that change requires not just a reward, but ensuring that people (workers) feel part of the community by having 'their name attached'. Amongst the techniques for changing the work behaviour of the representatives that Xerox implemented therefore were: testimonials from colleagues; mentoring by colleagues; senior management acceptance and identifying new work practices (allowing the individuals to work these out for themselves, individually, rather than imposing a solution).

What Xerox provided, on request, were laptops (which some 90% of their technicians took); CD-ROMs of service manuals; electronic bulletin boards with search engine and repository; off-line capability to search for and to author tips; and standard Web browser access to the knowledge database. It was estimated that by the year 2000, Eureka had saved Xerox around $100 million, through a 5% cost saving in parts and a 5% reduction in the length of repair time. Of the 1,300 service engineers in France, some 250 have authored tips, and now that the system has been rolled out worldwide, there are more than 35,000 solutions from more than 12 countries in the knowledge base. The knowledge base is still growing by some 400 tips per month, and Xerox estimates that the Eureka system solves around 150,000 problems each year (an average of 10 problem solutions per technician).

Whilst Eureka started as a grassroots problem-solving initiative that was later rolled out worldwide, it proved such a success that a knowledge management strategy was felt to be required. This strategy was founded on four major principles:

1.   The company should 'never create the same solution twice'—if a solution already exists, they should use it rather than recreating a new solution. In addition, they should focus on continuously improving 'existing' solutions.

2.   The company should make knowledge easily accessible in real time to their people (workforce), customers, and partners. Solutions should be made available to everyone as soon as they are created.

3. The company should create an environment where the organisation values continuous learning and development for the future.

4. The company should recognise and reward people who benefit the organisation by creating, sharing, and reusing knowledge rather than re-inventing known solutions (Xerox UK).

McDermott (1999) concludes that there are four challenges when building communities such as the Eureka community described above. The first challenge is that of designing the human and information systems that will help the communities think together. The second challenge is to actually develop the communities so that they will share this knowledge. The third challenge is to create an organisational environment that values knowledge, and the final challenge is related to a personal concept of being open to others and willing to share ideas. As we can see, the personal challenge was already overcome by Xerox representatives in their war-story breakfasts. Thus the second challenge was also overcome—the community was already in existence. What Xerox needed was to create the organisational environment and to support the community through human and information systems; this was done through the Eureka project and the peer review. Representatives valued their knowledge and saw that the organisation valued this also—the peer recognition being strategically important here. Again this is a sociotechnical viewpoint.

If we return to the principles for sociotechnology discussed earlier, we see that the Xerox system fulfils the following principles:

- The design of the new Eureka system was compatible with its objectives.

- It also permitted variance control as the representatives judged and inspected their own work through the system of peer review.

- As the boundary was extended through the Eureka system into the wider organisational community, it also fulfilled the principle that boundaries should not interfere with the sharing of knowledge of experience.

- In addition, as technicians were permitted to choose whether or not, and if so, how, they accessed the system, it also fulfilled the principle of power and authority devolved to the most appropriate level. Representatives were given the authority to decide what resources they wished to use and how, in order to undertake their work.

We can also assume that the system permitted the representatives to control the variances that affected their work by providing sufficient feedback and information, and that power games were not played in this instance. To some extent it also, through the peer recognition system, provided support congruence, as it emphasised what people knew, not just what they did, although no tangible reward was offered. Finally, for those who wanted, the Eureka system would provide responsibility, involvement, and growth in their work.

We can thus argue that, to a large extent, the Eureka system was a sociotechnical system as well as a knowledge management system. Remembering that Xerox understood that (in their own words) "knowledge management has both a social and technical dimension." Understanding that a good knowledge management system can be a sociotechnical system allows us to also infer that better knowledge management systems will also be better sociotechnical systems and vice versa. Thus, if we look again at the principles for sociotechnology discussed above, we can make some assumptions as to how they might apply to knowledge management and take us beyond the systems that are purely technical in specification, and that do not take account of the issues of how knowledge is formulated and maintained.

*Table 3.1: Cherns' Principles Adapted for Knowledge Management
(Adapted from Coakes, Willis, & Clarke, 2001)*

Principle	Knowledge Management Explanation
Compatibility	▪ Design for knowledge management has to account for the social construction of knowledge within an organisation. Conflicts may occur as organisational cultures may not be compatible with the sharing of knowledge. ▪ The objectives of the workers may not be in harmony with the objectives of the organisation. Knowledge management does not, however, demand consensus, although power plays are anti-organisational knowledge management, but these objectives may be individually appropriate depending on the organisational culture.
Minimal Critical Specification	▪ Knowledge is fluid and changing. ▪ The technology used and the design of such systems for assistance should also be fluid and capable of change. Any rigidity will stifle the necessary creativity. Rules of what should be done, and how, should be minimal. ▪ Systems should be permissive as opposed to mandatory.
Variance Control	▪ Knowledge management requires that the social system is the controlling factor in deciding what work should be done, how, and by whom according to their requisite knowledge. ▪ Decisions to a high level of independence and self-management of tasks, etc., should be devolved to the knowledge workers.
Boundary Location	▪ Boundaries should not impede the sharing of knowledge. ▪ The organisation structure should be such that knowledge can flow freely and easily as required, to where required.
Information Flow	▪ For knowledge management to work well, there must be no organisational barriers to the sharing of information and knowledge. This would include the breakdown of power plays and resistance to knowledge sharing. ▪ It would also imply a minimum level of checks and balances by management and especially of 'checking up'.

Table 3.1: Cherns' Principles Adapted for Knowledge Management (Adapted from Coakes, Willis, & Clarke, 2001) (continued)

Principle	Knowledge Management Explanation
Power and Authority	■ People require the necessary power and authority, in conjunction with the required responsibility, to decide what resources they need to undertake their work.
The Multi-Function Principle	■ A knowledge-based organisation needs to be fluid and adaptable to change, especially in relation to the external and internal environment. It would seem that a flat structure, with people working in teams across projects/processes, might be more appropriate. ■ The management of knowledge means looking at an organisation from a cognitive perspective, with the organisation seen as a knowing sentient organism and using its resources, both human and technological, to make sense of its environment.
Support Congruence	■ The suggestion is that we pay people for their scarce knowledge, not what they do. This obviously will have repercussions when organisations manage this knowledge. Who decides who knows most? How can one judge? Is one type of knowledge more useful to the organisation than another? How should the reward system be devised to be fair and equitable?
Transitional Organisation	■ Taking into account the above comments about the fluidity of the organisation that manages its knowledge in relation to the environment, it follows that the organisation is constantly in a state of transition. Management of staff in such a state of constant flux, and management of their knowledge, is clearly a challenging task.
Incompletion	■ As discussed in the transitional organisation above, redesign is continually happening as knowledge is constantly changing, and the resources that people require to perform their work activities is also in a state of flux. It is important to recognise this, and if at all possible, to embrace this state of flux as being the norm rather than the exception.

This sociotechnical perspective shows clearly that in order for organisations to manage and share their knowledge effectively, they must first consider, and then organise for, the following:

- ensuring that the organisational culture is developed for the easy sharing of knowledge and information;

- designing the organisational structure and form to minimise checks and barriers to the sharing of knowledge and information;

- organising the management role to permit a maximum devolution of responsibility and decision-making;

- designing the organisational structure and form to permit fluidity of this structure and form, as change will occur and will impact both the organisational knowledge and the required organisational output;

- developing the organisational reward system to encourage the development of learning and knowledge; and

- ensuring that the organisational technology infrastructure is designed in such a way as to permit all of the above.

Chapter IV

Systems Thinking and Knowledge Management

4.1   Introduction

In order to understand knowledge management (KM), reference has been made to the insufficient nature of knowledge seen as either a purely technical or purely social phenomenon. This has led to an argument for a sociotechnical view of KM, which in this chapter is further developed to consider KM in more depth, and to try to answer the question: What kind of system is a knowledge management system?

We begin by looking at organisations and their management, initially setting KM in a historical frame. Systems thinking, and its relationship to KM, is then reviewed, followed by a more in-depth analysis of social systems philosophy and theory, and the domain of epistemology. All of this points to a theoretical grounding for KM in the philosophy and theory of Kant and Habermas; in order to further develop this theme, social theory, and particularly critical social theory, is discussed. The outcome is an argument for KM to be grounded in critical social theory, and more specifically in Habermas' theories of communicative action. A framework for the application of these ideas within KM investigations is presented.

4.2 Organisations and Their Management

Our study of organisation theory begins with Frederick Taylor's scientific management (Taylor, 1947), initially formulated at the turn of the nineteenth to the twentieth century. Major subsequent developments have been administrative management theory (Fayol, 1949), where the management process is defined (to forecast and plan, to organise, to command, to coordinate and control), and bureaucracy theory (see Gerth & Mills, 1970).

Taylor's work may be loosely classified as time and motion or work study, and this, as well as the other theories noted above, adhere to the rational model, which views organisations mechanistically, seeing the attainment of maximum efficiency as achievable by putting together the parts in an effective way under the control of management. Hierarchy, authority, and rational decision-making are fundamental to this.

In the 1920s, largely as a result of the Hawthorne experiments, the human relations model began to gain ground, based on social structures of people at work and motivation. This model pointed to democratic, employee-centred management. More recent developments have seen the growth of the systems model of organisations, where they are viewed systemically as open systems responding to environmental changes and maintaining a steady state (Selznick, 1948; Katz & Kahn, 1978). This systems approach links well with empirical research in sociotechnical systems (Pasmore & Sherwood, 1978), and contingency theory (Lawrence & Lorsch, 1969).

Broadly, the systems model recommends that if an organisation is not functioning properly, the sub-systems should be examined to see that they are meeting organisational needs, and the organisation examined to see that it is well adjusted to its environment. These tasks are charged to a management sub-system.

From a systems perspective, business organisations today may be characterised as complex, adaptive, human activity (micro-social) systems. In so far as such systems are devoid of human interaction (in, for example, a robot assembly plant), focus on a purely mechanistic approach may yield valuable results. As system complexity, and particularly the degree of human activity, increases, this approach is seen to break down, and human viewpoints need increasingly to be considered.

4.3 Systems Thinking

In common usage, the term 'system' has come to mean very little. How, for instance, are we to make sense of a single definition of 'system', when it is applied to such diverse objects as 'a hi-fi system', 'the railway system', or 'the system of planets and stars we refer to as the Universe'? Clearly, before the idea of a knowledge management system is investigated, we need a common definition of 'system'. This is what this section aims to achieve.

To begin with, a system is more than a simple collection of components, since properties 'emerge' when the components of which systems are comprised are combined. So, for example, we may gather together all of the components that make up a bicycle, but only when they are assembled do we have the emergent property of a mode of transport. Further, all systems must have a boundary—try to envisage a system without a boundary, and it soon becomes clear that the concept is meaningless. When considering the nature and properties of any system, care should be taken when looking at the components of the system in isolation. These parts, or sub-systems, interact, or are 'interdependent', and so need to be considered as a whole or 'holistically'. In addition, there is likely to be a discernible structure to the way sub-systems are arranged—in a hierarchy, for example. Finally, there need to be communication and control with the system, and it has to perform some transformation process. So, in summary, a system may be defined according to its:

- Boundary
- Emergence
- Holism
- Interdependence

- Hierarchy
- Transformation
- Communication and Control

Further, and following Checkland (1981), it is possible to conceive of a typology of systems divided into:

- physical systems, which are either natural or designed; and
- human activity systems.

Generally, whilst physical systems might be *complicated*, and require significant skill and expertise to construct or even understand (hence the modern-day interest in the Universe), only human activity systems exhibit *complexity*. In essence, human activity systems are complex adaptive systems. In order to relate this understanding to knowledge management, it is necessary to determine how, according to the above classifications, organisational systems should be categorised. Are they designed physical or human activity systems, or some combination of the two?

Designed physical systems are mechanistic or deterministic, requiring a view of the world that is mechanical or technical, and typically rule based. By way of an example, think of an aeroplane. It is clearly a designed physical system, whose design depends on the laws of aerodynamics. Construction of, arguably, this most complicated of all machines requires considerable skill and knowledge, but it all accords to a set of rules, most of which are well known. It is these properties that have led to such systems being seen as closed in relation to their environment. By contrast, organisational systems, whilst they might make use of designed physical or even natural systems, are made up of human actors. They are open, complex, adaptive systems of activity.

Following this line of thought, knowledge management systems emerge fundamentally as systems of human activity, exhibiting voluntary behaviour (or 'free will'). Such systems take an interpretivistic or subjective view of the world—a view which sees not 'objective reality', but a series of human perspectives and opinions. They are probabilistic rather than deterministic. However, whilst KM systems may be primarily human activity systems, they may also contain sub-systems that are technological or organisational, and these sub-systems may have a role in better enabling the KM to function. A way of conceptualising this is to think of a KM system as a human activity 'lens' through which all knowledge activity is viewed, and in accordance with whose characteristics and properties that activity is interpreted (Figure 4.1).

Knowledge management and knowledge acquisition therefore consist fundamentally of human activity, and as a consequence are subject to human perception and agreement. The whole bounded KM system that this is seeking to manage or interpret may contain technological and structural elements, but the purpose of these is simply to better enable the human activity system to function.

This view is supported by research that highlights the complexity of social systems, and the inappropriateness of studying such systems using scientific methods. In effect, in the social sciences, there is a complexity that stems from the introduction of human activity. Such activity is not absolutely predictable, being based on intended and unintended actions that do not easily lend themselves to study by the reductionist rules of repeatability and refutation.

Figure 4.1: The Nature of Knowledge Management Systems

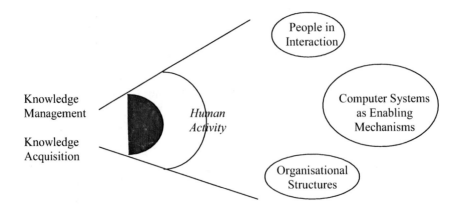

Systems thinking, then, may be seen as fundamental to an understanding of KM, which is a human (social and cognitive) activity, supported or enabled by structural and technological sub-systems. By way of a summary, each of the properties of systems can now be related directly to issues in KM (Table 4.1).

Table 4.1: Systems of Knowledge Management

System Property	Implications for Knowledge Management — Human Activity Systems	Enabling Mechanisms: Designed Physical Systems — Structure	Technology
Boundary	The limits of that which can be known	The organisation, or relevant part of it	Bounded technological sub-systems which enable the whole system of knowledge management to function more effectively
Emergence	Emergent properties of a knowledge system, e.g., decision-making	Structure and technology must be seen in terms of their contribution to the emergent properties of the whole KM system	
Holism	Encompasses technical, human (cognitive and social), and organisational factors	Must not be viewed in isolation, but only as part of the whole KM system	
Interdependence	Changes in part of the system (e.g., human knowledge acquisition) effect changes in other parts (e.g., the use of enabling technologies)	Technology, organisation, and human activity working together are the source of success in any KM system	
Hierarchy	As human beings we see structures in knowledge systems (hence the data structures in computerised systems)	Organisational structures help facilitate human knowledge acquisition and sharing	Technologies support the organisation and/or human actors
Transformation	The acquisition of knowledge always leads to changes, which may be perceived in organisational terms as transformation processes	The key in transformation achieved through knowledge management: technology and structure are enablers	
Communication and Control	These are fundamental to knowledge systems, and once more require understanding of the interactions between human, technical, and organisational issues	Used as aids to communication and control in the overall KM system	

4.4   The Philosophy and Theory of Social Systems

4.4.1 Some Philosophical Issues

The philosophical and theoretical perspective on which this study is grounded sees the world as socially constructed, and therefore argues that human issues are best seen from a socially constructed viewpoint. This section describes that viewpoint in more detail, and sets the context for the study.

Philosophically, this study is grounded in critical social theory, as derived specifically from the work of Kant (1724-1804), particularly as described in *The Critique of Pure Reason* (Kant, 1787). Whilst it might appear odd to underpin a twenty-first century study of knowledge management with the work of an eighteenth century philosopher, we contend that Kant's work has particular resonance for the domain of KM, and ask only that you bear with us for the time being, and suspend judgement until the end of this chapter. By tracing a route through philosophy and theory, we hope you will see the relevance of the underpinning chosen for this study.

4.4.2 Knowledge Management from its Philosophical and Theoretical Roots

Information from literature and empirical evidence suggests knowledge management (KM) to be a domain still at a rather immature stage of development. One of the key reasons identified for this is that the concept of *knowledge* lacks a clear definition. This chapter lays out an approach to underpinning the concept of knowledge, and thereby KM, from philosophical and theoretical perspectives, and from this underpinning reframes the domain of KM. The work is presented, not as a definitive study, but as something to promote what we see as an essential debate. Comments on the issues discussed here will be gratefully received by the authors.

It is common to come across ideas of knowledge that categorise it according to: explicit or implicit; explicit or tacit; more than data or information and less than wisdom; and so on. Whilst of value in themselves, such definitions lack something fundamental, as is evidenced by the fact that they commonly give rise to self-referential definitions (for example: 'knowledge is made up of explicit and implicit knowledge'). What seems to be happening here is that we are learning something about the nature of knowledge, having assumed that we already understand what it is *in its essence*.

In this study we meet the problem head on, but first a word of caution! There is no intention in a single book chapter to attempt a once-and-for-all definition that will satisfy everyone on the question of knowledge as a concept. We, as authors, would like to think that we can achieve the task of setting in motion an important debate, which will yield satisfactory outcomes to its participants: this chapter aims to be the beginning of that debate.

So to the question: What is knowledge? To answer this, our research has been on two complementary dimensions: philosophical and theoretical. First we have undertaken a very brief review of the KM literature in order to determine a rationale for the study. Following this, the chapter looks at what we might learn from epistemology, with the explicit aim of determining what the theory of knowledge has to tell us about its management. This particularly addresses how an understanding of such theory helps unravel the problem of what knowledge *is*, without which we argue that *management* of knowledge is impossible. We next take a deeper historical perspective on philosophical developments in the understanding of knowledge. Beginning with concepts taken from Greek philosophy, this history covers the thinking of early Western philosophers through to the most recent ideas of contemporary epistemology. Issues covered include scientific versus alternative forms of knowledge, knowledge as objective reality or subjective understanding, and Kant's transcendental philosophy. Where relevant, specific philosophical positions are addressed, examples being Locke's definition of knowledge according to its source in intuition, reason, or experience, and Hume's concept that knowledge is limited to sense experience.

A review of pre-critical philosophy is used as a backdrop to the philosophical perspective which forms the basis of this research, grounded on Kant. Specific theoretical developments seen to be relevant to an understanding of knowledge management are then reviewed, including work by Habermas on the 'subject-knower-object' problem, through which knowledge is defined both in relation to objects of experience and to the so-called *a priori* categories that the knowing subject brings to the act of perception. Through this and other theoretical perspectives, the social and reflective dimensions of knowledge are investigated in more depth.

The aim throughout is to relate these ideas to an understanding of knowledge that will inform contemporary knowledge management studies, and the final section of the chapter looks at the practical guidance for knowledge and its management which might be derived from these perspectives, and how this relates to selected recent approaches to KM.

4.4.3 A Brief Review of the Literature

The knowledge management (KM) literature seems, from our perspective, to lack certain fundamentals, which a review of some of the more recent publications will serve well to illustrate. There seems to be only a limited attempt to base the development of organisational KM systems on any explicit foundation. So, for example, in an otherwise excellent paper partially targeted at unearthing the 'conceptual foundations' of knowledge management, Alavi and Leidner (2001) discuss views of knowledge taken from IT and other literature, commenting that:

> *"The question of defining knowledge has occupied the minds of philosophers since the classical Greek era and has led to many epistemological debates. It is unnecessary for the purposes of this paper to engage in a debate to probe, question, or reframe the term knowledge...because such an understanding of knowledge was neither a determinant factor in building the knowledge-based theory of the firm nor in triggering researcher and practitioner interest in managing organizational knowledge."*

It is our contention that, by any reasonable standards, such a view is unsupportable. It seems that what is being said could be characterised in any of the ways listed below, none of which seems to us to be acceptable.

1.   The philosophical and theoretical foundation for the study of knowledge has nothing to tell us about how we should manage it.

2.   Philosophy and theory is of no value to the debate.

3.   We should accept there being no more to say about the underpinning to the domain, and it is therefore acceptable to proceed on a conceptual or pragmatic basis.

4.   All of the philosophical and theoretical issues raised in the past have been incorporated into current approaches.

However we should interpret this statement, it is our hope that, by the end of this chapter, you will be closer to our view: that philosophy and theory are central to an understanding of how to manage knowledge.

Not all writers exclude consideration of fundamental underpinning to the domain, but mostly the research can be characterised as eclectic and somewhat unconnected in character. So, for example, Sutton (2001) draws widely from philosophical and theoretical sources, including, for example, Heidegger and Wittgenstein. But the arguments and perspectives are presented in a rather disconnected manner.

For the most part, research in KM is primarily pragmatic or at best conceptual. In an essentially pragmatic study, Earl (2001) proposes a taxonomy of KM strategies. The problem is that, although the *practical* significance of the findings presented are without question of value, there seems to be nothing to tie the ideas together, with even the conceptual schema (unusually for Earl) being strangely fragmented. Other recent publications on KM seem to follow a similar tack. These include a *Journal of the Operational Research Society* special issue (Williams & Wilson, 2003) and a range of edited texts (see, for example: Coakes et al., 2001).

Having determined a rationale for the study, the next section now proceeds with an analysis of concepts drawn from epistemology.

4.4.4 What We Might Learn from Epistemology

It seems perhaps curious that so much of the writings in KM ignore (explicitly at least) epistemology, or the theory of knowledge.

> *"Philosophers have given a great deal of thought to ... what we can know—or mistakenly think we know—through perception or*

*through other sources of knowledge, such as memory as a store-
house of what we have learned in the past, introspection as a way
to know our inner lives, reflection as a way to acquire knowledge
of abstract matters, or testimony as a source of knowledge originally acquired in others"* (Audi, 1998, p. 1).

What seems to be put in play here is the dependence, for an understanding of
the concept of knowledge, on its generation and retention from and within a
number of sources. Certainly, any idea of managing knowledge that solely
focuses on material stored, for example, in databases, seems insufficient even
from this initial cursory inspection. Further to this, reason (Audi, 1998, p. 104)
may also be seen as a source of *a priori* truths, though such an approach has
been challenged by empiricist philosophers. This will be discussed in more
detail below, together with the position taken on these issues by this chapter,
which is essentially Kantian. Finally, from the domain of epistemology, we have
to consider (Audi, 1998, pp. 152-175) the process of inference, by which
basic knowledge is extended.

Within the limits of a chapter of this length, we will attempt to make sense of
these issues and their relation to KM in our contemporary 'Western World'.
But before that, we would like to delve a little deeper from a philosophical and
theoretical perspective.

4.4.5 Issues from Pre-Critical Philosophy

Some of the earliest and most influential Western evidence of civilisations
struggling with systems of thought is to be found in Greek philosophy, which,
at its most basic, might be seen as a search for *certain* knowledge. Central to
this is the concept that our senses may delude us, and a questioning of whether
we have any basis for believing that sense experience brings us into contact with
objective reality. This led early Greek philosophers to the central question of
what the world consisted of. Socrates (470-399 BC), for example, believed it
possible to achieve objective knowledge through conceptual analysis. It is here
that we first see the division of knowledge into *what is* and *what ought to be*:
factual and normative knowledge. Seeking knowledge through conceptual
analysis led Socrates to his 'theory of ideas', which was further developed by

Plato (427-347 BC). In essence, Plato considered ideas to have objective reality, and knowledge to be gained by a continuous cycling between ideas and perceptions. Plato argued that whilst the objects of our knowledge do exist, those objects cannot be attributed to anything in our world of perception. They existed in an ideal state in a world beyond our knowledge.

Aristotle's (384-322 BC) approach to determining knowledge takes into account the philosophies of nature, mathematics, and metaphysics. Here again we see the attempt to establish absolute truths through the process of reason.

Moving forward to the beginnings of our modern age, the reawakening of interest in the ideas which had absorbed the Ancient Greeks led, during the Renaissance and beyond, into what might be characterised as arguments over method. Emerging pre-eminent during the period of the Enlightenment was scientific method, within which knowledge was seen as objectively determined. To those espousing early scientific method, we live in a world that is realistic and deterministic, and that can be understood through reductionist method, using such approaches as induction, deduction, and experimentation. Truth was to be determined through repeatability, refutation, verification, and falsification.

Into this world came Descartes (1596-1650) as the first of the 'Continental Rationalists'. In terms of knowledge creation, the relevance of Cartesian method is that truth is judged according to rational criteria—even sense experience should be verified through reason. In opposition to this we might cast the British empiricists. Locke (1632-1704), as with the empiricists who followed him, accepted rationalism as giving an insight into *concepts*, but did not see that this necessarily gave an insight into *reality*. For the latter, acquisition of knowledge is attained in the empirical sciences.

We thus reach a position where the concepts of knowledge production through rational and empirical processes are in opposition, and to the philosophy of Immanuel Kant (1724-1804).

4.4.6 A Foundation in Kantian Critical Philosophy

Kant's critical problem, as first formulated in the letter to Herz (21 February 1772), concerns the nature of objective reality. Prior to Kant, all philosophical schema took objective reality as a 'given', and sought to explain how it was that we could have knowledge of this reality. If this were taken as definitive, it is easy to see how we might build (empirical) knowledge in the way suggested by Locke (1632-1704): that we are born with a 'tabula rasa' or 'blank slate' on which impressions are formed through experience. This explains the pre-Kantian debate of reason versus experience as the source of our knowledge. The rationalist view was that, by reason alone, we are able to formulate universally valid truths (for example, around such issues as God and immortality); empiricists, by contrast, see experience as the only valid source of knowledge.

Kant's insight, and unique contribution, was to bring together rationalism and empiricism in his new critical transcendental philosophy. The basis of this is his 'Copernican Revolution' in philosophy. Loosely stated, this says that objective reality may be taken as existing, but that, as human beings, we have access to this only through our senses: we therefore see this objectivity not as it is, but as we subjectively construct it. Unlike Berkeley (1685-1753), Kant does not claim that objects *exist* only in our subjective constructions, merely that this is the only way in which *we can know them*: objects necessarily conform to our mode of cognition.

For this to be so, Kant's philosophy has to contain *a priori* elements: there has to be an object-enabling structure in our cognition to which objective reality can conform, and thereby make objects possible for us. This is what lies at the heart of Kant's *Transcendental Idealism*.

1. Whilst objects may exist (be 'empirically real'), for us they can be accessed only through their appearances (they are 'transcendentally ideal').

2. Our cognition does not conform in some way to empirical reality; rather this 'objectivity' should be seen as conforming to our modes of cognition. In this way, we 'construct' our objective world.

3. Objects of cognition must conform to our sense experience. So, in this sense, knowledge is sensible, or the result of experience.

4. These objects must conform to the object-enabling structures of human cognition. The resultant transcendental knowledge is (at least) one stage removed from objective reality, and is, according to Kant, governed by *a priori* concepts within human understanding.

All of this gives a foundation for determining what knowledge is, and how it might be obtained, and is the subject of the following section.

4.4.7 Kant and Knowledge

The thinking with which Kant was grappling in trying to make sense of knowledge is well represented by the positions of Leibniz (1646-1716) and Hume (1711-1776). In effect, both saw knowledge as either necessary and *a priori*, or contingent and experiential. Kant's unique argument is that, whilst accepting these forms of knowledge, although all of our knowledge *begins with* experience, it does not follow that knowledge all *arises from* experience: in other words, experience may be simply the cue that gives rise to knowledge claims not derived from it. One of these key non-empirical knowledge claims is the concept of freedom.

A further claim made by Kant is that knowledge can be built only through the combined interactions of sensibility and intuition:

> *"Without sensibility no object would be given to us, without understanding no object would be thought. Thoughts without content are empty, intuition without concepts are blind. It is, therefore, just as necessary to make our concepts sensible, that is, to add the object to them in intuition, as to make our intuitions intelligible, that is, to bring them under concepts. These two powers or capacities cannot exchange their functions. The understanding can intuit nothing, the senses can think nothing. Only through their union can knowledge arise"* (Kant, 1787, p. 93).

Further, that which appears to us is not simply a collection of unconnected sensations: it consists of content as well as form, and without the latter would be meaningless. Form is intuitive, and cannot arise out of the sensation—it must be *a priori*. A sequence of auditory sensations, when heard by us, becomes a tune; but the tune is not inherent in the original data (this would be equivalent to empirical data supplying its own form, and even if there is seen to be an inherent form supplied with the data, there is no reason why we should see it as such; this requires apprehension)—it must be supplied by us.

> *"What objects may be in themselves, and apart from all this receptivity of our sensibility, remains completely unknown to us. We know nothing but our mode of perceiving them—a mode which*

is peculiar to us...Even if we could bring our intuition to the highest degree of clearness, we should not thereby come any nearer to the constitution of objects in themselves" (Kant, 1787, p. 82).

In summary:

1. Objectivity is conceivable only from the perspective of a thinking subject.

2. Central to Kantian philosophy is the question of how it is possible for subject and object to be so joined—what conditions must apply in order that this might be so?

3. In the Transcendental Deduction, Kant argues that subject and object make each other possible: neither one could be represented without the other.

4. All of this rests on their being: 1) a world of objects which is unknowable to us; 2) *a priori* concepts in understanding which enable representation of this world of objects.

Kant's philosophy has been the foundation for much of philosophical debate which continues to the present day, one of the primary themes of which is pursued below.

Whilst Kant's work, even within this one text of *The Critique of Pure Reason*, is complex and extremely diverse, certain strands of relevance to KM can be drawn out. Primary amongst these is the need to take a position on the way in which we see the World. As human beings, our viewpoint is essentially made up of two factors:

1. The concepts we are born with, which Kant called *a priori* concepts. An example of this, which seems particularly relevant to our research domain given its dependence on communication, is the idea that we are born with an ability to communicate through language. The actual language used is acquired empirically, but the ability to acquire it seems to be endemic to the human race.

2. An empirical understanding that we access through our senses. The relevance of this is that we do not have access to 'objective reality', only to that which our senses are able to show us (for Kant, this formed the basis of his theory of 'Transcendental Idealism', giving rise to 'objects for us' which differ from what objects might be 'in themselves').

Theoretically, this philosophical position leads to a grounding in those theories relevant to human understanding and interaction, which are to be found in the social and cognitive domains. Given that in KM we are seeking mutual understanding, those theories which best explain social interaction might be seen as especially relevant. Drawing again on the stream of social enquiry emanating from Kantian philosophy, this leads, through the critical social theory of the early twentieth century Frankfurt School, to contemporary social theorists such as Foucault and Habermas (see, for example, Habermas, 1971, 1987). It is to the latter that the fields of management science and, now, knowledge management, turned for support in the 1980s and beyond, and it is therefore strands of Habermasian theory that are used to underpin this study. The detailed range of these theoretical perspectives is too great for inclusion in a chapter of this length, but the principles will show its relevance to KM. Habermasian critical social theory is concerned with issues such as social inclusion, participation, and a view of how we *ought to* undertake intervention in social domains.

4.4.8 A Theoretical Perspective Grounded on Kant

Critical philosophy has been fundamental to a stream of thinking in the twentieth century to the present day, giving rise to forms of critical social theory, for which the primary contemporary theorist is Habermas (1929-).

Habermas (1971, 1976, 1987) follows Kant in arguing that reliable knowledge is possible only when science assumes its rightful place as one of the accomplishments of reason. Whilst the achievements of scientific study are not disputed, the problem perceived through the route followed by Kant and Habermas is that the methods of science which have grown out of modernity are effectively self-referential: that scientific study sets up rules and then tests itself against its own rules is a procedure that has given considerable advances to modern society, but to regard this as representing all knowledge is mistaken. Habermas refers to the worst excesses of this as 'scientism': that we must *identify knowledge with science.*

Habermas' argument is against the objectivistic illusion of unreflecting science (or otherwise modern positivism), in which, with (for example) approaches such as experimental method, rules are devised against which observations are then tested in an unreflective and self-supporting manner. Habermas argues that the scientistic (positivist) science community is unable to perceive self reflection as part of its process, and that such reflection must be built into an understanding of knowledge. As with Kant, Habermas' challenge is whether knowledge is reducible to the properties of an objective world, leading him to a definition of knowledge that is based on perception, but only in accordance with *a priori* concepts that the knowing subject brings to the act of perception.

Further, since the knowing subject is a social subject, all knowledge is mediated by social action and experience, leading to Habermas grounding his theories in communicative interaction, an issue we return to at the end of this chapter.

In essence, Habermas argues that these difficulties disappear once a scientific basis for our thinking is denied. For example, suppose science (as is suggested by Kant and Habermas) is seen as just one form of knowledge, which in any case is simply a convenient human perception of how the world works. Now, all human endeavour becomes mediated through subjective understanding. However, this problem has been replaced with another, which may be stated as follows:

1. Accepting all human actions as mediated through subjective understanding leads to the possibility of a basis for knowledge management in the universal characteristics of language.

2. There is no longer a dichotomy between subject and object.

3. The difficulty we are now left with is essentially a practical one, of how to incorporate these ideas into management practice.

To address this, Habermas' (1976, 1987) theory of communicative action presents a universal theory of language, which suggests that all language is oriented toward three fundamental validity claims: truth, rightness, and sincerity. What is most compelling about this theory, however, is that all three validity claims are *communicatively mediated*. This viewpoint is most radically seen in respect of the truth claim, where it is proposed that such a claim results not from the content of descriptive statements, but from the Wittgenstinian approach casting them as arising in language games which are linked to culture: truth claims are *socially contextual*.

In the following section, these ideas are taken forward to provide an approach to KM that is grounded theoretically and philosophically.

4.4.9 What Does This Mean for Knowledge Management?

Knowledge management has been defined by some as the extraction and conversion of 'tacit' knowledge on an individual and organisational level into 'explicit' knowledge. Further, it is argued, this explicit knowledge often takes the form of specific electronic 'tools' or 'assets' that can be manipulated for competitive gain, examples being intranets, groupware, and knowledge repositories. 'Tacit' knowledge, by contrast, is often described as the 'hunches, intuition, and know-how' of people, or their 'skills, routines, and competencies'. The aim of KM as regards tacit knowledge might be seen as an attempt to make this often highly subjective knowledge explicit, thereby facilitating its management through such enabling media as technology.

Additionally, a number of studies have called for a more holistic, systemic approach to KM. One such example is the division into the 'know-why, know-what, know-who, know-how' questions of KM. Know-how might be seen as technologically focused, know-who as socially constructed and depending on

Figure 4.2: Early Lessons from Philosophy and Theory

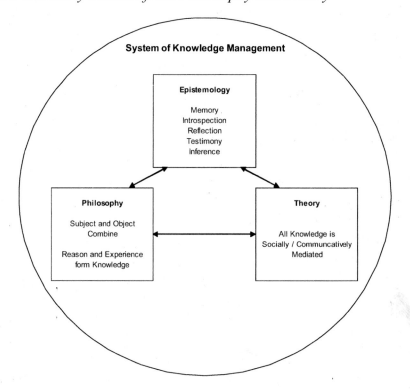

processes of debate, whilst know-why and know-what relate to issues of power and coercion in societal structures.

Finally, there are numerous classifications which aim to demystify KM. Included in these, for example, is the division into socialisation, externalisation, combination, and internalisation.

But what does 'managing knowledge' infer from the standpoints discussed in this chapter (see Figure 4.2)?

Epistemology, philosophy, and theory all have a part to play in determining the elements of a system of knowledge management.

4.4.9.1 Epistemology

Knowledge derives from perception, memory, introspection, reflection, and testimony. It is subject to *a priori* concepts, and is extended by inference.

4.4.9.2 Philosophy

From the time of Greek philosophy, there have existed fundamental arguments regarding knowledge being a search for truth, or for normative agreement. Initially the argument raged between rationalism and empiricism, and one of Kant's unique contributions, through the 'Copernican revolution in philosophy', was to unite subject and object in knowledge production: subject and object, according to Kant, make each other possible.

4.4.9.3 Theory

Following the thinking of Habermas, in which can be seen the echoes of Kant, science produces only one form of knowledge—believing all knowledge to be scientific is an 'objectivist illusion'. What Habermas does that is so helpful to us is he cites knowledge as mediated by social action, and subject to reflection, without which we end up with self-referential systems that are in danger of producing 'knowledge' based on disputable 'facts'. To misquote an anonymous source: "The problem ain't so much what we know, as what we know that ain't so."

4.4.10 Summarising the Issues from Philosophy and Theory

The philosophical and theoretical investigation conducted in researching the content of this chapter indicates that knowledge is a human construct, inseparable from the *a priori* understanding that we, as human 'actors', bring to its formation. Epistemology shows us that, for example, 'knowledge as a storehouse' is at best a partial view, and one which, for the purpose of KM, must be supported by other knowledge sources and processes. So, as human 'actors', the *a priori* conceptual understanding we bring to the knowledge process, if omitted from the management of knowledge, leaves that management impoverished.

The primary philosophical concerns in relation to KM may be summarised as:

1.   We see knowledge both in terms of 'truth' and 'normative understanding'. Knowledge is not solely concerned with those irrefutable truths or facts that might be scientifically proven.

2.   Reason and experience contribute to our knowledge store and our understanding.

3.   The 'objectively real' and our 'subjective understanding' are interlaced, each providing the conditions for the other.

KM, therefore, must be addressed *through* a human perspective: there is no sense in a KM process focused only on the 'objectively real'. Following the Kantian stream of critical social theory into the twenty-first century, the most significant theorist, and one on whom much management systems development has been based, is Habermas. From Habermas' theoretical approach to communicative action, it is possible to see a way forward through knowledge derived from a communicatively mediated rationality, in which normative understanding is privileged ahead of 'objective truth'.

The remaining objective of this chapter is therefore to ground KM in a more comprehensive view of social theory. To this end, the following section discusses issues in social theory and a potential approach to KM.

4.5 Social Theory

This section is a search for the relevant theoretical underpinning to knowledge management research and practice, further expanding the philosophical and theoretical discussion above. Information is sought from two sources. In the first place, there is the underpinning social theory itself. Secondly, the holistic intent of knowledge management is pursued through a review of systems theory.

A study is undertaken of social theory, reviewing the paradigmatic arguments and assessing potential future directions. To establish the theoretical underpinning, the relevant philosophical, ontological, epistemological, and methodological issues are outlined and placed in context with the development of the natural sciences and systems science. Difficulties encountered in management science are reviewed, providing a basis for development of the relevant theoretical underpinning to knowledge management.

Critical social theory has been applied extensively in information management (Hirschheim, 1986; Hirschheim & Klein, 1989; Lyytinen & Hirschheim, 1989; Clarke, 2000; Clarke & Lehaney, 2002) and offers potential as a way forward for knowledge management. This chapter aims to determine a practical approach to knowledge management by exploring work already undertaken in the domain of management science, where the relevant ideas have been a subject of debate since the 1960s.

This exploration begins with an outline of the branch of critical social theory to be applied, and pursues this line of reasoning through critical systems thinking, relating each approach to the paradigm problems encountered. These views are then synthesised to produce an approach to knowledge management that is true to the principles of critical social theory.

4.5.1 Social Theory: The Paradigm Problem

This section reviews the work of Burrell and Morgan (1979), which is used to provide a framework for understanding the development of knowledge management within this chapter.

Figure 4.3: Four Paradigms for the Analysis of Social Theory (Burrell & Morgan, 1979, p. 22)

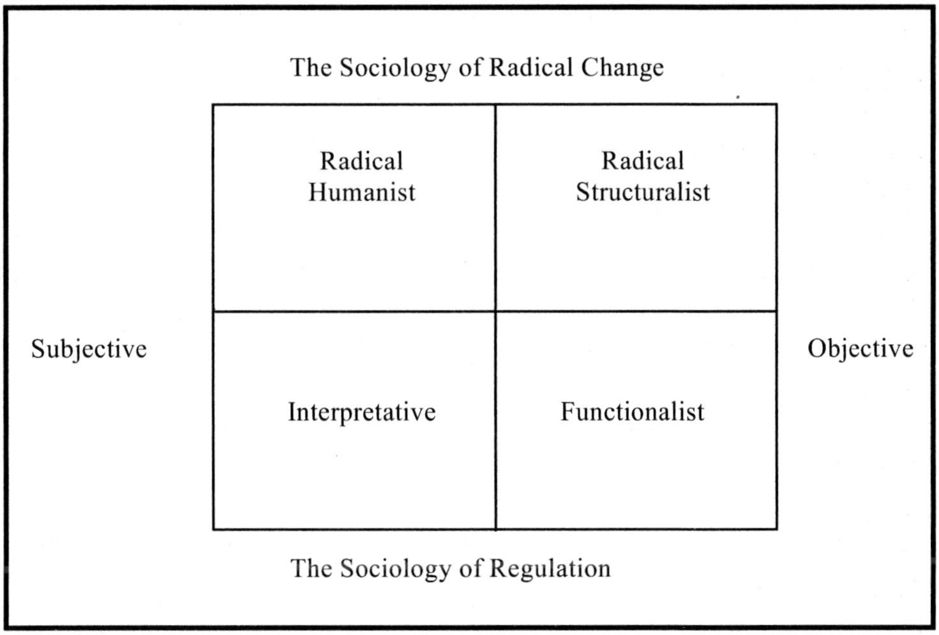

The Sociology of Radical Change

Radical Humanist	Radical Structuralist
Interpretative	Functionalist

Subjective   Objective

The Sociology of Regulation

Burrell and Morgan positioned all social theories into one of four paradigms: functionalist, interpretivist, radical humanist, and radical structuralist (Figure 4.3), according to the extent to which they were subjective versus objective or regulative versus radical.

The subjective-objective dimension can be seen in terms of four elements: an ontology, an epistemology, a view of the nature of human beings, and methodology.

The ontological debate concerns the nature of reality, the two opposing extremes of thought being: *realism*—that reality is external to the individual and is of an objective nature; and *nominalism*—that reality is a product of individual consciousness. Epistemology is concerned with the grounds of knowledge, or how the world might be understood, and this understanding is

Table 4.2: The Subjective-Objective Dimension (Burrell & Morgan, 1979, p. 3)

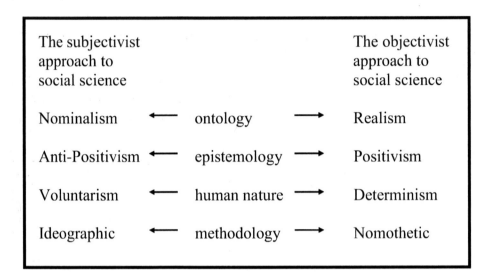

communicated as knowledge. The two opposing extremes are: *positivism*—knowledge is hard, real, and capable of being transmitted in a tangible form; and *anti-positivism*—knowledge is soft, more subjective, based on experience and insight, and essentially of a personal nature. Human beings may be viewed on a scale from *deterministic*—determined by situations in the external world and conditioned by external circumstances—to *voluntaristic*—they have free will, and create their environment.

The view taken of ontology, epistemology, and the nature of human beings directly influences the methodological approach that is adopted. A realist ontology, positivist epistemology, and view of human beings as largely deterministic leaves nomothetic methodologies as the appropriate choice. Such methodologies are characterised by a search for universal laws that govern the reality that is being observed, leading to a systematic approach. A nominalist ontology, anti-positivist epistemology, and view of human beings as largely voluntaristic indicates ideographic methodologies as appropriate—the principle concern would be to understand the way an individual interprets the world, with a questioning of external 'reality'.

The regulation-radical change dimension (Table 4.3) was the result of Burrell and Morgan recasting the then-prevalent order-conflict debate. The sociology of regulation emphasises a view of society based on preservation of the status quo, whilst the sociology of radical change is "concerned with man's emancipation from the structures which limit and stunt his potential for development" (Burrell & Morgan, 1979, p. 17).

The functionalist paradigm is, in Burrell and Morgan's terms, regulative in nature, highly pragmatic, often problem orientated, and applying natural scientific methods to the study of human affairs (Burrell & Morgan, 1979, p. 26).

The early application of functionalism to business organisations is to be found in functionalist organisation theory, which can be traced from the work of F.W. Taylor (e.g., 1947). This laid the foundation for the 'classical school', contributors to which have been, for example, Fayol and Gulick. In Fayol's work, organisations are characterised in terms of a reality that can be investigated systematically, taking a highly mechanistic view of human beings, informed by an objectivist ontology and epistemology.

Table 4.3: The Regulation-Radical Change Dimension (Burrell & Morgan, 1979, p. 18)

The sociology of regulation is concerned with:	The sociology of radical change is concerned with:
The status quo	Radical change
Social order	Structural conflict
Consensus	Modes of domination
Social integration and cohesion	Contradiction
Solidarity	Emancipation
Need satisfaction	Deprivation
Actuality	Potentiality

Functionalist organisation theory can be identified anywhere from the most objective to the most subjective margin of the paradigm, and, from a social theoretical perspective, the objective-subjective dimension does not automatically imply a paradigm shift. The relevance of this to KM goes back to the earlier arguments for KM as a human-centred domain. A functionalist approach to knowledge management does not exclude human action, but risks functionalist issues such as structure becoming the main focus of attention: a 'real world' that is seen to exist independently of human perception.

As with the functionalist paradigm, the interpretative paradigm is also regulative, seeing social reality as "…little more than a network of assumptions and intersubjectively shared meanings" (Burrell & Morgan, 1979, pp. 29-31). Burrell and Morgan argue that the ontological assumptions of interpretative sociologists led them to seek an understanding of the existing social world from an ordered viewpoint, and do not allow them to deal with issues of conflict or coercion. Interpretivism suffers criticism from all sides. Functionalists see it as finding out about problem situations without any means of solving problems or, in effect, producing any 'hard' output. Radical thinkers criticise interpretivism for its support of the status quo—the existing power base: interpretivism is fine for achieving consensus, provided the conditions required for consensus-seeking pre-exist; it has no means of overthrowing existing power structures or of resisting coercion.

The radical humanist paradigm has much in common with the interpretative paradigm, being nominalist, anti-positivist, voluntaristic, and ideographic, but unlike interpretivism "emphasises the importance of overthrowing or transcending the limitations of existing social arrangements" (Burrell & Morgan, 1979, p. 32). Radical humanism aims to help humans achieve their true potential. The emphasis is on radical change and the attainment of potentiality through human emancipation, or release from 'false consciousness':

> "…the consciousness of man is dominated by the ideological superstructures with which he interacts, and these drive a cognitive wedge between himself and his true consciousness. This… 'false consciousness' inhibits or prevents true human fulfilment" (Burrell & Morgan, 1979, p. 32).

Radical humanism is the position from which critical theory may be taken as a perspective. In relation to the earlier discussions, interpretivism offers an alternative to functionalism in so far as it does not accept there to be an objective reality but only socially constructed reality, but that its relativist stance makes it unable to view itself as the target for reflection. The radical humanist paradigm offers a way forward. Through critical social theory there is the possibility of moving beyond a debate located firmly in the sociology of regulation to a critically reflective, radical position.

Habermas (1971) provides the primary theoretical support that management science has taken to underpin interventionist approaches based on radical humanism. Habermas' Theory of Knowledge Constitutive Interests sees all human endeavour as undertaken in fulfilment of three knowledge constitutive or cognitive interests: technical, practical (in satisfaction of human interaction or communication), and emancipatory. Jackson (1993) follows the cognitive categories of Habermas, and argues that in Western industrialised society, the technical interest has been accorded too much primacy. Jackson goes further in asserting, again after Habermas, that, in fact, practical questions are re-defined as technical ones, effectively blocking the separation of what we ought to do from questions of how we ought to be doing it.

The radical structuralist paradigm shows similarities with functionalist theory, but advocates radical change through structural conflict (Burrell & Morgan, 1979, p. 34). Whilst this may be a tenable view for organisational theorists, its value to this study is limited, since this discussion is not about revolution in that sense.

These paradigmatic considerations carry implications for KM that will now be investigated in more depth in the following section.

4.5.2 Social Systems Theory: Its Application to Knowledge Management

In the study of social systems, where the key to the functioning of the system is human activity, functionalist views are questioned. Experimentation is of limited value in such systems: the utility of problem solving, functionalist techniques, is diminished when dealing with ill-defined, highly complex human activity systems. As a result, 'softer' methods of approaching the issues are seen to be of value.

Social systems are therefore where the reductionist, functionalist approach meets its most severe challenges, and where systems views are seen to be of increasing relevance. Social science involves increasing complexity—a complexity that derives from the systemic nature of the objects of study and the introduction of human activity. The limitations of functionalism are demonstrated in the study of social systems, where predictive models may be seen to have only limited value. Social action does not lend itself to study by reductionist methods, but is determined by the meaning that individuals attribute to their actions.

This brings the discussion back to the functionalist-interpretivist debate, but now, with the support of social theory, this debate can be taken further and a foundation developed for KM. This is the direction that has been pursued by part of the systems movement, from its origins in the so-called Singer/Churchman/Ackoff school (Jackson, 1982; Britton & McCallion, 1994), through to present-day systems thinkers. Jackson (1982) has shown how the soft methods of Ackoff, Checkland, and Churchman all adhere to some degree to the assumptions of the interpretative paradigm, and identifies a third position that distinguishes hard, soft, and emancipatory systems thinking (Jackson & Keys, 1984; Jackson, 1985). The argument is for a pluralist approach, which sees the strengths and weaknesses in each of the three areas and argues that each one must be respected for those strengths and weaknesses.

All of this is mirrored in KM, where the argument, which from a Habermasian (Habermas, 1971, 1976) perspective is seen as a critical social problem, is wrongly cast within the sociology of regulation. The effect of this may be illustrated through Figure 4.3, where KM is best perceived from a radical humanist perspective. Seen from social theory, for example, the concept of a KM system contained within a computer database might be seen as excessively functionalist, though perhaps with some evidence of interpretative analysis. But interpretative approaches alone would be seen as insufficient to deal with the complexity of human interaction, which critical social theory, whilst addressing the functionalist and interpretivist, also signals progression to a more radical approach. Much work in this area has already been undertaken in the management science domain, and it is from here that further support will be sought in formulating an alternative framework for KM.

4.5.3 Critical Social Theory—The Theoretical Underpinning

Critical social theory (CSoT) can be traced from the work of Kant, through Marx and the Frankfurt School. The two most widely accepted modern theorists are Foucault and Habermas, and it is to the latter that management science turned in the 1980s in order to develop a more human-centred view of its domain.

CSoT applied to the field of KM is appealing for its denial of a grounding in solely natural scientific principles. Seen through a scientific framework, KM appears as objective: the same for all involved since it is independent of human perception. CSoT refutes this, seeing our understanding of the world as determined by *a priori* conditions that are uncritically accepted. Critical theory seeks to expose these, and thereby release human beings from their 'false consciousness' to a position from which true potentiality can be attained. An alternative to the current functionalist and interpretivist approaches to KM may be found in developments based on the work of Habermas (1971, 1976), in particular his theory of knowledge constitutive interests (Table 4.4).

Habermas' three cognitive interests—technical, practical, and emancipatory—are identified in labour, interaction, and power, and provide conditions for the three sciences—empirical/analytic, hermeneutic, and critical. The empirical/analytic, served by the natural sciences, is therefore seen as satisfying only the technical interest. Since, as has been argued, traditional approaches to KM might be seen as having their roots in the natural sciences, or at best in an interpretative ontology, they appear from a Habermasian perspective as an insufficient basis for KM. What is needed in addition is critical science to deal with issues of power and domination, serving the emancipatory interest.

From these roots came the development, in the domain of management science, of critical systems thinking, which is detailed below before moving onto the development of a critical framework for KM.

4.5.4 Critical Systems Thinking

Critical systems thinking (CST), it is argued, accepts the contribution of both hard and soft approaches, and, through critique, enhances awareness of the

Table 4.4: The Theory of Knowledge Constitutive Interests (Oliga, 1991)

Knowledge Constitutive Interest	Basis of Human Interest	Type of Interaction	Underlying Paradigm	Methodological Approach
Technical (control)	Labour (instrumental action)	Man-Nature	Functionalist	Empiricism
Practical (understanding)	Communicative Interaction	Man-Man	Interpretative	Hermeneutics
Emancipatory (freedom)	Authority (power)	Man-Self	Radical/Critical	Critique

circumstances in which such approaches can be properly employed. The pragmatism of functionalist approaches and the lack of theoretical reflection in interpretivism allow CST to expose both as special cases with limited domains of application. The value of CST to KM can be demonstrated through the Burrell and Morgan grid (after Burrell & Morgan, 1979, p. 22). Burrell and Morgan's work, together with contributions from Oliga (1991), may be interpreted as shown in Figure 4.4.

This perspective further supports the view that traditional views of KM largely emerge as serving the technical interest, focusing on purposive-rational action. The alternative, evident in this domain since the 1970s but still limited in acceptance, is the service of the practical interest from the interpretative paradigm, relying on the communication of perceptions and consensus forming.

The key to the value of critical systems thinking to KM rests on the value of an approach based on critical pluralist method. This is admirably summarised by Jackson (2000, pp. 364-367), and the following section seeks to build this into a KM framework.

Figure 4.4: The Social Validity of Hard, Soft, and Critical Approaches

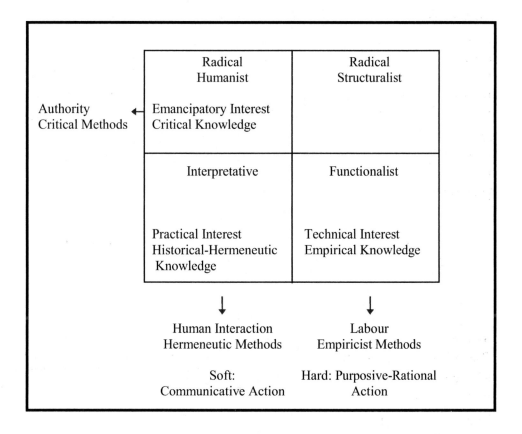

4.6 A Critical Systems Framework for Knowledge Management

As has been argued, the foundations of a critical systems approach to organisational studies owes much to the work of Churchman (1968), which was built on foundations laid by Singer, and has been continued by Ackoff and other adherents to the systems school (Britton & McCallion, 1994). In the rest of this chapter, we will attempt to draw together the issues from organisational theory, systems theory, social theory and philosophy, and critical theory, to provide a foundation for KM. In short, the objective is to construct a critical systems framework for knowledge management.

The route we have chosen to this is a review of the progress in critical systems thinking within the domain of management. As the objective is an *action* framework, the initial approach is to assess the various means by which critical systems has been applied in management settings, before drawing this together at the end to form a framework for KM action.

The work of Jackson and Keys (1984) proved a major turning point in the development of a critical framework that is true to the commitments of critical systems thinking. By looking at the range of problem contexts and at the systems methodologies available for addressing these contexts, Jackson and Keys provided a unified approach that draws on the strengths of the relevant methodologies, rather than debating which method is best, and argued for a reconciliation focusing on which method to use in which context, controlled by a 'system of systems methodologies'.

4.6.1 The System of Systems Methodologies

A convenient starting point for KM is to be found in the work of Jackson and Keys (1984) and the 'system of systems methodologies' (SOSM: Figure 4.5).

The SOSM (Figure 4.5) is used as the basis for an argument that organisational intervention can be understood through determination of the problem contexts within which it is conducted. The SOSM is therefore, first and foremost, a problem context classification, through which it is argued that problem contexts can be categorised according to the extent to which they exhibit a 'people complexity', from unitary to coercive, and a 'systems complexity', from simple to complex. So, for example, a 'problem' may be seen as 'simple-unitary': 'simple' in the sense that it has few elements and few interactions between elements; 'unitary' in terms of people complexity in that there is only one agreed viewpoint. Such 'problems', it is argued, do not require discussion and can be 'solved' using hard, scientific, 'design-based' methods. By contrast, a 'complex-coercive' context not only exhibits system characteristics of high complexity (many elements, many interactions), but also cannot be progressed until the power issues (hence high 'people complexity') dominating the context are resolved (for a more detailed analysis applying the use of the SOSM, see Clarke & Lehaney, 1999).

In use, this problem context classification forms a basis for determining the methodology to be used in the intervention. So, for example, a 'simple-unitary' problem context will demand the use of a methodology that focuses on design

Figure 4.5: The System of Systems Methodologies (Based on Jackson & Keys, 1984; Jackson, 1990, 1995)

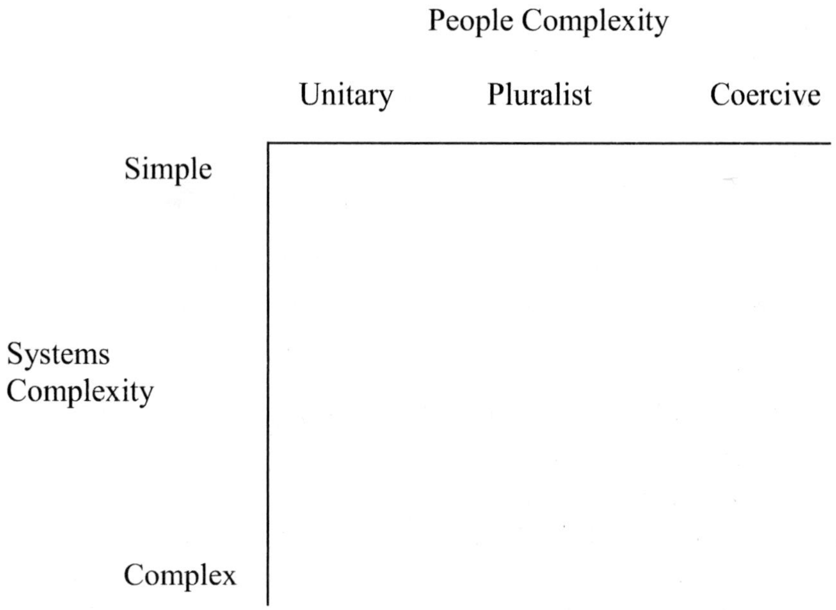

People Complexity

	Unitary	Pluralist	Coercive
Simple			
Systems Complexity			
Complex			

issues, and does not seek to address multiple viewpoints, since these are seen not to exist within the context identified. For KM, our earlier analysis would seem to place it at complex-pluralist/coercive on this classification.

4.6.2 Total Systems Intervention and the Complementarist Framework

In the early development of total systems intervention (TSI), the paradigm position taken by the SOSM was core to the approaches recommended. That is to say, it was accepted that different problem contexts 'inhabited' different paradigms, and further that communication across paradigms was difficult if not impossible. So, for example, a problem context characterised by high levels of disagreement among participants, in which debate might be seen as a way forward, might prove difficult to combine with a requirement to produce a technical system, where the focus is on design, and agreement as to means and ends is typically assumed.

Whilst 'paradigm incommensurability' was the normal view in these approaches, a way out of the problem was proposed through Habermas' theory of knowledge constitutive interests. In essence, this theory was that, at a fundamental level, human beings, in carrying out any task, seek to satisfy three interests: technical, practical, and emancipatory. If this could be shown to be so, then the incommensurability of paradigms becomes a human construction, rather than something fundamental to human activity, and by acceding to approaches that take account of Habermas' interest constitution theory, such incommensurability could be overcome.

By the early 1990s, the most comprehensive attempt at applying this theory to organisations was undertaken through total systems intervention (Flood, 1995), where 'complementarism' was promoted as a way forward, enabling methodologies from different paradigms to be used together in a single intervention, applied to the same problem situation (for an example of TSI in use, see Clarke & Lehaney, 2000).

TSI offered a 'critical complementarist' approach, which was seen to be capable of resolving both the theoretical and practical difficulties. This Habermasian perspective sees the functionalist view of organisations as an insufficient basis, serving only the technical interest. What is needed in addition is social science, to service the practical (hermeneutic) interest in achieving communication and consensus, together with critical science to deal with issues of power and domination, serving the emancipatory interest. Critique is applied in a Kantian (Kant, 1787) sense, aiming to: 1) free participants from purely instrumental reason; 2) enable practical reason, to examine and re-examine assumptions made; and 3) inform the choice and mix of methodologies in relation to the changing nature of the problem contexts, and the strengths and weaknesses of the available methodologies.

The process of TSI is shown in Figure 4.6 and described in summary in the following text. TSI is iterative and recursive. Iteration implies that the process is continuous, rather than a start-end method. The TSI ideology explicitly recognises the part played by both technical and human activities in organisations, and the extent to which human interpretation may in some instances so distort the so-called 'real world' that study of the latter may become meaningless.

TSI provides a critical framework within which choice and implementation of methodologies in an intervention can be managed pluralistically. The problem

Figure 4.6: The Process of Total Systems Intervention (Flood, 1995)

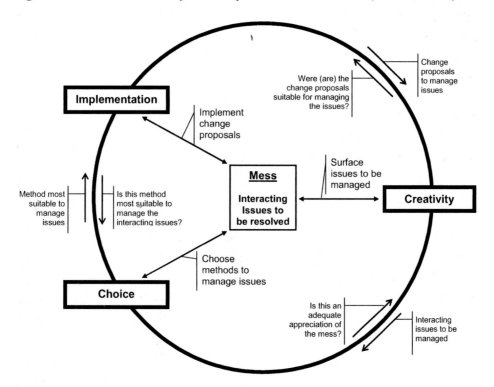

context is viewed as a 'mess' within which creativity (e.g., brainstorming, metaphor) is used to surface the issues to be managed (Figure 4.6); reflection on creativity then seeks to critically determine whether an adequate appreciation of the 'mess' has been gained.

Originally, the SOSM was used to inform methodological choice (Flood & Jackson, 1991). Latterly, it has been recommended (Flood, 1995) that this be replaced by the complementarist framework. In this, first metaphor is used to determine whether the key concern is one of design (technical), debate (practical), or disimprisonment (emancipation); then a methodology or mix of methodologies may be chosen to address the problem context, with critical reflection on whether these methodologies are indeed the most suitable being carried out prior to implementation.

4.6.3 The Creative Design of Methods

Midgley (1997a) and Ulrich (1983) focus on boundary critique as the key to mixing methods. Boundary critique has a long history, but it is from Ulrich (1983, 1996) and Midgley (1992) that the recommendation to critically challenge what should or should not be considered part of any system is drawn. Midgley's approach is to begin with a boundary definition that is accepted as arbitrary, and progress by "…looking for grey areas in which marginal elements lie that are neither fully included in, nor excluded from, the system definition."

The critical choices made at the boundary are of truth and rightness: truth being represented by questions of what is, and rightness by questions of what ought to be. Critical assessment of the system boundary should be undertaken by a representative sample of participants in the system. Typically, an arbitrary system definition is presented for discussion in, for example, a brainstorming session (DeBono, 1977). Critique can be informed by a combination of Midgley's and Ulrich's approaches to boundary critique: Midgley's (1992) approach to examining what is in the margin for elements that support the secondary boundary or the primary boundary; Ulrich's (Midgley, 1996) approach to challenging system boundaries through 12 'critically heuristic boundary questions' that address issues of motivation, power, knowledge, and legitimisation (see Clarke & Lehaney, 2000, for an example of the use of boundary critique).

Boundary critique has led to Midgley's promotion of the creative design of methods (Midgley, 1997b), which was originally conceived as an improvement to SOSM, but is now promoted as addressing issues which SOSM deals with insufficiently. For example, whilst SOSM promotes the idea that there is only one interpretation of each method, creative design of methods sees methods as subject to multiple interpretations. Also, importantly, Midgley argues that SOSM restricts boundary judgement to simple coercive problem contexts, whereas it is a primary concern of creative design of methods to free up boundary judgement for use in all contexts.

Applying the creative design of methods requires that the interventionist maintain a multiplicity of participant viewpoints, together with the potential mix of methods or parts of methods required to address them, within an ongoing critical framework. The boundaries must be critically challenged throughout an intervention, and the approach will be continually changing in response to this and participant feedback.

4.6.4 Diversity Management

Flood and Romm (1996) promote diversity management and triple loop learning as an improved way to deal with mixing methods. In essence, triple loop learning is seen as a way to manage the diversity of methodologies and theories available, in addressing the diversity of issues to be found in organisational intervention.

In application, diversity management is about managing design, debate, and might-right issues, and so is a complementarist approach to the perceived hard, soft, and critical factors which Flood and Romm see as pervading organisational problem contexts. The overall objective of diversity management might be seen as the enhancement of emancipatory practice.

4.6.5 Critical Systems Practice

In his most recent work, Jackson (1999, 2000) continues to promote critical pluralism, but now sees this in terms of developing TSI into critical systems practice. Pluralism in the use of methodology is advocated: "...to make the best use of the methodologies, methods, models, and techniques...to tackle diverse and difficult problem situations while...ensuring their continual improvement through research" (Jackson, 2000, p. 382). This pluralism must: encourage flexibility in the use of methodologies, enabling practitioners to decompose approaches and tailor them, within a critical framework; encourage paradigm diversity, using methodologies from different paradigms in the same intervention (for a critique of a range of methodologies, see Clarke, Lehaney et al., 1998).

What is clear in Jackson's recommendations is his view that it is no longer possible to rely on Habermas, but, rather, pluralism calls for a meta-methodology, for which Jackson lays out nine "constitutive rules" (Jackson, 2000, p. 393). This "critical systems meta-methodology" is seen by Jackson as a "structured way of thinking which understands and respects the uniqueness of the functionalists, interpretative, emancipatory, and post-modern theoretical rationales, and draws upon them to improve real-world problem situations." It is recommended that methods for enhancing creativity are applied, at least, from these perspectives, and that methodologies are used as appropriate.

Critical systems practice, Jackson recommends, should be embedded within a systems and action research approach; should ensure a pluralism of 'clients', theoretical and methodological pluralism, pluralism in the modes of representation employed, and pluralism in the facilitation process; and should be sensitive to the organisational context in which it is operating.

Further, the claim to be using a generic system methodology, according to the particular theoretical rationale it is designed to serve, must be justified according to the principles and guidelines established for the use of each generic systems methodology.

In essence, critical systems practice calls for an improved version of TSI, but it is as yet unclear how these ideas are to be applied. In essence, a set of constitutive rules are provided, but a framework within which these might be operationalised is not given.

4.6.6 Critical Pluralism

In critical pluralism, Mingers and Gill (1997) promote what they see to be missing in critical approaches to the use of a mix of methodologies: multi-paradigm multimethodology. From a discussion of current dilemmas in critical systems thinking, Mingers and Gill promote emphasis on engagement with agents in a social context as the basis for their approach. The focus, they suggest, should be on the relationship between three notional systems seen to form the multimethodological context: the problem content system, or real-world situation of concern; the intellectual resources system, or available theories and methodologies; and the intervention system, or agents undertaking the intervention.

In theoretical terms, the work is strongly grounded on Habermas' theory of communicative action (Habermas, 1987), but with the added consideration of knowledge being linked to power.

Mingers and Gill use this thinking to develop a framework for mapping methodologies against the four phases of appreciation, analysis, assessment, and action, based on Habermas' three worlds (Mingers & Gill, 1997, p. 431). The actual process of critical multimethodology, they argue, "will be a continual cycle of reflection, judgement, and action" (p. 437).

4.6.7 Pragmatic Pluralism

Taket and White (1996) offer pragmatic pluralism as a means of mixing methods from an essentially postmodernist perspective. Their approach is strongly grounded theoretically, with the suggestion that guidelines, examples, stories, and metaphors are of more value than prescribed frameworks for action. The approach is expressly holistic, and sees pluralism as a means of addressing diversity. Pluralism, they argue, should be applied to the roles of the interventionist, modes of representation, and the nature of the client. It is explicit that work with the disempowered should be seen as fundamental within any intervention context.

In application, it is argued that, in any intervention, there will be multiple rationalities to be managed, and that, whilst guidelines may be offered for addressing these, there is little to be gained from a prescriptive approach. The approach is therefore largely left open to the practitioner, who should follow a strategy of mix and match, operationalising what feels good in accordance with the guidelines provided: the interventionist should recognise differences in methodologies and match these with variety in the local context. Triangulation, the use of parts of methodologies in combination, a flexible and adaptive stance, and critical reflection are all fundamental to the application of this approach.

This completes the review of perspectives on KM. In the following section, discussion and critique is conducted, reflecting the issues raised by these theoretical and practical perspectives.

4.7 Discussion and Critique

Each of the approaches outlined above have in common the aim of addressing diverse (or 'pluralistic') problem contexts with a diversity of methods. One of the approaches, that of Ormerod, however, stands apart from all others in expressly recommending that theory is not considered as relevant to the domain. However, it might be argued that progressing in this purely ad hoc or contingent way turns the risk of trying to use a method in a way that actually contradicts the assumptions on which it is based:

> *"Different methodologies express different rationalities stemming from alternative theoretical positions which they reflect. These alternative positions must be respected, and methodologies and their appropriate theoretical underpinnings developed in partnership"* (Flood & Jackson, 1991, pp. 47-48).

The inference to be drawn from the other approaches outlined is that theoretical work in this domain is too important and relevant to be ignored. The system of systems methodologies originally presented an approach to matching problem context to methodologies seen to be applicable to that context, and was expressly based on Habermas' theory of knowledge constitutive interests (KCI). Total systems intervention initially operationalised SOSM into a process for intervention, similarly based on KCI; arguably, diversity management has continued this theme, being essentially an improved application of KCI. With the creative design of methods came an approach which sought to develop the ideas of SOSM and TSI, enabling the use of parts of methodologies, synthesised to address a unique problem context, within an expressly critical framework. The creative design of methods also introduced the idea of a basis in Habermas' theories of communicative action, rather than the theory of knowledge constitutive interests.

The recent critical systems practice advocated by Jackson also moves away from KCI, recommending instead that any claim to be using a methodology according to its theoretical rationale must be justified "according to the principles and guidelines established for the use of each…methodology" (Jackson, 2000, p. 393). In this, Jackson might be seen as returning to the need to recognise the distinctive background and theory of each methodology (see, for example, Jackson & Keys, 1984; Flood & Jackson, 1991; Brocklesby, 1995).

Pragmatic pluralism draws on a very broad theoretical range, but much is premised on critical social theory. Finally, critical pluralism provides a framework for intervention grounded on Habermas' theory of communicative action.

If we seek to summarise much of the work in KM in terms of theoretical development, the primary basis is to be found in critical social theory, with the main theories being applied in determining intervention approaches having been Habermas' theory of knowledge constitutive interests, and his theory of communicative action. Of these, communicative action seems the most promising arena in which to ground future development of the domain. An outline of the arguments in this respect might be as presented.

4.8 A Future for Knowledge Management

The ability to communicate by use of language is something that human beings bring to the world by nature of their existence: that is to say, it is not developed empirically, but is a priori. To the extent that any theoretical position can be grounded on such an a priori ability, then such a position may be seen as fundamental to us as communicative human actors.

In so far as communication, at least partially, may be oriented toward mutual understanding, it might be argued as the foundation of knowledge creation and sharing. In these terms, knowledge is not reducible (as is so often seen in scientific or pseudo-scientific study) to the properties of an objective world, but can be defined both objectively and according to the a priori concepts that the knowing subject brings to the act of perception. This knowing subject, being social, mediates all knowledge through social action and experience: subject and object are linked in the acts of cognition and social interaction, and the so-called subjective and objective 'paradigms' may be represented as just a convenient tool for understanding, which has been accorded too much primacy as a form of reality.

Rather, then, than relying on the concept of paradigms, this concept, and particularly the idea of paradigm incommensurability, should be opened up to challenge. Consider the so-called subjective/objective dichotomy. According to the paradigm argument, viewed (say) from an epistemological perspective, one who sees a problem context as positivistic, and seeks, for example, a technological solution, will be unable to communicate and share knowledge with another who views the same problem context as existing in the views and opinions of those participants involved in and affected by the system of concern. There are at least two fundamental difficulties with this:

1. It contradicts common human practice, and, dare it be suggested, common sense. Human participants in social groups commonly combine technical ('positivistic') and interpretative ('anti-positivistic') activity, seemingly denying the paradigm incommensurability thesis from an epistemological standpoint.

2. Theoretically, the paradigm incommensurability view seems to have dubious support. At its most basic level, it derives from the idea that technical, scientific, functionalist activity cannot be conducted together with interpretivistic, subjective activity. But if, theoretically, subjective and objective are inseparable, paradigm incommensurability becomes much less compelling.

In essence, then, it is the argument of this chapter that these difficulties disappear once a scientific basis for our thinking is denied. For example, suppose science (as is suggested by Kant and Habermas) is seen as just one form of knowledge, which in any case is simply a convenient human perception of how the world works. Now, all human endeavour becomes mediated through subjective understanding, and the paradigms as impenetrable barriers disappear. So, the problem of interest constitution theory being no longer defensible is resolved, since it is no longer being relied on. However, this problem has been replaced with another, which may be stated as follows:

1. Accepting all human actions as mediated through subjective understanding leads to the possibility of a basis for KM in the universal characteristics of language.

2. The dichotomy between subject and object has gone, and with it, paradigm incommensurability.

3. Organisational intervention is recast as an entirely communicative issue. For example, the so-called technical interest of knowledge constitution theory becomes instead a question of how technology may further enable human interaction, all within a framework of human intercommunication.

4. The difficulty that now arises is essentially a practical one, of how to incorporate these ideas into management practice.

Work by Habermas (1976, 1987) on communicative action presents a universal theory of language that suggests that all language is oriented toward three fundamental validity claims: truth, rightness, and sincerity. What is most compelling about this theory, however, is that all three validity claims are communicatively mediated. This viewpoint is most radically seen in respect of the truth claim, where it is proposed that such a claim results not from the content of descriptive statements, but from the Wittgenstinian approach, casting them as arising in language games that are linked to culture: truth claims are socially contextual.

'Truth' can therefore be assessed by reference to communication: truth is what statements, when true, state! Rightness is about norms of behaviour, which are culturally relevant, and are therefore to be determined by reference to that which is acceptable to those involved and affected in the system of concern as a cultural group. Finally, sincerity is about the speaker's internal world: his/her internal subjectivity.

These ideas can now be taken forward to provide a KM approach, or set of approaches, which are theoretically grounded, and closer to that which is experienced in action. The conclusions below begin this process.

4.9 Conclusions

The issues raised in this chapter can now be used to design a critical action framework for KM interventions, based on critical theory.

The review of KM undertaken in this chapter indicates the potential for approaches explicitly grounded in critical social theory, and points to a possible future direction through a Critical Action Framework for knowledge management (Figure 4.7). The research project of which this is part is now moving on to apply this framework and report on its use in action.

Figure 4.7: A Critical Action Framework for Knowledge Management

Investigation of	Investigation Through	Outcome—Knowledge to be Managed
Knowledge as:	Subject and Object investigated through Participative Analysis	"Manage" as a systemic process of participative inquiry
Memory	Tests of Communicative Rationality:	Outcomes in the form of:
Introspection	Truth	Systems Descriptions
Reflection	Rightness	Process
Testimony	Sincerity	Content
Inference		
	Involves Application of	Leads to Understanding of
	Methodologies for Problem Context Analysis	Context in which KM is to be Applied
	Methodologies for Participative Analysis	Processes for Knowledge Exchange to be embedded within the organisation
	Critical Method for Tests of Communicative Rationality	Knowledge Explicated to be Recorded for Shared Use
		Knowledge for which dissemination is to be Restricted

Chapter V

A Review of Knowledge Management Frameworks

5.1 Introduction

This research is concerned with developing a framework for the evaluation of an organisation's potential to engage in knowledge management (an organisation's 'KM-readiness', or KMR). To recap, Chapter 3 offered background information and empirical evidence of issues that need to be considered in organisations, Chapter 4 provided an overview of knowledge management, and Chapter 5 explored organisational structure, strategy, and culture in the context of knowledge management. Discussion thus far would not be sufficient to provide a robust and reasoned framework. This chapter is intended to accumulate some further and more focussed ideas as to what should be in a KMR framework, and to assist in the understanding of the material presented here and further on in this thesis. This chapter, therefore, provides a comprehensive review of published knowledge management frameworks that purport to address evaluation, implementation, and other connected areas.

Before continuing, it is important to set this exercise in context. The review of frameworks is distinct from a review of literature in which the frameworks are presented. The latter is not intended here. For example, a review of a paper may involve a comprehensive critique, which includes exploration into the general area of research, clarification of the hypothesis, detailed examination of research methods and methodology, literature review, and comprehensive examination of data representation and quality. Such a review would consider the presentation of the paper, and it would critically reflect on the overall purpose of the paper and contribution made to new knowledge, either conceptual or practical. This review focuses solely on the frameworks presented in a paper and in particular those that may address evaluation of knowledge management in an organisation.

This review is important in two major ways, both of which form the key objectives:

- First, by showing that there is no single existing framework that addresses KMR, gaps in concepts and practice are highlighted. This helps to demonstrate that a new framework for the evaluation of an organisation's potential to engage in knowledge management will contribute to knowledge; the shortfall is clearly demonstrated in this chapter.

- Second, the review highlights useful elements and concepts that ought to be in the framework being developed; this is also achieved.

More than 3,000 papers were found by means of the usual search methods. From these, based on titles, abstracts, and keywords, a total of 267 articles were identified as having potential relevance to this research. However, 107 of these focus solely on technology and technical aspects of information, and these were not considered suitable for the purposes of this research. The remainder of the papers were considered in more detail, and eventually 40 papers were considered to have frameworks of kinds that were worth serious evaluation.

The approach taken to this review is a qualitative interpretivist approach and as such specific issues require attention, such as reliability and validity. For example, Decrop (1999, p. 158) states that methodological introductions are "mostly limited to describing the research design or mentioning reliability and validity criteria, but without showing how these criteria are implemented." In an attempt to address such issues, this approach has been structured carefully by establishing the criteria up front and offering as consistent, systematic, transparent, and valid a review as possible, involving a three-stage process:

1.   The establishment of a set of keywords to conduct the initial search.

2.   An initial review of knowledge management frameworks and a process of elimination.

3.   A systematic review of the remaining and most appropriate frameworks with the help of an evaluation grid that has been developed as part of this work.

There are many euphemisms that might be used for the word 'framework'. These include process, approach, method, methodology, procedure, system, scheme, and structure, amongst others. Similarly the word 'evaluation' has many alternatives, and frameworks that address implementation, for example, may have a lot that could contribute to the process of evaluation. In order to avoid missing relevant frameworks, a set of euphemisms and variants was developed for the literature search (see Appendix 6.1). The literature search includes books, journals, conference papers, and Web-based materials.

An initial review of knowledge management frameworks and process of elimination was conducted to maintain focus and to avoid lengthy reviews of frameworks that were clearly not relevant, or of frameworks that are so embryonic that there is little to review. For example, after a review it may be discovered that a framework is clear in structure, methodologically robust, theoretically and empirically underpinned. However, if it addresses only one aspect of knowledge management (such as technology for example), it offers very limited possibilities in terms of evaluating an organisation's overall potential to engage in knowledge management. The latter is the purpose of this review, and as far as it has been possible, only papers that address this area have been selected for the next stage of more detailed review. Some approaches may be too simplistic or too theoretical and fail to offer a reasonable and coherent set of activities in any connected form that could be described as a framework (triviality criteria). Such papers were purposely excluded from the structured review.

Papers that presented a framework that focused on, or that contained associated concepts and elements that may be helpful in evaluating the extent to which an organisation is KM ready, and that did not fall foul of the triviality criteria (from 2), were subjected to a third level review. Such frameworks may not necessarily be designed explicitly, specifically, or solely to evaluate an organisation's KMR, but they appear to be directed toward assisting managers to assess their organisations' current situations and to suggest what might be addressed in order to introduce knowledge management into the organisation. This third level review is a systematic, structured, and consistent process undertaken with the help of the grid shown in Table 5.1.

Table 5.1: Generic Review Grid for Knowledge Management Frameworks

Score Key	1 = lowest possible score; 5 = highest possible score				
Total Score	**Explicitness**	**Clarity**	**Reasoning**	**Theory**	**Empirical Work**
Purpose	*Has the purpose of the framework been explicitly stated?*	*Has the purpose been discussed with clarity?*	*Is there reasoning to support the purpose of the framework?*	*Is there theoretical underpinning to support the purpose of the framework?*	*Is there empirical underpinning to support the purpose of the framework?*
Process	*Is the KM process explicitly stated?*	*Has the KM process been presented with clarity?*	*Is there reasoning to support the KM process?*	*Is there theoretical underpinning to support the KM process?*	*Is there empirical underpinning to support the KM process?*
Activities	*Are KM activities explicitly stated?*	*Have the KM activities been presented with clarity?*	*Is there reasoning to support the KM activities?*	*Is there theoretical underpinning to support the KM activities?*	*Is there empirical underpinning to support the KM activities?*
Develop & Test	*Is it explicit that development and testing has been undertaken?*	*Have the methods of development and testing been presented with clarity?*	*Have the methods of development and testing been reasoned?*	*Has development and testing been theoretically underpinned?*	*Has development and testing involved empirical evidence?*

This grid has been developed as part of this research and forms a major part of the review. It is intended to help offer an easily comparable and accessible review that is as consistent, objective, systematic, transparent, and valid as possible. To achieve this, the categories against which the review is conducted are established up front, and specific criteria, identified by Lincoln and Guba (1985, in Decrop, 1999, p. 158) is taken into consideration. Lincoln and Guba established four criteria that should be addressed when undertaking qualitative research:

1. *Credibility (internal validity):* How truthful are particular findings

2. *Transferability (external validity):* How applicable are the research findings to another setting or group?

3. *Dependability (reliability):* Are the results consistent and reproducible?

4. *Confirmability (objectivity):* How neutral are the findings (in terms of whether they are reflective of the informants and the inquiry, and not a product of the researcher's biases and prejudices)?

Applying these criteria specifically to the grid, credibility (internal validity) has been achieved through the process of assessment on an individual basis and according to each cell and the categories identified. Transferability (external validity) was introduced in two ways, first by iteration and comparing the outcomes of individual frameworks at a collective level within the scope of the overall review, which then provided more dependability, ensuring that the measures used were consistently applied in the broader sense. Second, the grid and its findings have been exposed to external critique. Feedback has indicated that the grid could be applied to other types of research, and the findings in this case seemed consistent and if undertaken by another could be reproduced as long as the objective remained consistent.

Confirmability was addressed through iteration and by reviewing the overall exercise with external input from practitioners and critique at the KMAC Conference at Aston (Coakes et al., 2003). Discussion at this conference highlighted that it is impossible to achieve a totally objective approach because a professional bias has to be maintained to achieve the objectives of the exercise. However, it has been possible to reduce personal biases and prejudices, achieving a more neutral approach than would otherwise be the case. The following section provides further detail of the grid and how it was used.

5.2 Generic Review Grid for Knowledge Management Frameworks

The left-hand column identifies elements that were considered when reviewing the frameworks and assists in understanding the structure of proposed frameworks and how they have been developed. The elements are purpose, process, activities, development, and testing. These were established through an initial literature search to clarify the areas that knowledge management frameworks include and represent key significant strategic elements or concepts expected in most systematic approaches to knowledge management. Development and testing has been included because without appropriate development and testing, a framework may not achieve what it is intended for. The row headings help to assess the credibility and quality of the elements in the left-hand column that are considered in the frameworks; these are explicitness, clarity, reasoning, theory, and empirical work.

The grid was applied by considering the frameworks being reviewed in the context of each cell, and by cross-referencing and asking the relevant questions; scores were then applied. Each individual cell is scored according to the extent to which the requirements of the cells have been met. The score key is based on a simple 1-5 Likert scale. A score of 1 shows that the specific cell was considered to be extremely poor in regard to the criteria indicated, and a score of 5 shows that the specific cell fully met the criteria. The highest possible score per framework is 100, the lowest possible score is 20. It is important to recognise here that if this is to be conducted in a constructive and critical manner, then it is important to ask the right questions in each cell, as Ulrich (2003, p. 326) indicates: "It is usually better to ask the right questions without having the answers than to have the answers without having asked…competence depends more on the questions we ask than on the answers we find." The following describes and explains the cells and applications in more detail.

Purpose

The purpose is to some extent self-explanatory because without purpose it is questionable as to why a framework would be proposed. By clearly stating the purpose of the framework, this ensures that the reader or potential user understands the overall objective.

Knowledge Management Process

There may be diverse approaches to knowledge management process and different terms used, for example: strategy, stages, system, and elements. Recent discussion on the 'Knowledge Forum' highlights this further (Husig, 10 March 03, Processes and Knowledge). Husig recognises that there are different understandings of the term process and explicitly defines knowledge management process as an integral part of the organisation's business process. Knowledge management process is defined as the broad linkages within which knowledge management operates and has been selected to determine the extent to which a framework has been structured.

Knowledge Management Activities

Knowledge management activities are the actions that are taken within the process, and here it was important to identify the distinction between process and activities, because the interchangeable use of the term's process and activity can cause confusion about the structure and layers within a framework. For example, as with knowledge process, activities may also be referred to in different ways; for example, some frameworks may have strategy as the process, and processes as the activities. Exploring this further using the grid helps to organise variable language about the frameworks into a logical structure for consideration.

Development and Testing

Development and testing is important in establishing the extent to which a framework has been developed and its readiness to be used following testing and validation. If appropriate testing has not been undertaken, the framework may not achieve what the author purports the purpose to be, and therefore remains conceptual or aspirational.

Explicitness

Explicitness explores the extent to which the different elements are presented intelligibly, so that the reader or potential user can distinguish what the framework's purpose is and the extent to which the elements have been clearly stated.

Clarity

Clarity relates to ongoing discussion about the different elements of the framework and measures the extent to which discussion is transparent and well structured; for example, this relates to how and where the elements of the framework might be used, which increases understanding, confidence, and the ability to apply or adapt the framework independently and successfully.

Reasoning

Reasoning is intended to establish the rationale behind the chosen elements of the framework and measures the extent to which the elements have been discussed with justification and with effective use of literature. If well reasoned, the discussion about the framework answers how and why questions that users may have when attempting to understand the ethos behind a framework.

Theory

Theory may be drawn from any area as long as it is relevant and appropriate to provide principles of analysis or an explanation of the elements of the framework. If properly justified and referenced, theoretical underpinning can provide a more robust structure and foundation for each aspect of the framework.

Empirical

Empirical underpinning relates to the extent to which the elements have been compiled and tested by some form of evidence drawn from 'real-world' experience. For example, survey research to consider what process or activities could be included, and the application of the framework to a given organisation to test fitness for purpose.

The individual cells and column headings will be discussed next, and explanations and reasons will be provided to assist in understanding the grid and its context.

Purpose/Explicitness

This is intended to assess the extent to which the purpose of the framework has been explicitly stated. There may be several intended purposes and the importance here is that these are clearly stated. This cell therefore measures the extent to which this is achieved.

Purpose/Clarity

In some cases discussion may be embarked upon in a disjointed manner and contrary to the purpose of the framework. This can result in ambiguity and misunderstanding obstructing the ability to use the framework. This cell measures the extent to which discussion is applied with clarity.

Purpose/Reasoning

This is an assessment of the extent to which authors include relevant literature in discussion effectively and how this is applied to the overall purpose. It also establishes why the framework has been produced and why different approaches have been adopted.

Purpose/Theoretical Underpinning

This cell measures the extent to which theory is applied to the purpose of the framework. There is no prescription about any particular theory, but it should be clearly stated and an overall theoretical foundation established. For example this could be systems theory, decision-making theory, organisational behavioural theory, and so on.

Purpose/Empirical Work

This measures the extent to which research has been undertaken to justify the need for a framework, rather than relying on a literature review only.

Knowledge Management Process/Explicitness

This is a measurement of the extent to which knowledge management process has been made clear in the framework. For example, by explicitly recognising process, the structure of a framework may be more coherent, transparent, and understandable. The user is then in a position to understand what the process is and how it may be used.

Knowledge Management Process/Clarity

Having established what the process is, bearing in mind that use of language may vary ranging from strategy, systems, stages, and so on, this cell measures the extent to which the process is discussed and presented with clarity.

Knowledge Management Process/Reasoning

This measures the extent to which literature is applied in discussion to underpin the chosen process. Although each approach may be relevant, the extent to which this has been reasoned is important to assist with understanding the chosen approach.

Knowledge Management Process/Theory

This cell identifies whether theoretical underpinning has been applied to the knowledge management process and if so, it measures the extent to which it has been used and explained.

Knowledge Management Process/Empirical Work

This cell measures whether empirical work has been undertaken to develop the chosen process.

Knowledge Management Activities/Explicitness

This cell is a measurement of the extent to which knowledge management activities have been made clear in the framework. As with knowledge management process, use of language may vary, for example steps, tools, actions, sub processes to meet the overall process, strategy, or system of a framework.

Knowledge Management Activities/Clarity

This cell measures the extent to which the activities are discussed and presented with clarity.

Knowledge Management Activities/Reasoning

This cell measures the extent to which literature and its application to the development of activities within the framework has been undertaken.

Knowledge Management Activities/Theory

This cell identifies whether theoretical underpinning has been applied and, if so, measures the extent to which it is used and discussed.

Development and Testing/Explicitly Stated

This cell measures the extent to which development and testing has been clearly stated in a structured way.

Development and Testing/Clarity

If development and testing has been undertaken, this cell measures the method by which it has been undertaken and whether it has been discussed and presented in a clear and constructive way.

Development and Testing/Reasoning

This cell measures why a particular method of development and testing has been undertaken and the extent to which literature (if appropriate) has been used and applied through discussion.

Development and Testing/Theory

Development and testing will be enhanced further if underpinned by theoretical and methodological principles. This is the extent to which theory and methodology has been applied in development and testing.

Development and Testing/Empirical Work

Development and testing should by implication involve empirical work. If not it is questionable as to what kind of development and testing has been undertaken. This cell measures the extent to which this has been achieved.

5.3 Framework Review

Mullich (2001)

Purpose

Overall, the introduction and discussion about any proposed framework is unstructured, with weak links and no conclusions, which makes it extremely difficult to ascertain the purpose of any intended framework (if it exists). It is in fact unclear if there is a framework at all. The importance of distinguishing between knowledge management and information management is stated, with

no further discussion about the differences between the two or the consequences if the distinction is ignored. A subsequent comment points to the need
to provide better information to achieve positive results, yet the focus is about
growing a knowledge management system. Initially, slow incremental implementation of a knowledge management system by means of pilot projects is
proposed, but the perspective shifts quickly to being organisational-wide.
Discussion therefore is ambiguous and there is little or no reference to literature.
There is no theoretical underpinning or empirical work throughout.

Knowledge Management Process

There is no explicit knowledge management process discussed, although
components are mentioned that might be considered implicitly to be activities
within a knowledge management process. No explicit links are made between
the activities. Reference is made to project processes and business processes,
and the process of providing information, but there is no focus on the
knowledge management process.

Knowledge management is regarded as impacting on business process, rather
than being regarded as an integral part of the process; one comment explicitly
states that during the implementation of a knowledge management system,
people want information about using technology more than the knowledge
management process.

Knowledge Management Activities

Apart from brief comment about knowledge transfer and collaboration, knowledge management activities are not evident and have not been discussed in a
structured manner. However, there is a set of bullet points, which the author
promotes as a means to involve people, and consequently, as a means to
successful knowledge management initiatives.

Development and Testing

The author has not presented a specific framework or proposal for testing.

Results and Conclusions

There are no real results or conclusions. A list of bullet points is presented that appear to be the factors that could be considered in the development of a knowledge management system.

Summary

This is an anecdotal presentation of a knowledge management system with an ambiguous purpose. Throughout, there is no explanation, very little discussion, and no real evidence or reasoning to support any of the assertions made. Statements are unsupported by explanation, discussion, evidence, or reasoning. There is no overall research design, and no theoretical underpinning or empirical support is provided.

The list of bullet points are the nearest this gets to a 'system', and, given the previous comments, these cannot be considered to be robust or reliable.

Score Key	1 = lowest possible score; 5 = highest possible score				
Total Score 20	Explicitness	Clarity	Reasoning	Theory	Empirical Work
Purpose	1	1	1	1	1
Process	1	1	1	1	1
Activities	1	1	1	1	1
Develop & Test	1	1	1	1	1

Robertson (2002)

Purpose

The purpose of this approach is explicitly stated as a description of two knowledge sharing systems and exploration as to why they were used differently. However, the author refers to knowledge sharing systems, knowledge management systems, and information systems, using the three terms interchangeably, making no explicit distinction between these concepts. A comprehensive description of an IT system is provided that was implemented in a first case scenario and modified in a second, as a result of a merger between two companies. As discussion progresses, it loses clarity and appears to be more about one IT system that has been modified and developed rather than two systems. There is no overall theoretical underpinning, and empirical work is limited to the boundaries of the merging organisations, presented in a retrospective and descriptive manner.

Knowledge Management Process

The author draws on his experience of developing and implementing an IT system, providing clear detail about the capabilities of software. There is no reference to the overall knowledge management process and little use of literature in discussion about the use of the chosen software. Although the importance of people, teams, and collaboration is explicitly stated, there is no further discussion and the focus is on IT-based information sharing and interaction with the IT system. There is no reference to theory and empirical work specifically in relation to the knowledge management process.

Knowledge Management Activities

Knowledge management activities have not been referred to except in the context of implementing a system and accessing information through the use of ICT. The author expressly includes hard data-based activities such as document storage, search capability, security features, and Web-based software. There is no reference to theory, and empirical work is based on the author's perspective within the context of the merging organisational IT systems.

Development and Testing

The approach used in development and testing involves a description of the author's experience in developing an IT system, which is company focused and incremental. The author highlights the need for a participative approach with optimal user groups to design and develop the system, but there is no overall design for this development and no indication of testing or benchmarking beyond the confines of the organisation. The author highlights issues that are related to the implementation and evaluation of a knowledge sharing system, which he suggests have been collected through interviews with users, however there is no methodology and context in which this information has been collected and no reference to theory.

Results and Conclusions

The author provides results to indicate increased use of the second stage modified IT system and reasons as to why this has been achieved. These include participation and discussion with users to achieve the most relevant design of the system and maintenance of a website with living documents to ensure continued contribution. Although the results indicate a high level of human issues including communication, there is no discussion about this aspect of knowledge management apart from interaction with the system. In the final conclusion the author identifies a list of activities that relate to information sharing, but again confuses the reader by explicitly referring to knowledge management, when in fact the content is about an IT system.

Summary

Overall, the purpose of this approach does not fully reflect the content, which is further exacerbated by the interrelated use of terms, for example knowledge management, information systems, knowledge sharing system. This is an experiential and descriptive account of the implementation of an IT system, based in a specific organisation. Although explanation, reasoning, and evaluation are provided to a limited extent, there is little empirical support beyond the organisation, and reference to empirical work contains no indication of how this information was collected. There is no overall research design and theoretical underpinning. A description of the development and implementation of an IT system and software is provided, with the implication that knowledge management is an IT system, yet there is no reasoning to underpin this perspective.

The main contribution this model offers to the development of an evaluation framework is the need for a participative approach when assessing the current situation, and designing and implementing an IT system for information sharing in an organisation. This approach implicitly contains evaluation and in this case is specifically focussed on an IT system.

Score Key	1 = lowest possible score; 5 = highest possible score				
Total Score **30**	**Explicitness**	**Clarity**	**Reasoning**	**Theory**	**Empirical Work**
Purpose	3	1	1	1	2
Process	2	1	1	1	1
Activities	2	2	1	1	2
Develop & **Test**	2	2	1	1	2

Gao, Li, & Nakamori (2002)

Purpose

The purpose of this framework is stated as a new systematic perspective on knowledge and a toolbox for practical knowledge users, however as discussion continues, confusion emerges. A review of literature and exploration into knowledge theory informs discussion and development of the author's perspective on knowledge management. From this, the authors indicate that there is a softer trend in the knowledge management process, in addition to new technology such as the use of the Web, information technology, and expert systems.

Discussion becomes disjointed when the authors propose a new systematic perspective on knowledge, using critical systems thinking and soft systems thinking, which when applied to knowledge management is intended to provide a useful toolbox for practical knowledge users. Although a toolbox is provided, discussion in relation to development loses clarity because the author then refers to two sets of systems. The final outcome presents a framework that relates a proposed knowledge system to eight systems methodologies applied to different knowledge processes. The authors refer to this as being the tool kit, however there is limited discussion as to why each systems methodology might be appropriate and no indication of how this tool kit might be used in practice.

Knowledge Management Process

The knowledge management process is organised and defined by the authors in the first instance by separating the management of work process from the management of knowledge workers, to classify knowledge management into two dimensions, which are hard conditions and soft environments. This is clear and well reasoned out, and the authors propose two sets of systems method-ology to underpin these dimensions:

- the organisational knowledge system (explicit and cultural knowledge);
- the human being as part of an organisation and personal knowledge (explicit and tacit).

The authors define the organisational knowledge system or process as the management of existing knowledge, which includes developing knowledge repositories and knowledge compilation arrangements and categorisation. The human being as part of an organisation is defined as the management of specific knowledge management activities. There is no reference to empirical work, and theory is drawn from systems thinking.

Knowledge Management Activities

Knowledge management activities are explicitly stated and include managing knowledge acquisition, creation, distribution, communication, sharing, and application. The authors propose that to sustain these activities, it is important to create the right hard and soft environments, for example the hard environment relates to technology and the soft environment relates to people issues such as teamwork and the learning climate. The authors distinguish between knowledge objects and process, defining knowledge objects as entities that exist in their own right over time in a hierarchical system which includes data, facts, information, experience, learning, and expertise. The knowledge is then used as a tool to underpin people's theoretical and practical work in the social organisational setting. Again there is no reference to empirical work to substantiate this approach.

Development and Testing

There is no indication of testing of this framework. With regard to development of the framework and theoretical underpinning, the authors explicitly state the need for two sets of systems to underpin knowledge management. They propose that various systems methodologies enable knowledge to be applied systematically by employing soft systems methodologies generically or as a lens according to the knowledge management approach and methodology that demonstrates most synergy. Although initially the distinction between the use of two sets of systems methodologies is made, the application of various soft systems methodologies is applied in the final framework. At this stage, the paper loses clarity, because there is no specific focus and, for the practitioner, no indication as to how to apply and use each methodology.

Results and Conclusions

There is no indication that this framework has been tested, therefore, there are no results. The authors conclude by asserting that this framework could be used as a whole or a lens to systematically apply knowledge. This includes decision-making, engendering working relationships, and facilitating knowledge sharing. There is no indication of how this could work in practice.

Summary

The purpose in this case is to provide a new systematic perspective on knowledge and a useful toolbox for practical knowledge users. As discussion unfolds, however, discussion loses clarity and the extent to which the purpose is achieved is questionable. Theoretical underpinning is drawn from the area of systems thinking, however, because the authors refer to several different approaches in systems thinking, discussion remains at a general level. This does not provide the opportunity to understand and justify why a particular soft systems approach might be used at a particular point of the knowledge management process. There is no indication of empirical work in the development and testing of the framework, therefore it remains conceptual. Further, the authors intend this framework to be a toolbox for practical knowledge users; if, however, practical knowledge users do not have prior knowledge and understanding of each systems thinking approach, the purpose of the framework may not be achieved. This framework contributes a conceptual overview of systems thinking to knowledge management and indicates that such an approach may be an effective way forward in the development of an evaluation framework.

Score Key	1 = lowest possible score; 5 = highest possible score				
Total Score 43	**Explicitness**	**Clarity**	**Reasoning**	**Theory**	**Empirical Work**
Purpose	*4*	*2*	*3*	*3*	*1*
Process	*4*	*2*	*3*	*3*	*1*
Activities	*3*	*2*	*3*	*3*	*1*
Develop & **Test**	*1*	*1*	*1*	*1*	*1*

Connell, Klein, Loebbecke, & Powell (2001)

Purpose

The purpose here is the introduction of a Knowledge Management Consultation System (KMCS), in which the authors provide the characteristics of the structure and functioning of such a system. This is clearly stated, and a model of the KMCS and the purpose of the model is presented and discussed in the context of knowledge transfer. The distinction is made between knowledge, the need for knowledge, and the carriers of these components, including the complexities of transferring tacit to explicit and tacit to tacit knowledge. The authors clearly state that the model has not been empirically validated and therefore remains conceptual.

Knowledge Management Process

The knowledge management process is made clear, with the emphasis of discussion on the process of knowledge transfer from person to person, and person to machine. The authors highlight weaknesses in the use of IT, and propose that the KMCS considers the organisational implications of a knowledge management system. Discussion is presented with clarity focussing on two key components of the KMCS—a human expert or computer that holds knowledge, and a user with a need to consult the knowledge, each defining the other. The authors refer to the sociotechnical approach as an indication of theoretical underpinning, and point out that either way, both components comprise one element of a sociotechnical system. This incorporates explicit foreground knowledge such as facts, rules, formal heuristics, and social norms, and implicit background knowledge, which is routine or instinctive, tacit and intuitive. The authors propose that the KMCS attempts to bring together the social domain and knowledge-based systems to develop and integrate both with the same consideration in one process.

Knowledge Management Activities

Knowledge management activities have been referred to as the components of the KMCS, and are clearly defined and categorised according to the type of action or activities within the overall process of consultation. These include the participants in different roles within a system, for example, those who are experts to be consulted and those who require knowledge.

The author asserts that participants within the system—whether an expert or client—have their own conceptual structures and definitions of the world which are carried out through social constructs from which rules are developed through social interaction. The consultation activity is, therefore, subject to interpretation, norms, values, and beliefs, and there is no guarantee of accuracy in any exchange. Although coherently discussed, there is no empirical work to support this perspective.

Development and Testing

The approach taken to development and testing of the KMCS has not been explicitly stated and appears to have been undertaken through discussion, reasoning, and contribution from literature. There is no empirical evidence to validate the KMCS, and there is no indication that it has been tested. It, therefore, remains aspirational.

Results and Conclusions

There are no specific results in relation to this framework, as it has not been empirically tested. The authors conclude by declaring that the KMCS could have implications for the functionality of computer-based knowledge management systems.

Summary

The purpose of the KMCS is discussed in a coherent and balanced manner. In some areas, theoretical underpinning is drawn from literature to support ideas and discussion, however this is very limited and general, and there is no empirical work. The knowledge management process is discussed directly in relation to knowledge transfer, and focuses on consultation between people, and between people and IT. Knowledge activities include communication only, and are referred to within the scope of the consultation. Although this is well reasoned and clear, the inadequacy of robust empirical and theoretical discussion, in addition to the fact that no further development and testing have taken place, weakens the system.

The main contribution that this system makes to the development of an evaluation framework is the distinction and interaction between people and IT, and the recognition that a sociotechnical approach may be a relevant underpinning theory providing a more holistic view of knowledge management.

Score Key	1 = lowest possible score; 5 = highest possible score				
Total Score **51**	**Explicitness**	**Clarity**	**Reasoning**	**Theory**	**Empirical Work**
Purpose	*5*	*5*	*5*	*2*	*1*
Process	*5*	*5*	*5*	*2*	*1*
Activities	*3*	*2*	*2*	*2*	*1*
Develop & **Test**	*1*	*1*	*1*	*1*	*1*

Bhatt (2002)

Purpose

The purpose of this framework is clear and is intended to explore the differences between individual and organisational knowledge, and how individual knowledge can be transformed into organisational knowledge. A review of knowledge management sets the context in which the author presents this framework, providing clarity and understanding of what the author is attempting to achieve. Use of literature is limited, and there is no theoretical or empirical underpinning.

Knowledge Management Process

The distinction between process and activities is not made clear. In general the author argues that it is through organisation, including procedures, information, rules, and ideas, that knowledge is realised, and knowledge management is defined as a process of facilitating knowledge. The process includes two approaches, the first being the relationship between individual and organisational knowledge, and the second relates to knowledge management strategies. Each approach is discussed, logically reasoned, and visually illustrated. Both provide a continuum of the process from individual to formal knowledge management and an underpinning strategy to manage this. In addition the author makes the distinction between independent and inter-dependent interactions, and the nature of tasks between routine and specifiable, and non-routine and non-specifiable. There is no reference to theoretical or empirical underpinning for the knowledge management process, and because each approach is referred to as a process, this can cause some confusion in attempting to understand the structure.

Knowledge Management Activities

The author does not clearly and explicitly identify knowledge management activities within the process, but refers to learning, diverse tasks, and the use of information systems such as the Internet, intranets, and extranets. Again there is no reference to theoretical or empirical underpinning.

Development and Testing

This framework has been developed through discussion and reference to literature. There is no indication of empirical research and testing of the framework.

Results and Conclusions

There are no specific results, and the author concludes by emphasising the importance of creating organisational knowledge through individual interactions and the importance for management to provide the right environment to achieve this. There is no further discussion or indication of how management might achieve this.

Summary

The purpose of the framework and subsequent discussion is clear, however the author does not distinguish between knowledge management process and activities, but uses these terms interchangeably, with emphasis on process. The main focus is on the transfer of individual to organisational knowledge, and this is clearly reasoned. There is no explicit theoretical underpinning or empirical research, with the exception of reference to literature to justify the author's perspective. There is no evidence of testing, therefore this framework remains conceptual. The main contribution from this framework is the recognition of the continuum within which knowledge is transferred from individuals to the organisational level, and in terms of evaluating an organisation's readiness for knowledge management, this continuum may already be in place, but not necessarily made explicit in the business process.

Score Key	1 = lowest possible score; 5 = highest possible score				
Total Score 41	Explicitness	Clarity	Reasoning	Theory	Empirical Work
Purpose	5	5	5	1	1
Process	3	3	3	1	1
Activities	2	2	2	1	1
Develop & Test	1	1	1	1	1

Hlupic, Pouloudi, & Rzevski (2002)

Purpose

The purpose of the framework proposed here is clearly stated for use in research into knowledge management. The framework is intended to provide a systematic and interdisciplinary approach to research in knowledge management through technical and hard, organisational and soft, philosophical and abstract perspectives.

Discussion is well structured and set in context by reviewing previous management approaches such as Total Quality Management and Business Process Reengineering, in addition to knowledge management. The authors propose that in the past, too much emphasis has been placed on technology and inadequate research has been undertaken into people's experiences of the interaction between business and people, and technology factors. The authors explore what knowledge management is and recognise that although the benefits to organisations are clear, there is still confusion about what knowledge management means and literature is diverse with no agreed definition behind the term knowledge management. There is no explicit reference to theoretical underpinning or empirical work.

Knowledge Management Process

Drawing on knowledge management literature, the authors provide a unified definition of knowledge management, identifying and emphasising people, technology, and the interplay between both. A clear distinction is made between hard and soft aspects, and comprehensive discussion is undertaken in relation to knowledge management processes from different perspectives. For example, the technical perspective includes tools, technology, and processes. The human and organisational perspective includes organisational learning, business intelligence, culture, human resource management, and operational management. The ontological and epistemological and psychological perspectives include definitions of knowledge management and appropriate methods for investigating knowledge management phenomena.

Knowledge Management Activities

This paper does not explicitly emphasise knowledge management activities. The focus is primarily on process.

Development and Testing

The development of this framework is undertaken through a comprehensive review into previous knowledge management literature. There is no indication of empirical work, therefore the framework remains conceptual.

Results and Conclusions

The authors provide an integrated framework based on knowledge management as an interdisciplinary approach for use in research into knowledge management. There are no results presented in this paper. The authors conclude by highlighting that there is little empirical and theoretical work that provides an integrated and systematic exploration into knowledge management, proposing that their framework will meet this need.

Summary

The purpose of the framework is clearly stated and the content is clear with well-reasoned discussion. The authors draw on previous knowledge management literature to develop this framework. There is no empirical work and the authors indicate that theory underpinning knowledge management remains inadequate. Knowledge management processes are reviewed to consider the potential approaches to research knowledge management in an integrated and coherent manner. Knowledge management activities are not explicitly referred to. The framework is clear and understandable, however there is no testing, therefore the framework remains conceptual. Although the framework is not appropriate for knowledge management in an organisational context, it does contribute to this review by confirming the weaknesses in previous literature in relation to theoretical underpinning and the need for an integrated approach to knowledge management. It also organises the different perspectives to knowledge management in a structured manner.

Score Key	1 = lowest possible score; 5 = highest possible score				
Total Score **46**	**Explicitness**	**Clarity**	**Reasoning**	**Theory**	**Empirical Work**
Purpose	5	5	5	2	1
Process	5	5	5	2	1
Activities	1	1	1	1	1
Develop & **Test**	1	1	1	1	1

Holsapple & Joshi (2002)

Purpose

The purpose of this framework is to describe knowledge manipulation activities that may occur during the process of knowledge flow, termed by the authors as an episode. This is clearly stated, and the authors propose that the framework can be used as a common language for debate about knowledge manipulation, and practitioners could use the framework to consider activities in relation to the design, measurement, control, and support of an organisation's knowledge management episodes. The authors provide a robust methodology and empirical work in the development of this framework, but there is no overall theoretical underpinning.

Knowledge Management Process

Overall the authors state that the knowledge management process is directed and shaped by managerial influences, and facilitated or obstructed by environmental influences and organisational resources. Discussion is clear and well reasoned, with the authors describing knowledge as a process by which an organisation's joint human-computer system changes the organisation's state of knowledge and produces outputs. They recognise the extent to which a system of knowledge management can be either complex or in some cases fairly straightforward, independent or interdependent. The term knowledge episode is used to define the process of identifying knowledge need through to satisfying that need, or not as the case may be. This episode can be independent or interdependent with other episodes and will occur at any given time in an organisation. The authors provide a clear methodology, which supports this approach to knowledge management process, however there is no theoretical underpinning.

Knowledge Management Activities

Knowledge management activities are explicitly stated and the authors distinguish between elemental level and higher-level knowledge activities. Elemental refers to the knowledge cycle, for example sharing, creating, identifying, collecting, adapting, organising, and applying knowledge. Higher level relates more to strategic approaches. This framework focuses on elemental activities and sub-activities, which directly manipulate knowledge and produce knowledge flows within a knowledge management episode. Overall the framework concentrates on activities such as the acquisition, selection, internalising, and utilisation of knowledge in addition to the internalisation and externalisation of knowledge and generating new knowledge. This is broken down further by exploring the sub-activities involved, for example, during the acquisition of knowledge, activities to capture include extracting, collecting, and gathering valid knowledge, which is then organised by distilling, refining, orienting, interpreting, packaging, assembling, and transforming. Transferring the knowledge includes activities such as communication channel identification, selection, scheduling, and sending. Internalising involves assessing and valuing the knowledge to be internalised and identifying the knowledge resources that are to be impacted by the knowledge flow produced. The description of activities is clear and well reasoned using empirical work gathered through the Delphi process. There is no theoretical underpinning.

Development and Testing

Development and testing has been clearly stated and structured using the Delphi approach. This includes a combination of concepts, best practices, and literature leading to an initial framework, which was then critiqued and evaluated by a panel of knowledge management practitioners and academics. During the development phase, the authors carried out a comparative analysis of knowledge management frameworks, identifying various knowledge management activities, which confirmed for them the need for a generic framework of knowledge manipulation activities. During the preliminary phase, evaluation criteria and standards were determined prior to starting development of the framework. Three boundaries were defined—business, descriptive, and detail. The business boundary focused on the development of knowledge management within business organisations. The descriptive boundary purely described knowledge manipulation activities in the process of knowledge management. The detail boundary was set as two levels, the first to identify basic knowledge manipulation activities at one level and their sub-activities at the second.

An iterative approach was used in developing the initial framework to account for notions of elemental knowledge found in a survey of literature, matching concepts, ideas, language, and their inter-relationships, which were compared, organised, and unified in an inductive fashion over many iterations. The framework was empirically evaluated using questionnaires and feedback received from a panel of academics and practitioners.

Results and Conclusions

The results and conclusions of the development of this framework are explicitly stated and underpinned with empirical research. A selection of responses are presented and commented upon further by the authors, adding to the robustness of this framework. The authors conclude by identifying implications of the framework, within which they discuss the activities that the framework could be used for such as exploring tacit and implicit knowledge, using it as a structure for discussing knowledge management issues, and as a basis for communication and sharing of ideas. The authors finally point out that they do not advocate a particular methodology or process to coordinate such activities, but the various configurations can be combined to define a process or methodology.

Summary

The purpose and subsequent discussion of this framework is explicitly stated, well structured, and clear. The methodology based on the Delphi process used by the authors provides validation and adds to the credibility of this framework.

Knowledge management process, activities, development, and testing are all well reasoned and empirically robust. Theoretical underpinning is applied to specific knowledge activities such as generating knowledge and the sub-activities involved in this process. Overall, however, the framework is not underpinned by any specific theory. The main contribution to be taken from this framework relates to the process and activities that should be considered to implement knowledge flow and manipulation. The empirical research undertaken is robust and provides perspectives on knowledge management that are useful to consider as secondary research in the development of a framework for the evaluation of an organisation's readiness to engage with the concept of knowledge management.

Score Key	1 = lowest possible score; 5 = highest possible score				
Total Score **92**	**Explicitness**	**Clarity**	**Reasoning**	**Theory**	**Empirical Work**
Purpose	5	5	5	1	5
Process	5	5	5	2	5
Activities	5	5	5	4	5
Develop & **Test**	5	5	5	5	5

Newman & Conrad (2000)

Purpose

The purpose of this framework is clear, to characterise knowledge management tools such as methods, practices, and technologies available to knowledge management practitioners. The authors describe the framework as a classification framework that incorporates principles, theories, and models that have been refined to support the author's approach to knowledge management. Theory, however, is not explicitly applied. Discussion continues with clarity and recognition of the association between people and technology, and consideration of knowledge management as more of an integrating practice than a new management practice. The authors assert that the framework has its theoretical roots in complex systems and human knowledge interactions, though they do not expressly discuss this. They propose that the framework can be used to: support internal development efforts to map specific tools and technologies according to their potential roles in knowledge flows, identify functional gaps, determine integration points, and endorse efforts that seek to develop technologies with a specific function. There is no evidence of empirical work to underpin this.

Knowledge Management Process

The knowledge management process is drawn out in relation to the knowledge flow, with activities to produce, manipulate, and use knowledge. There is no theoretical and empirical underpinning in relation to process.

Knowledge Management Activities

The author organises knowledge flows into four activities—knowledge creation, retention, transfer, and use. These activities are clearly described in more detail individually. In addition, explicit, implicit, and tacit knowledge artefacts are described. Explicit knowledge artefacts include hard-based information, for example reports, books, and files. Implicit knowledge artefacts are described as information that cannot be explicitly captured but can be inferred. Tacit knowledge artefacts are those which cannot be codified; these include unconscious awareness as much as knowledge that one is consciously aware of.

The authors assert that individual, automated, and organisational agents make knowledge artefacts active. Individual agents relate to people and may function independently or as part of a team, and are core to the knowledge process. Automated agents refer to technology, and organisational agents are more complex because they relate more to the organisation's retention and transfer of knowledge, which can be both technical and human, and incorporate culture.

The authors continue by discussing the behavioural differences between agent types and how different agents may deal with knowledge, whether codifying, contextualising, or sharing. The framework organises, applies, and integrates knowledge artefacts and agents to enable relevant selection of tools, and the development and deployment of knowledge. Although rationally described, there is no evidence of empirical work or theoretical underpinning, and little reference to literature.

Development and Testing

There is no indication of empirical testing of this framework and little reference to previous literature. The framework therefore remains conceptual.

Results and Conclusions

There are no specific results and the author concludes by proposing how the framework could be used, encouraging the reader to apply it and feedback to the authors. At this stage comment is made that further descriptions of the theoretical underpinnings will be undertaken in the future.

Summary

The purpose of this paper is explicitly stated and discussion continues with clarity and in a logical manner; however, there is an absence of theoretical and empirical underpinning and little reference to literature throughout. The knowledge process is briefly mentioned, but the majority of content focuses on knowledge management activities, which are described in some detail. It appears that development has been progressed from the author's own perspective and the framework has not been tested. The authors conclude by challenging the reader to apply the framework and feedback to their perspectives. The most interesting contribution to be gained from this framework relates to the author's perspective on the various agents, which are individual, automated, and organisational agents. The recognition that individual agents may function differently when in a team-based situation, when interacting with technology or at an organisational level, may be an important consideration when evaluating an organisation's readiness to engage with knowledge management. For example, the impact could require different management approaches and different levels of appreciation in terms of the dominant and sub-cultures of the organisation.

Score Key	1 = lowest possible score; 5 = highest possible score				
Total Score 44	Explicitness	Clarity	Reasoning	Theory	Empirical Work
Purpose	5	5	3	1	1
Process	2	3	2	1	1
Activities	5	5	3	1	1
Develop & Test	1	1	1	1	1

Arora (2002)

Purpose

The purpose of this framework is clear and is based on the Balanced Score Card to align management processes, introduce performance measurements, and focus an organisation to implement knowledge management. The author establishes the context by highlighting concerns that managers have in managing and institutionalising knowledge, and recognises the need for a structured and systematic approach. The authors assert that successful facilitation of knowledge management in this respect requires a long-term strategy with a clear vision, objectives and approaches that focus on the human side, and culture change more so than technology. There is no evidence of empirical work or theoretical underpinning to support this framework.

Knowledge Management Process

The authors explicitly highlight the knowledge management process, through three main objectives, which are knowledge exploitation, innovation, and skill enhancement. Each objective is broken down further. With regard to knowledge exploitation, the author highlights reasons for inefficiency and some proposals to rectify these. Knowledge innovation is discussed in the context of communities of practice, and in relation to skill enhancement, the author suggests some activities such as job rotation and communication to improve competence. Overall the author proposes that the Balanced Score Card provides a process to identify parameters and monitor knowledge management. The Balanced Score Card provides four perspectives that are considered, which are the financial perspective, the customer perspective, learning and growth, and the internal business process. Essentially this is the application of the Balanced Score Card as a financial management process, and there is no reference to theory or empirical work.

Knowledge Management Activities

Knowledge management activities are indicated through generic parameters that reflect the progress of knowledge management. These primarily relate to different types of communication such as discussion, communities of practice, feedback, team-based activities, and collaboration. The author also includes codification, products that have been introduced and measurement of intellectual capital, recognition and reward.

The author presents a matrix to show examples of how the Balanced Score Card can support an organisation to align its management processes and focus the organisation to implement them. The author asserts that it provides a performance measurement system, structured in a way that may lead to a least resistant path and places the main emphasis on people. Although this is logically discussed and makes practical sense, it appears to be less about knowledge management and more about a general financial management approach. There is no empirical work or theoretical underpinning that would validate the approach.

Development and Testing

The development of this framework is based on the author's own perspective. There is no evidence of benchmarking or feedback in relation to development, and there is no indication of testing.

Results and Conclusions

There are no specific results and no conclusion. The author finishes by recommending the next steps that can be taken when implementing the framework and asserts that the Balanced Score Card provides a framework for implementing knowledge management.

Summary

This is a practical discussion and conceptual application of the Balanced Score Card to general knowledge management in an organisation. The purpose is clear and discussion progresses in a rational and logical manner, however there is little evidence to support whether the approach chosen is appropriate or that the Balanced Score Card would make the impact suggested by the author, because there is no empirical work to substantiate this. There is no evidence of theoretical underpinning, and the knowledge management process and activities have been selectively applied to the Balanced Score Card, rather than a robust discussion about what knowledge management is, followed by discussion as to whether the Balanced Score Card could be adapted.

Despite the foregoing, this framework contributes to a potential evaluation framework for knowledge management, because with further empirical work and theoretical underpinning, a Balanced Score Card may provide an effective tool to progress an organisation to shift the emphasis from accountancy based on tangible, easily measurable items to more intangible and value-driven performance measures.

Score Key	1 = lowest possible score; 5 = highest possible score				
Total Score 39	Explicitness	Clarity	Reasoning	Theory	Empirical Work
Purpose	5	5	3	1	1
Process	2	2	2	1	1
Activities	3	3	3	1	1
Develop & Test	1	1	1	1	1

Hylton (2002)

Purpose

This framework is based on a knowledge audit (K audit) for knowledge valuation by exploring the tacit knowledge in people's heads and explicit knowledge in the organisation storage systems. The purpose is reasonably clear and structured, however discussion becomes ambiguous particularly in relation to process. The K audit is described as an evaluation of explicit and tacit knowledge resources, and purports to be a systematic and scientific procedure to diagnose the organisational health of knowledge and provide evidence to establish whether organisational knowledge is being maximised. There is no evidence to confirm that this has been achieved. The author refers to two case studies, using these as examples where employers do not know the extent of their knowledge value, and asserts that the K Audit would be beneficial, however there is no explicit empirical work to qualify this and there is no reference to theory.

Knowledge Management Process

The author recommends that the K audit should be the first stage of a knowledge management process because it involves explanation of the entire cycle of corporate knowledge. The emphasis is not on knowledge management process, but how it is assessed. The author asserts that the K audit, therefore, measures efficiency of the knowledge flow, storage, and return on investment and establishes when particular knowledge is no longer required.

The process comprises three main elements. The first is the HyA-K-Audit, which focuses on people and the knowledge process, and includes a survey of people in the organisation. The second is an inventory of current knowledge and is conducted through one-to-one interviews. The inventory also includes measurement of tacit and explicit knowledge. The third is a knowledge map that illustrates the structure and flow of knowledge, providing the opportunity to identify gaps and weaknesses.

Knowledge Management Activities

Knowledge management activities are referred to in the context of audit activities. These include indexing and categorising tacit and explicit knowledge by establishing the number and categories of knowledge workers, where they are located in the company, what job they do, and what professional and academic qualifications they have achieved. Again there is no evidence of empirical work or theoretical underpinning.

Development and Testing

There is no indication of the approach taken to develop this framework, and although the authors imply that the framework has been successfully used, in reference to the Case Studies, this has not been discussed or referenced.

Results and Conclusions

There are no specific results and the author concludes by emphasising the importance of the audit.

Summary

The purpose of this paper is reasonably clear and presented with clarity, however discussion becomes ambiguous. There is no theoretical or explicit empirical underpinning throughout the paper. The proposal to introduce a process for auditing knowledge in an organisation is logical and practical, however many of the assertions made by the author are not reasoned, and the absence of development and testing and robust empirical underpinning do not engender confidence in what the framework is intended to achieve. This is particularly relevant in relation to the author's 'scientific' measurement of intangible aspects of knowledge management and the extent to which this could be successful. The framework is interesting from an evaluation perspective because it is generally based around an audit procedure, in particular the reference to categorising knowledge workers, where they are located in the company, what job they do, and what professional and academic qualifications they have achieved, as well as the knowledge mapping approach.

Score Key	1 = lowest possible score; 5 = highest possible score				
Total Score 33	Explicitness	Clarity	Reasoning	Theory	Empirical Work
Purpose	4	3	2	1	1
Process	3	3	2	1	2
Activities	1	1	1	1	2
Develop & Test	1	1	1	1	1

Firestone (1999)

Purpose

The purpose of this framework is clearly stated. The introduction embarks on a fairly complex definition of Enterprise Knowledge Management, Natural Knowledge Management System, Artificial Knowledge Management System, and Distributed Knowledge Management System, with a brief overview of the interactions. The author then states the purpose as being an examination of the relationship between the Distributed Knowledge Management System and Enterprise Knowledge Management System. Discussion continues in a disjointed manner with assertions that are not fully reasoned with clarity. There is no clear reference to theory or empirical work. The use of technical language and acronyms impede understanding. The author produces a matrix that identifies knowledge and a knowledge management process, activities within the process, and a Distributed Knowledge Management System. This matrix is useful and helps to provide some clarity.

Knowledge Management Process

The knowledge management process is explicitly drawn out in the context of Enterprise Models. The Enterprise Model is defined as a network of rules intended to explain and predict interactions in the organisation and its environment. The author states that knowledge management production processes produce Enterprise Models, and there are three high-level knowledge processes that can be modelled in Enterprise Models. These are knowledge production, acquisition, and transmission. There does not appear to be any specific theory or empirical work to justify this perspective. The author continues by discussing each high-level knowledge process, explicitly identifying activities within each area.

Knowledge Management Activities

Knowledge management activities are clearly drawn out as activities to meet the requirements of the high-level knowledge process, though again there is no theory or empirical work. The author clearly illustrates the knowledge production and acquisition processes, and discusses the associated activities further. With regard to knowledge production, activities include generating new knowledge, revising and refining existing knowledge, and re-generating previously produced knowledge. Knowledge acquisition activities include gathering external data and information and knowledge, filtering it, testing, and storing. The process of knowledge transmission includes knowledge sharing activities both IT based and human based.

Development and Testing

There is no indication of empirical research in the development and testing of the framework, and no theoretical underpinning.

Results and Conclusions

There are no results. The author very briefly concludes that the Enterprise Knowledge Management System is an improvement on the Distributed Knowledge Management System.

Summary

Overall it is difficult to follow what the author is attempting to achieve with this framework, partly because the author does not set the context, which is further exacerbated by disjointed discussion. This model is developed under the auspices of Enterprise Models, however because this paper does not have a natural flow and logical links between sections, it is difficult for the reader to follow the author's discussion and ultimately what is attempting to be achieved. The use of technical language and acronyms appears to complicate what emerges as a fairly straightforward description of a knowledge management model.

Knowledge management processes and activities are clearly stated and logically discussed from the author's perspective. There is no indication of theoretical or empirical underpinning, or testing of this framework.

The main contribution is the discussion about different knowledge management systems.

Score Key	1 = lowest possible score; 5 = highest possible score				
Total Score **40**	**Explicitness**	**Clarity**	**Reasoning**	**Theory**	**Empirical Work**
Purpose	2	1	2	1	1
Process	5	4	3	1	1
Activities	5	4	3	1	1
Develop & **Test**	1	1	1	1	1

Duru Ahanotu (1998)

Purpose

This framework is explicitly and clearly presented, and is intended to demonstrate how production knowledge can support core competencies in manufacturing. and balance the activities of production workers between creation and maintenance of knowledge and production. The author provides a comprehensive literature review, and applies the principles and theories associated with learning and knowledge management to manufacturing processes. In doing so, the author challenges perceptions that place greater emphasis on the importance of knowledge workers (e.g., those who design) over production workers, arguing that the skill of production workers is equally essential to learning and innovation.

Knowledge Management Process

The author refers to a continuum ranging from learning through action to innovation or creation, which he refers to as knowledge development in the manufacturing industry. Although he does not explicitly state so, the implication is that this is the knowledge process. Drawing on theories of learning, discussion continues and the author concludes by recognising that the iterative process of innovation, continuous improvement, and translating these cycles into core competencies provides long-term sustainability for the organisation. This is a limited approach to the concept of knowledge management, representing only one aspect. There is no evidence that empirical work has been undertaken.

Knowledge Management Activities

The author explicitly identifies three activities to improve the knowledge development of production workers, which should be balanced with the need to maintain product output. These are production/operations defined as all activities that directly manipulate a product; experimentation defined as the discovery of knowledge, which is separate from production/operations; and absorption, which is the acquisition of knowledge. The author continues by discussing these in more depth and highlights the importance of time for production workers to undertake these activities in a product cycle, identifying slack time as an opportunity to learn and innovate. Having established knowledge activities, the author categorises workers into two sections—core workers who have established expertise and are active seekers of knowledge who lead innovation, and "peri core" workers who are sub-divided into three types. The first are those who currently lack knowledge but will develop to eventually join the core. The second are those who are active innovators when required, and the third are interested in specific assignments only. The author continues by discussing the importance of cross-organisational working and communities of practice to ensure that diverse viewpoints are taken into consideration. This is a description of an organisational structure from a knowledge management perspective; there is no empirical work or theory to underpin this approach, nor is there reference to organisational literature to provide a reasoned discussion.

Development and Testing

Development of this framework is based on one aspect of knowledge management drawn from literature and applied to the manufacturing industry, and is a description from the author's perspective. There is no empirical work to test the framework, therefore it remains conceptual.

Results and Conclusions

There are no specific results. The author concludes by drawing together discussion and pointing out that the framework is not intended to resolve issues. It presents methods to consider knowledge development and product creation for ongoing evolution of core competencies, and to highlight that production workers can successfully engage with the processes of creation, learning, and innovation.

Summary

The purpose in this case is clearly stated, and discussion focuses on the recognition that all employees have something to contribute to learning and development in an organisation if given the opportunity. In this sense, the author's discussion is well reasoned with theoretical underpinning derived from theories of learning and learning organisations. The knowledge management process is identified in relation to learning-by-doing and innovation. Knowledge management activities are explicitly stated and discussed with clarity, but there is no indication of empirical development and testing. When considering an organisation's knowledge management readiness, the main contribution this framework offers is recognition of the need for horizontal and vertical participation, and the contribution that every employee may have to creativity and improvement in the organisation.

Score Key	1 = lowest possible score; 5 = highest possible score				
Total Score 50	Explicitness	Clarity	Reasoning	Theory	Empirical Work
Purpose	4	3	4	4	1
Process	3	3	3	3	1
Activities	5	3	4	3	1
Develop & Test	1	1	1	1	1

Pervaiz, Kwang, & Mohamed (1999)

Purpose

The purpose of this framework has been made clear and is intended to measure knowledge management through screening and evaluation, incorporating tactical and strategic elements, measuring and leveraging knowledge management for competitive advantage. Following a brief introduction to knowledge management, the author continues by discussing measurement, including definitions of measurement, development of measurement, performance measurement, and measurement systems. The paper continues with the author applying knowledge management to a measurement system, in particular the Deming "Plan, Do, Check, Act" model, but does not adequately reason why this approach is better than others. Overall discussion is weak, with descriptions of techniques used in measurement taking precedence over knowledge management. There is no evidence of theory and empirical work.

Knowledge Management Process

The authors refer to the knowledge management process in the context of applying the Deming measurement model:

- Capturing or creating knowledge (plan)
- Sharing knowledge (do)
- Measuring the effects (check)
- Learning and improving (act)

The main emphasis is on measurement and not on the knowledge management process. There is no discussion as to why the Deming model would be chosen over other measurement techniques, and this appears to constrain the broader aspects of knowledge management. These, however, seem to be picked up by applying another measurement model, the cost model, when considering activities.

Knowledge Management Activities

The authors identify knowledge management activities by applying a cost model, which includes customer, organisation, suppliers, and technology, and provides examples of activities associated with each area. From this a measurement matrix for knowledge is introduced. The authors assert that the matrix provides a deeper understanding of knowledge management, including hard and soft aspects, and links knowledge management to policy and strategy. There is no discussion or evidence to substantiate this, no theoretical underpinning or empirical work. Additional activities that relate to potential areas for measurement are presented, though these are not included in the matrix and are speculative in nature.

Development and Testing

Development of the framework has been undertaken based around measurement techniques, and there is no indication that empirical work and testing has been undertaken. There is no evidence of theoretical underpinning.

Results and Conclusions

There are no specific results, and the authors conclude by presenting more questions in relation to measurement, additional knowledge management performance measures, and a list of bullet points to reinforce the importance of knowledge management.

Summary

The purpose of this framework is clearly stated, and the authors present models of measurement, intended to screen and evaluate knowledge, but the approach overall appears to be fragmented. The knowledge management process is referred to in the context of measurement using Deming, and the authors apply a cost model to knowledge management activities. This approach appears to ignore the broader complexities and richness of knowledge management, which the authors appear to recognise in their conclusion, when they introduce further knowledge management performance measures, highlighting the fragmentation and incompleteness of this framework, rendering the final matrix as unconvincing.

The authors have not clearly discussed and clarified why they have taken a particular approach to either their choice of measurement or approach to knowledge management. There is no theoretical or empirical work throughout, or any clear approach to development, and the framework has not been tested. Considering this framework in the context of an organisation's readiness to engage with knowledge management, the key contribution relates to measurement of the organisation's ability with a view to undertaking knowledge management, rather than assuming that the organisation is already fully engaged with knowledge management.

Score Key	1 = lowest possible score; 5 = highest possible score				
Total Score 34	Explicitness	Clarity	Reasoning	Theory	Empirical Work
Purpose	4	3	1	1	1
Process	4	2	1	1	1
Activities	4	2	2	1	1
Develop & Test	1	1	1	1	1

Merali (2002)

Purpose

The purpose of this framework is not entirely clear at the outset. In the first instance, the author proposes a cognitive congruence framework intended to reconcile contentious issues in knowledge management literature. It is then proposed that the framework could be used to explain the relationship between cognitive, action, and social aspects of the knowledge management process in the organisational context and can be used as a management tool. The framework has been developed in the context of differing views on knowledge management. As discussion unfolds, it becomes clearer that the framework emphasises individual and collective knowledge sharing. Although theory is referred to, it is not robustly applied in this case. Empirical work has been undertaken in a case organisation, though the approach used has not been made explicit.

Knowledge Management Process

The knowledge management process is considered in the context of socially situated processes of knowledge management by connecting the cognitive, social, and action dimensions. The framework contains a cycle that includes:

- *Schema,* which is the knowledge structure representing organised knowledge about an information domain and includes how knowledge is retrieved and used. Overall, schema contains a collection of interconnected beliefs and perceptions.

- *Self-concept,* which is a perception of one's identity in relation to other individuals or groups.

- *Relationship scripts,* which refer to relationships between individuals, inter-organisational knowledge networks, credibility, and filtering of information. This can be divided into a macro level and a micro level. The macro level is useful for understanding how an organisation perceives itself within its environment, and the micro level helps make sense of the social learning processes.

- *Relationship enactment,* which links the individual with the social dimension and is scaleable from the individual to the collective. Collective enactment is the process by which the self-concept is realised, experiences are formed, and learning takes place.

The process is confusing, because it is not clear how schema, relationship scripts, and relationship enactment differ from each other in practice. Theory is referred to, but not adequately discussed in a clear and reasoned way.

Knowledge Management Activities

Knowledge management activities are not referred to in this framework.

Development and Testing

The framework was applied to three different organisations and used to identify gaps in current levels of collective knowledge as compared to that which was necessary for success in circumstances of change and development in each organisation. The authors do not explicitly indicate the methodology used, and in essence offer a descriptive and retrospective assessment of the success of applying the framework. There is no critique, and the absence of a methodology obstructs understanding of this framework and how to apply it.

Conclusion

The authors conclude by stating that the framework is a sense-making device for studying organisations in dynamic contexts, and reconciling and coordinating individual and collective actions. As a framework for studying organisations, it may be effective, but the absence of the methodology and critique means that the extent to which this was achieved is questionable. Further, the authors originally proposed that this was a cognitive congruence framework intended to reconcile contentious issues in knowledge management literature. There is no evidence to suggest that this was achieved.

Summary

Although the purpose of this framework was made clear, as discussion unfolds it become less evident as to what is being proposed. This is further exacerbated by weak discussion and an expectation that the user would know how to utilise the framework; for example, there is no explicit methodology to explain how the framework was used in case organisations. Further, there is no indication of how knowledge management could be implemented in an organisation. The framework appears to be based on social psychology and for the standard practitioner offers little support in application except as an exploratory exercise, which in itself is limited. The authors do recognise the shortcomings of the framework and point to the dangers of ignoring environmental issues, but offer little indication as to how to address these.

There is no explicit theory underpinning many of the assertions that the authors make, but reference is made to learning theory, and through the literature review various other theoretical underpinnings are briefly referred to. This is not, however, robust and structured in such a way that the reader easily understands the author's perspective in the development of this framework.

In relation to evaluation of an organisation's readiness to engage with knowledge management, this framework appears to be a useful tool for the assessment of current knowledge and identification of new knowledge needed in the change and development of an organisation. However, further work would be necessary to realise its full potential.

Score Key	1 = lowest possible score; 5 = highest possible score				
Total Score 47	**Explicitness**	**Clarity**	**Reasoning**	**Theory**	**Empirical Work**
Purpose	5	2	2	2	2
Process	4	3	3	2	3
Activities	1	1	1	1	1
Develop & Test	3	3	3	2	3

Kamara, Chimay, & Carrillo (2002)

Purpose

This framework has been developed using previous studies into knowledge management processes in the construction and manufacturing industries. The purpose of the framework is explicitly stated as being a tool for the selection of a knowledge management strategy appropriate to the organisational and cultural context of an organisation, and was developed within a project context. Drawing on previous literature, the authors review knowledge management, presenting a clear and reasoned discussion. There is no reference to any theoretical underpinning.

Knowledge Management Process

The CLEVER framework includes four stages, which may be regarded as the overall process:

- *Definition of the Knowledge Management Problem*—This stage is descriptive and the characteristics of the knowledge under consideration are defined, the potential users and sources of knowledge, and enablers and prohibitors for users and sources.

- *Identify 'To Be' Solutions*—This is essentially a gap analysis of where the organisation is and where it wishes to be in relation to strategy and policy. The outcome at this stage is a set of knowledge management concerns or issues that the user wishes to focus on.

- *Identify Critical Migration Paths*—This stage defines how the user wishes to proceed and is synonymous with a critical path analysis.

- *Select Appropriate Knowledge Management Processes*—This stage relates to the implementation stage and the most relevant path that should be chosen from a standard list of processes to proceed with a selected strategy. Although the authors refer to processes, this may be more relevant to activities.

Empirical work has been undertaken through a study of knowledge management processes, and the methodology used was explicitly stated, but there is no reference to theory. The outcome of this study highlighted that knowledge management in the construction and manufacturing industries lacked formal proactive knowledge management processes. There were, however, some examples of good practice such as the use of project management tools, documentation systems, regular revisions of project plans to learn from lessons of the past, and use of certain procurement options. The missing processes derived from this study include identification of high-grade knowledge, making high-grade knowledge explicit and highly controlled, and assistance in selecting appropriate strategies for knowledge management. The authors continue to refer to processes within the process, which can cause some confusion. They then identify tools of application, which are regarded in this case as activities.

Knowledge Management Activities

Knowledge management activities are not explicitly defined. The authors discuss the application of the framework within which three main tools are described:

- A *Problem Definition Template (PDT)* is used to identify types of knowledge, and knowledge management processes are referred to again in addition to those above. These processes are knowledge generation, knowledge propagation, knowledge transfer, knowledge location and access, and knowledge maintenance/modification.
- A *Knowledge Dimensions Guide* is introduced that identifies the current situation and potential future situation.
- A generic *Knowledge Management Process Model* is used to facilitate or identify resistors to develop the organisation toward the desired situation. This includes tacit/explicit, individual and shared knowledge and people, and IT- and paper-based knowledge sharing.

There is no reference to theory and, with regard to empirical work, this was conducted and has been referred to under Knowledge Process.

Development and Testing

The main aims to develop and test the framework were explicitly stated at the outset. These are:

- To explore current knowledge management practices in manufacturing and construction industries.
- To draw out generic structures for knowledge management practices by cross-sector comparisons.
- To develop a viable framework for knowledge management in a multi-project environment.
- To evaluate the framework using real-life projects and scenarios supplied by the participating companies.

Drawing on literature the authors reviewed definitions of knowledge management and established the framework for project research. The authors state that the development of CLEVER was undertaken based on empirical research and testing with participating organisations. However, there is no further reference or discussion to support this.

Results and Conclusions

The authors conclude by summarising the purpose of the framework which is derived from literature and studies in collaborating organisations, though these are not identified. The authors recognise that there are many solutions in relation to various processes of knowledge generation capture and transfer, and it was not their intention to introduce another process; however, this appears to be exactly what they have done.

Summary

The purpose of this framework is clear and discussed in a coherent manner, although it does appear to be complicated by the interchangeable use of terms, which for the practitioner can cause some confusion. The knowledge management process is identified and activities are referred to as processes within a process with an additional set of activities, which are tools to implement

Score Key	1 = lowest possible score; 5 = highest possible score				
Total **Score 54**	**Explicitness**	**Clarity**	**Reasoning**	**Theory**	**Empirical Work**
Purpose	5	5	5	1	2
Process	4	3	3	1	3
Activities	4	2	2	1	3
Develop & **Test**	3	2	2	1	2

knowledge management. The structure and dual use of the term process can result in ambiguity. The framework is weakened by the lack of theoretical underpinning, and although reference to empirical work in the form of case studies through collaborating organisations has been made, there is no further discussion about these. The main lesson to be learned from this framework is the need for clear structure and consistent use of language when developing a layered approach to knowledge management. The approach taken provides a reasonable example to draw ideas from the Knowledge Dimensions Guides.

Balasubramanian, Kumar, Henderson, & Kwan (1999)

Purpose

The purpose of this framework is initially unclear, and as discussion unfolds, it eventually emerges that the purpose is twofold. The first aspect of the purpose focuses on a framework entitled 'Knowledge Mill', which is intended to describe the knowledge management process. This is then underpinned by a schema for modelling and leveraging knowledge elements in the specific context of decision-making to implement process knowledge within an organisation. Implementation is undertaken using a software package called 'Thoughtflow'. Discussion is ambiguous and unstructured, resulting in the reader having to decipher the exact purpose. There is no theoretical underpinning, and empirical work is limited to one case study.

Knowledge Management Process

The authors define knowledge management as a community capability to share knowledge that creates value for the organisation and its customers, within which the knowledge management process is referred to. For example, to deliver capability the authors identify operating drivers, which are technology, organisation, and processes. Technology relates to the knowledge management system. Organisation is the relationship with other firms, the culture and internal management structure and knowledge management processes are initially explicitly defined as procedures, workflows, management controls, and human resource management within the context of capability as indicated above. The authors continue to explain that their approach is split into two parts. The first is a goal-oriented modelling schema, which is centred on decision-making. This is intended to enable the organisation to define its knowledge objects, find and organise information, store and re-use it. The second is the Knowledge Mill framework, which describes the activities that are performed during the conceptualisation, design, development, and use of knowledge management applications. There is no reference to empirical work or theoretical underpinning to validate this approach.

Knowledge Management Activities

The authors identify activities within the Knowledge Mill framework that begin with senior management decision-making to identify the goals of the application system and continue to include capturing, transforming, classifying, maintaining, discovering, and disseminating knowledge.

These activities are referred to as a set of primary activities that need to be performed for all activities in the knowledge management process. The following offers more detail:

- Capturing brings together data/information including experience and lessons learned from inside and outside the organisation.

- Transformation relates to validation and contextualisation of information so that it is easier to access.

- Classification includes indexing, filtering, and linking new information.

- Maintenance relates to content and technical support using IT.

- Discovering identifies information from the knowledge base to make recommendations to different stakeholders in the organisation.

- Dissemination determines how people gain access to the content.

The authors proceed by discussing technical aspects of software deemed appropriate to support the knowledge management process and discuss the process of decision-making and its cognitive elements including power and politics. There is no further discussion about this, and no theoretical or empirical underpinning to support the assertions made.

Development and Testing

Development and testing is undertaken through a case study exercise and primarily focuses on the technical aspects of the process. The software 'Knowledge Flow' is applied to strategic planning and deployment, and the authors clearly state that the next step will be to undertake qualitative evaluation with users through interviews. At this stage, therefore, testing is incomplete, and although the authors refer to empirical work in the development stages vis á vis the case study, they do not discuss the approach taken any further.

Conclusions

The authors conclude by highlighting further work that is necessary to develop the framework and goal-oriented schema. They state that from evaluation and lessons learned, the intention is to develop a methodology for designing knowledge management systems, but there is no methodology as to how the evaluation was undertaken. The authors recognise the complexities of power and politics in relation to decision-making; highlight that a purely rational approach that ignores the subjectivity and personal and organisational dimensions is doomed to failure; and propose that a framework that gives consideration to these issues is more realistic. In this sense they propose that their framework considers this, however there is inadequate reasoning in the discussion to support this conclusion. There is no clear theoretical underpinning to support the framework, and empirical work focuses mainly on technical aspects.

Summary

The purpose of this framework is initially unclear, and as discussion progresses, it emerges that the purpose is twofold. The authors introduced a framework, 'Knowledge Mill', that is descriptive and an underpinning schema for using software that is based specifically on capturing and organising knowledge around decision-making. They discuss the cognitive elements of decision-making, highlighting the complexities of power and politics, but there is inadequate discussion and no theoretical underpinning. Overall discussion about the framework is confusing because of the interchanging use of terms relating to process and processes that underpin the process. With the exception of discussion about the software, it is difficult to visualise the nature of the framework being proposed here. There is no explicit reference to theoretical underpinning and a case study scenario is used to apply the framework; the emphasis is mainly on technology. In regard to an evaluation framework, this example explicitly indicates the importance of considering power and politics, though no further discussion or guidance is offered.

Score Key	1 = lowest possible score; 5 = highest possible score				
Total Score 50	Explicitness	Clarity	Reasoning	Theory	Empirical Work
Purpose	4	3	2	1	3
Process	5	3	2	1	3
Activities	5	2	2	1	3
Develop & Test	3	2	2	1	2

Binny (2001)

Purpose

The purpose of this framework is clear and is stated as being a framework intended to assist organisations in balancing their knowledge management focus, and to establish and communicate their strategic knowledge management. This includes two main aims: The first is to review the diverse knowledge management literature and provide a framework for the discussion of knowledge management, which is intended to minimise confusion and assist in planning and investment in knowledge management in organisations. The second main aim is to provide a checklist of knowledge management applications and technologies, which can be used to assess an organisation's current level of knowledge management and related activities. Entitled the Knowledge Management Spectrum (KM Spectrum), it is also intended to provide understanding of the range of knowledge management options, applications, and technology. The idea to develop the KM Spectrum has arisen from the author's previous experience of working with executives and strategists who are attempting to engage with knowledge management, and in this sense provide general empirical work. There is no theoretical underpinning to support the purpose or any other aspect of the framework.

Knowledge Management Process

The authors divide knowledge management into six main categories, which can be viewed as the process. The six categories, termed 'Elements', are:

- *Transactional Knowledge Management* refers to the application of technology, for example, customer services applications, order entry applications.

- *Analytical Knowledge Management* is the interpretation or creation of new knowledge from various sources of materials and data, and includes, for example, data warehousing, data mining.

- *Asset Management* focuses on processes associated with the management of knowledge assets, for example, intellectual property, document management. This involves two key areas, which are explicit knowledge assets and processes relating to identification, exploitation, and protection of intellectual property.

- *Process-Based Knowledge Management* covers codification and improvement of processes or work practices, procedures, and methodologies.

- *Developmental Knowledge Management* focuses on increasing the competencies or capabilities of the organisations' knowledge workers. This covers transfer of explicit knowledge through training, and the development of tacit knowledge through communities of interest and engendering a learning culture.

- *Innovation/Creation Knowledge Management* concentrates on providing an environment in which knowledge workers can come together in teams to collaborate in the creation of new knowledge.

Developmental, innovation, and creation appear to be one and the same, as both involve collaboration and learning from which creativity emerges. The author does not adequately explain why these have been split into different categories.

It is indicated that empirical work has been drawn from the author's personal experience of working with organisations. There is no theoretical underpinning.

Knowledge Management Activities

Apart from the reference to the activities indicated within the elements referred to in the foregoing, knowledge management activities are not explicitly discussed. The author does, however, highlight that existing knowledge management activities need to be acknowledged, understood, and considered when developing strategies and plans, but makes no further reference to them.

Development and Testing

Development of this framework is based on the author's experience of working with executives and strategists. Whilst the author states that the framework has been developed with executives, this has not been substantiated with real evidence or references. In addition there is no evidence of testing the framework and no theoretical underpinning.

Conclusions

The author concludes by emphasising that the purpose was not to establish what knowledge management is, but to ensure that all available approaches, applications, and technologies are considered.

Summary

The purpose of this framework is clear, and discussion progresses with clarity and reasoning. There is no theoretical underpinning and no indication that the framework could actually achieve what is intended, because it does not appear to have been tested empirically. The framework may offer practitioners guidance and a categorisation of approaches about what might be available to consider in relation to knowledge management. The knowledge management process provides the main focus, and knowledge management activities are not explicitly referred to. Neither process nor activities are underpinned by theory, and empirical work has been drawn from the author's experience of working with strategists and executives; however, there is no methodology or constructive approach.

Score Key	1 = lowest possible score; 5 = highest possible score				
Total Score 39	**Explicitness**	**Clarity**	**Reasoning**	**Theory**	**Empirical Work**
Purpose	5	4	4	1	3
Process	4	3	2	1	2
Activities	1	1	1	1	1
Develop & **Test**	1	1	1	1	1

McAdam & Reid (2001)

Purpose

The purpose of this framework is clear—to identify and describe the key dimensions of knowledge management using a socially constructed knowledge management model, with the intention of determining perceptions of knowledge management in SMEs and large organisations. The authors have classified knowledge management into three categories—Intellectual Capital Models, Knowledge Category Models, and Socially Constructed Models—for the knowledge management process. The Socially Constructed Model was chosen because of the breadth of definition of knowledge and the intrinsic link with the social and learning processes in organisations. Discussion, reasoning, and theoretical underpinning as to how the three categories have been chosen is very brief, though what is available is presented with clarity. The final model that the authors propose has been adapted from Demarest (1997).

Knowledge Management Process

The knowledge management process is clearly referred to in the context of four key dimensions in the model. The process, therefore, is:

- *Knowledge construction,* which includes scientific and socially constructed knowledge.
- *Knowledge embodiment,* which includes the process of social interchange where knowledge is embodied within the organisation.
- *Knowledge dissemination,* which is the process of sharing knowledge throughout the organisation and its environment.
- *Knowledge use,* which is the process of using knowledge to economic advantage in regard to organisational outputs.

This is presented with clarity and reasoning, and empirical work has been undertaken to determine perception of knowledge management. There is no theoretical underpinning.

Knowledge Management Activities

Knowledge management activities are not referred to.

Development and Testing

This model is used as a framework to undertake research into perceptions of knowledge in SMEs and large organisations through research survey and workshops. The model is adapted from Demarest (1977), but there is no indication of what adaptations have been made. Within the scope of the model, 296 questionnaires were distributed and 95 returned, of which 49 were SMEs and 46 were large organisations. From the results of the survey, eight workshops were held and the results presented. There is no evidence to indicate the effectiveness of the model over and above the questionnaire. In terms of considering perceptions of knowledge management, the questionnaire approach may be useful in relation to assessing knowledge management readiness, but the model itself does not appear to provide anything more than the questionnaires.

Results and Conclusions

The conclusions from this model and associated survey identified the usefulness in establishing organisational perceptions of knowledge management. The authors propose that the four key dimensions in the model are representative of approaches to knowledge management in both large organisations and SMEs. When comparing large organisations and SMEs, the model was used to draw out differences in approaches, identifying that large organisations are more people-based knowledge-oriented and SMEs were more mechanistic.

Summary

The purpose of this model is clearly stated, and discussion progresses with clarity and reasoning. The categories of knowledge management that the authors propose appear to be limited, and there is inadequate discussion to justify why the three categories have been chosen. The socially constructed model is an adaptation from Demarest (1997), but there is no indication of what adaptations have been made, therefore the development of the actual model has not been adequately discussed. A research methodology based on survey research and workshops is presented, but there is no evidence to indicate the effectiveness of the model over and above the use of a questionnaire, which explores perceptions of knowledge management in large organisations and SMEs. Knowledge management processes have been referred to within the context of four key dimensions of the model, and knowledge management activities have not been included. Considering this framework in the context of an evaluation of an organisation's knowledge management readiness, the distinction between category models, such as Intellectual Capital Models, Knowledge Category Models, and Socially Constructed Models, provides a useful perspective to consider and explore further.

There is no explicit theoretical underpinning in relation to the model.

Score Key	1 = lowest possible score; 5 = highest possible score				
Total Score 47	Explicitness	Clarity	Reasoning	Theory	Empirical Work
Purpose	5	5	3	1	1
Process	4	3	3	1	1
Activities	1	1	1	1	1
Develop & Test	5	5	3	1	1

Abou-Zeid (2002)

Purpose

The purpose of this model is explicitly stated and discussed with clarity and reasoning to provide a basis for identifying the processes to be supported by any Knowledge Management Support System (KMSS). It was developed in recognition of a paradigm shift in knowledge management, which has been divided into three key areas:

- From regarding knowledge as a commodity to knowledge creation and recreation.
- From the management and technical approach to an enabling and social approach.
- From knowledge as being possessed by people to knowing, which is associated with acting and doing.

The model, known as the Knowledge Management Reference Model (KMRM), is intended to provide a comprehensive framework that transcends these three areas. The KMRM consists of a three-layered approach to knowledge management systems in an organisation. The three layers are cognitive domains, functionality, and resources, with an additional conceptual construct used to model the constituents of the functional layer. There is no reference to theory and empirical work at this stage.

Knowledge Management Process

The knowledge management process is made explicit and referred to within the three layers. The cognitive layer relates to the organisation's cognitive domain and all possible relationships both internal and external. The external cognitive domain includes customers, suppliers, partners, and competitors. The internal cognitive domain is the set of all things that relate to organisation and includes business purpose, processes, outcomes, and rules.

The functional layer explicitly refers to the knowledge management process and comprises two comprehensive categories. These are the knowledge manipulating process and knowledge enabling process. The knowledge manipulating process is described as the process that would lead to change in the current state of a 'K-thing'. Simply explained, a K-thing relates to knowledge that is, for example, identified or required by the organisation. The knowledge manipulation process includes activities such as knowledge identification, generation, elaboration, preservation, mobilisation, presentation, and evaluation.

The knowledge enabling process relates to cultural and organisational issues, and includes inculcating the knowledge vision, managing conversion, mobilising knowledge activists, creating the right context, and globalising local knowledge.

Knowledge management resources include the organisation's ICT tools that support the knowledge manipulating and enabling process, however these have not been specifically included in the model. This illustrates the author's priority in relation to knowledge management, particularly because an explanation is offered indicating that technology should support and keep track of work, provide customised solutions for individuals and groups, and use language that relates to the organisational knowledge. In this sense it can be viewed as an enabling process or activity, which is dynamic and flexible to support knowledge manipulation. There is no indication of theory or empirical work in the establishment of process.

Knowledge Management Activities

Knowledge management activities are clearly referred to as the activities that underpin the process as indicated above. Additional examples in relation to the knowledge manipulating process include knowledge identification such as determining the knowledge gap by comparing need with existing knowledge, assessing the knowledge and activity to convert it, and identifying internal and external resources.

With regard to knowledge enabling processes, activities are made explicit, for example the process of cultivating or inculcating the knowledge vision, which includes activities such as developing mental maps of the environment in which the organisation exists and setting normative, operational, and strategic goals.

There is no empirical evidence to underpin the choice of activities and no reference to theory.

Development and Testing

The KMRM has been developed based on a robust review of literature and varying approaches to knowledge management. There is some ambiguity in relation to development within a real organisation, for example testing of the model seems to be a retrospective application in Matsushita's "Home Bakery," previously used as a case by Nonaka and Takeuchi (1995). The author does not indicate whether the case was revisited in reality or used conceptually, therefore it may be empirically weak. Although this appears to be a systems approach to modelling knowledge management, this has not been explicitly stated, nor is there any apparent theoretical underpinning.

Results and Conclusions

The author concludes that the proposed KMRM provides a basis for developing a hybrid descriptive and prescriptive model for knowledge management systems. The prescriptive element identifies knowledge processes and different ways an organisation can engage. The descriptive element offers an opportunity to characterise organisational knowledge and the connection between manipulating and enabling processes. The model achieves this understanding.

Summary

The purpose of this model is explicitly stated and discussed with clarity and reasoning using a broad review of previous and current knowledge management literature. The knowledge management process and activities have been clearly presented and structured. Although the authors appear to have taken a systems approach to knowledge management, this has not been explicitly stated, nor is there any theoretical underpinning. Use of the framework has been illustrated by application to a previous case study (Nonaka & Takeuchi, 1995). However, this is ambiguous in that there is no indication as to whether this has been undertaken retrospectively and is therefore conceptual, or whether the framework has been freshly applied in the present by revisiting the organisation and undertaking action research to test the framework.

This model contains a level of evaluation of the organisation in relation to knowledge identification by determining the knowledge gap between what exists and what is needed by the organisation. Although it does not address the organisation's overall readiness to engage with knowledge management, it is useful to draw from this model when developing an evaluation of the activities and process framework.

Score Key	1 = lowest possible score; 5 = highest possible score				
Total Score 66	Explicitness	Clarity	Reasoning	Theory	Empirical Work
Purpose	5	5	5	1	1
Process	5	5	5	1	1
Activities	5	5	5	1	1
Develop & Test	4	3	4	1	3

Achterbergh & Vriens (2002)

Purpose

The model presented here is based on Beer's (1979) Viable System Model (VSM), which is applied to knowledge management to support the diagnosis, design, and implementation of knowledge processes, and therefore provides the theoretical underpinning for this model. The purpose is clear in that the VSM is intended to make and maintain viable knowledge. The authors set the model in context by highlighting two specific areas that should be addressed in an organisation. The first is to establish what kind of knowledge an organisation needs to remain viable. The second is how to manage knowledge to address these issues. Although the purpose is clear, discussion is disjointed and it is not until after significant discussion that the reader or user deduces that the model is divided into three core elements, which illustrate the overall structure.

Knowledge Management Process

Three core elements that identify the structure and contain the process are:
1.   Five functions that comprise the VSM.
2.   Knowledge domains, which contain activities to meet the requirements of the five functions.
3.   Knowledge processing, which includes generating, retaining, sharing, and applying knowledge.

The knowledge management process is referred to in the context of producing or processing viable knowledge and includes generating, retaining, sharing, and applying knowledge. The process is cross-referenced, using a matrix, with the five functions of the VSM and associated activities (discussed further under knowledge activities).

Dependency diagrams are used to illustrate the relationship between viable knowledge and the knowledge process, highlighting where viable knowledge is generated, shared, and applied between functions. Management of viable knowledge is discussed which includes diagnosing the knowledge process to ensure that various elements are effective and efficient, and whether the technological, social, and infrastructure domains are suitable for processing viable knowledge. As indicated in the foregoing, theoretical underpinning is derived from the VSM. There is no indication of empirical work at this stage.

Knowledge Management Activities

The authors explicitly refer to knowledge management activities within the context of Beer's (1979) five functions necessary for organisational viability. Each function of the VSM is considered as an activity that requires knowledge as a background to solve a specific system-related problem. This includes assessment of performance and signals in relation to goals, perceived facts, and gaps, and the necessary action to achieve positive outcomes. The VSM is an iterative and layered model that deals with relations between functions and relations between different levels of iteration. Organisations are considered as social systems, and communication links the five functions of the VSM. The five functions are:

- *Organisational Primary Activities,* which are the core activities of an organisation that demonstrate its main reason for existence. Each department or business unit of an organisation needs knowledge about organisational goals and other business units or departments goals. In this sense, the four functions that follow below ensure synergy of primary activities and a holistic approach to safeguarding the viability of the organisation.

- *Coordination* ensures that the interdependencies between primary activities are managed through planning, quality standards meetings, and so on, and knowledge about business units or departments is needed to assess the loss of performance.

- *Control* relates to the current goals of the organisation and includes activities such as monitoring whether the goals are achieved through direction to and reports from managers and auditing procedures, and reviewing new proposals to assess the potential for change.

- *Intelligence* ensures that the activities of the organisation are aligned with environmental developments and is based on knowledge about the environment, including trends, changes, or other initiatives that could be adapted to meet new organisational goals.

- *Policy* relates intelligence to control, ensuring that the organisation defines its identity in such a way that fits developments in its environment. This includes activities such as reviewing new proposals for innovation and balancing discussion about adaptations necessary to achieve results.

As indicated, theoretical underpinning is derived for the VSM, and there is no indication of empirical work at this stage.

Development and Testing

Development of the model is clear and well reasoned. The authors review knowledge management concepts, processes, and instruments and definitions of knowledge, and apply Beer's (1979) VSM relating this to domains of viable knowledge using a case study to demonstrate the application of the model. Through the case study, the authors illustrate how the application of the VSM can organise and define activities to establish a system of knowledge management. Empirical work is limited to one company, and there is no methodology to explain how the VSM was applied to the company. Descriptive examples are offered, with little analysis of the empirical work.

Results and Conclusions

The authors conclude by highlighting what the model is capable of achieving in terms of managing viable knowledge, and draw out the benefits and importance of a systems approach using the VSM. They emphasise that using the VSM provides a theoretical contribution to knowledge management. The model is regarded as generic and can therefore be applied to any organisation or organisational goals.

Summary

The purpose of this model is clearly stated and theoretically underpinned using the VSM. The functions and activities in the model are well reasoned, and dependency diagrams help to illustrate the relationship between functions and knowledge process. The knowledge process is clearly stated as the actual management of viable knowledge rather than knowledge management—in other words the knowledge that is needed to maintain the viability of an organisation. In this sense the model seems to have less emphasis on knowledge management and more on organising and deciding what knowledge needs to be managed and the knowledge required to actually manage, using the five functions to achieve this.

Development of the model is based on a review of knowledge management literature. Empirical work and testing is undertaken using a case study based on an ICT company, however there is no actual reference to the company. In relation to an organisation's knowledge management readiness, this model provides an excellent example to consider evaluation that could be undertaken based on the five functions of the VSM and associated activities, and demonstrates that a systems approach provides a robust underpinning to knowledge management. The model proposed here considers organisations such as Social Systems and refers to the importance of communication, but there is no reference to influencing factors such as power, politics, and complexity of communication.

Score Key	1 = lowest possible score; 5 = highest possible score				
Total Score 82	Explicitness	Clarity	Reasoning	Theory	Empirical Work
Purpose	5	5	5	5	3
Process	5	4	4	5	2
Activities	5	5	5	5	2
Develop & Test	4	3	3	2	5

Bolloju, Khalifa, & Turban (2002)

Purpose

The authors introduce an approach for integrating decision support and the knowledge management process using knowledge discovery techniques. They present an integrative framework for building enterprise decision support environments. The context in which this framework is introduced is based on decentralised decision-making and the requirements of decision-makers to combine different types of data and knowledge (both tacit and explicit) available in organisations. The purpose is ambiguous in that further into discussion, the authors then state that they are introducing two frameworks—the first for developing enterprise decision support environments as initially highlighted, the second for conducting research in the fields of decision support and knowledge management. However, the second framework does not appear to be explicitly referred to from this point onwards. There is no reference to empirical work throughout, and theory is specifically drawn from decision support.

Knowledge Management Process

The knowledge management process is referred to in relation to decision-making, however the main focus is more on the decision-making process. Reference to the knowledge management process is limited in that the authors categorise knowledge into general domain knowledge, organisational knowledge, and problem-specific knowledge, and how this knowledge is necessary to support decision-makers. They continue by focussing on the knowledge creation process and using Nonaka's (1994) model of knowledge creation, which includes socialisation, externalisation, combination, and internalisation, which they then apply to decision-making.

The authors propose that the integration of decision support and the knowledge management process has three characteristics that facilitate knowledge conversion through automated techniques. These are:

- The application of knowledge discovery techniques for knowledge externalisation.
- The employment of repositories for storing externalised knowledge.
- The extension of knowledge discovery techniques.

The authors do not fully discuss and reason the connection from a knowledge management perspective, but from a systems modelling and decision support perspective, nor do they provide empirical work to support the three characteristics chosen. The concept of the knowledge process deteriorates as the model unfolds, because in describing how the model will operate, the authors appear to consider tacit and explicit knowledge in the same vane as data and information. In this sense, they seem to have disregarded the complexity of tacit knowledge, despite using Nonaka's (1994) knowledge creation model.

Knowledge Management Activities

Knowledge management activities are not explicitly referred to.

Development and Testing

The development of this framework has been undertaken based on decision support systems, and the application to knowledge management is weak with very limited reference to knowledge management literature. This is reflected in discussion and is demonstrated by a superficial level of understanding about tacit and explicit knowledge. There is no indication of empirical work to test this framework.

Results and Conclusions

There are no results and the authors' conclusion is weak with assertions made about how the framework will assist decision-makers, however there is no indication of testing to justify this. The authors highlight implications for research, which is primarily based on modelling, IT, and decision-making.

Summary

The purpose of this framework is a little ambiguous because the authors refer to two frameworks and produce one, which purports to provide an integrative approach to decision-making and knowledge management. Clarity of discussion and reasoning is weak, and the outcome does not fully meet the initial purpose. The main focus is on decision-making with little regard to the concept of knowledge management overall. The knowledge management process is referred to through integration with decision support systems, but this appears to be at a superficial level. Knowledge management activities are not included.

Development is undertaken from a decision support systems perspective, and testing has not been undertaken. Theoretical underpinning is drawn from decision support systems, however the application of this does not address the overall concept of knowledge management and is general. There is no reference to empirical work throughout. The contribution that this framework may make to an evaluation of knowledge management readiness relates to the decision-making process as one aspect and raises ideas about understanding in relation to why decisions may be taken, and in what context.

Score Key	1 = lowest possible score; 5 = highest possible score				
Total Score 31	Explicitness	Clarity	Reasoning	Theory	Empirical Work
Purpose	4	3	2	4	1
Process	3	2	2	2	1
Activities	1	1	1	1	1
Develop & Test	2	1	2	3	1

Snowden (1998)

Purpose

The purpose of this framework is to provide a context for the practices of knowledge management and a perspective for the role of intellectual capital assets within an organisation. In establishing the purpose of the framework, the author clearly distinguishes between knowledge and information, and establishes the dimensions of knowledge management from individuals and judgement to communities on one axis and from tacit to explicit knowledge on another axis. The author then continues to consider a perspective on knowledge management through decision-making, highlighting that the balance between tacit and explicit knowledge needs a model of decision-making, for example the uncertainty matrix. The uncertainty matrix contrasts uncertainty of objective with uncertainty of cause and effect, providing four environments, each requiring a different balance of tacit and explicit knowledge. Further discussion is not undertaken about this matrix, nor is it referenced. There is no explicit theoretical underpinning or empirical work.

Knowledge Management Process

The author refers to four key elements, as the process within which knowledge management is progressed. The elements are:

* knowledge mapping,
* competence creation,
* intellectual capital systems,
* organisation change.

Knowledge mapping is a process of discovery through the use of knowledge, and includes judgements and decisions. For example, decision-making creates a picture of how information flows, and the results can be mapped linking different decision processes in the organisation. Knowledge mapping also includes consideration for participation, communication, team formation, and creation. The author recognises that whilst this is appropriate for explicit knowledge, the process for tacit knowledge is more complex and in this sense considers competence creation.

It is the authors' view that tacit knowledge assets can be made explicit, and obstructions to this process may include the mystification of an individual's knowledge, whereby the individual wishes to maintain an authoritative position. However, other tacit knowledge can be made explicit through communities, and as such the author proposes 'competence creation', which relates to communities of tacit knowledge holders. Communities can be developed according to the needs of the organisation and based around individuals who have a natural professional affinity. This can be seen in organisational structures, however the author recommends that such communities should be time-dependent. If they exist too long, they are likely to become part of the organisation structure; this should be avoided, as the process of knowledge sharing will diminish. The recommendation is that communities should be formed around a time-dependent task. The author provides no empirical evidence or theoretical underpinning to justify this assertion.

Intellectual capital systems are stated by the author as one of the most common knowledge management projects. Intellect capital systems are generally IT based, but should be developed through effective knowledge mapping and creation of communities of competence to ensure effective use of IT.

Organisation change is the final stage of the process and relates to the creation of an organisation that is knowledgeable and capable of sustained learning. This process includes specific activities that are highlighted below.

Knowledge Management Activities

Knowledge management activities are referred to within the context of organisation change only. Activities include learning contracts, mentoring, self-development, and network management, training audits, and best-practice exchange. The author points out that best practice exchange is a beneficial covert method of knowledge exchange and recommends this as an entry level to knowledge management in an organisation. This approach is relatively inexpensive and encourages both tacit and explicit knowledge exchanges. There is no indication of empirical work or theoretical underpinning to support this perspective.

Development and Testing

There is no indication of the methodology used to develop this approach, and there is no evidence of empirical work and testing having been undertaken in relation to testing.

Results and Conclusions

The author does not provide a conclusion, but notes are provided and intended to introduce the knowledge management practitioner to further reading.

Summary

The purpose of this framework is clear, and discussion progresses with clarity, however the reasoning and depth of discussion is brief. The knowledge management process is made explicit, and knowledge management activities are limited to the context of organisational change only. There is no indication of development and testing, and there is no theoretical or empirical underpinning. Overall, the approach taken is at an introductory level and remains conceptual. Having stated this, the framework still contributes ideas to consider in relation to the evaluation of an organisation's readiness to engage with knowledge management, particularly the communities of practice and the extent to which an organisation engages in initiatives such as this to share, create, and improve knowledge and learning.

Score Key	1 = lowest possible score; 5 = highest possible score				
Total Score 42	Explicitness	Clarity	Reasoning	Theory	Empirical Work
Purpose	5	5	3	1	1
Process	5	5	3	1	1
Activities	5	5	3	1	1
Develop & Test	1	1	1	1	1

Carneiro (2001)

Purpose

The purpose here is explicitly stated to be the development of a conceptual model of knowledge management efficiency in organisations. The model is clear and reasoned, and is divided into two areas. These are technical tools for specification of intelligent systems resources and intelligent agents (people) who focus their roles on the organisation's performance. The model is developed based on a set of factors that justify the relationships among knowledge management efficiency, intelligent agents, and technological resources. In addition the authors purport to develop a framework for the roles of intelligent agents and technical tools in a conceptual knowledge management model. There is no reference to theory or empirical work to underpin this.

Knowledge Management Process

The knowledge management process is explicitly regarded as knowledge acquisition, use of technical tools, and organisation of people, all of which contribute to organisational effectiveness. The model is presented as a sequential process, with knowledge sources feeding into technical tools and intelligent agents, both of which contribute to knowledge development and result in knowledge management and organisational efficiency. The dynamics and complexity of knowledge management are not demonstrated, and there is no empirical evidence or reference to theory to support this approach.

Knowledge Management Activities

Knowledge management activities are not explicitly referred to.

Development and Testing

Development of this model is based on a literature review and personal experience. There is no evidence of empirical work. The author emphasises the advantages that decision support systems and IT can bring to the effectiveness of the organisation and knowledge management. Although in each case discussion is well reasoned and clear, the final conceptual model appears to be an afterthought, with no indication as to how the model operates or could be applied in an organisation.

Results and Conclusions

The author concludes by highlighting that the model needs to be validated through empirical work and that future research should explore specific areas such as the measurement of factors that affect intelligent agents and use of technical tools, and assessment of managers' attitudes regarding the usefulness of strategic decision support systems and IT to improve knowledge management efficiency. There is no mention of the development of theoretical underpinning.

Summary

The purpose of this model is clearly stated as being conceptual and remains so, with no empirical evidence throughout. Discussion is presented with clarity and a certain amount of reasoning using literature to contribute to the overall development. The knowledge management process has been explicitly referred to as three key elements of the conceptual model, but these are not discussed in any detail. Knowledge management activities have not been referred to. Emphasis is placed on decision support systems, however there is no further discussion, no theory in relation to decision support or knowledge management. This framework is a reasonable example and standard approach which does not contribute anything significantly different when considering an organisation's readiness to engage with knowledge management.

Score Key	1 = lowest possible score; 5 = highest possible score				
Total Score **42**	**Explicitness**	**Clarity**	**Reasoning**	**Theory**	**Empirical Work**
Purpose	5	5	5	1	1
Process	5	3	2	1	1
Activities	1	1	1	1	1
Develop & **Test**	2	2	2	1	1

Goh (2002)

Purpose

The purpose, introduction, and discussion about this framework are clear. The author prescribes an integrative conceptual framework that links key factors in literature that relate to knowledge transfer. This includes managerial implications and organisational characteristics. The author reviews key issues that relate to knowledge transfer including organisational learning, technology to facilitate transfer, cultural issues, and structure. Discussion is clear and presented with clarity, however it lacks depth, remaining at a general level.

Knowledge Management Process

The author briefly distinguishes between hard organisational processes and soft people-oriented processes. From the literature review, the integrative framework includes the process of leadership, problem-solving/seeking behaviours, support structures, absorptive and retention capacity, and types of knowledge. Each process is underpinned by a description of approaches that would facilitate knowledge sharing, and this is presented in a prescriptive manner, with no contrasting debate.

A summary of management approaches to achieve effective knowledge transfer is provided. There are many assertions made by the author with no theoretical underpinning or empirical work, and assumptions are made that an organisation will generally be compliant. This is despite a comment about power and knowledge, which receives no further consideration.

Knowledge Management Activities

Knowledge management activities are not explicitly referred to.

Development and Testing

This is a conceptual framework that has been developed from a review of literature, though it lacks depth and reasoning. Testing and associated empirical work has not been undertaken.

Conclusions

The author concludes by stating that the framework contributes to the elaboration and integration of some key factors that influence the knowledge transfer process and re-emphasise the prescriptive approach presented.

Summary

This is a presentation of a knowledge management framework based on a literature review that focuses on aspects of knowledge transfer. The purpose and discussion is clear, however reasoning is weak with little contrasting discussion and overall a prescriptive approach. There is no overall research design, and although theory is referred to, this remains at a general level. Empirical work has not been undertaken. An important contribution that this framework may offer to the concept of an organisation's readiness to engage with knowledge management is the right management approach and organisational design to facilitate knowledge transfer.

Score Key	1 = lowest possible score; 5 = highest possible score				
Total Score 37	**Explicitness**	**Clarity**	**Reasoning**	**Theory**	**Empirical Work**
Purpose	5	5	3	2	1
Process	3	2	3	2	1
Activities	1	1	1	1	1
Develop & **Test**	1	1	1	1	1

Pérez Pérez, Sanchéz, Carnicer, & Jiménez (2002)

Purpose

The purpose of this framework is explicitly stated: to study the potential feasibility to telework knowledge tasks and jobs. Analysis of knowledge tasks is undertaken according to the knowledge process, which includes generation, codification, storage, and transfer. Overall discussion progresses clearly and is well reasoned, based on a review of literature and previous empirical research in relation to teleworking. The methodology used to develop the framework is presented, resulting in a clear and understandable framework, with the exception of one area of discussion relating to an analysis model of knowledge tasks or processes in relation to variables and values. This element of the framework is disjointed and ambiguous. There is no theoretical underpinning provided.

Knowledge Management Process

The author assesses and discusses knowledge management literature to establish the most appropriate knowledge management process for the framework. The knowledge management process is explicitly stated as being:

- Knowledge Creation
- Knowledge Acquisition
- Knowledge Retention
- Knowledge Distribution

This is clearly discussed with the addition of ICT and information in the context of supporting the process. There is no theoretical underpinning or empirical work.

Knowledge Management Activities

Knowledge management activities are referred to as the activities undertaken in order to achieve the requirements of specific roles in the context of knowledge roles and in relation to the feasibility of these roles for teleworking. The author states that the choice of roles and tasks has been derived from knowledge management literature, but no further empirical work appears to have been undertaken to validate this choice.

Development and Testing

Development of this framework has been undertaken through literature review, and empirical work has been undertaken specifically in relation to teleworking. There is no evidence of empirical work having been undertaken to test the final framework.

Results and Conclusions

The author concludes by summarising the purpose and potential benefits of the framework, and proposes further research to empirically test it based on case study and surveys, to both validate and extend the framework.

Summary

Overall the purpose of this framework is clear, and although well discussed and reasoned through reference to literature, there is no explicit theoretical underpinning. The knowledge management process is established from a review of literature, and knowledge management activities are referred to as knowledge tasks associated with specific jobs. Development has been undertaken in a clear and reasoned way, based on literature and empirical work in the area of teleworking. The authors provide a brief methodology, which assists in understanding the approach taken. Empirical work to test the final framework has not been undertaken, and there is no theoretical underpinning. This framework is useful because it contributes to one aspect of the modern organisation that relates to mobile working, telecommunicating, and virtual working in the context of knowledge management.

Score Key	1 = lowest possible score; 5 = highest possible score				
Total Score 55	Explicitness	Clarity	Reasoning	Theory	Empirical Work
Purpose	5	5	3	1	2
Process	5	5	5	1	3
Activities	3	3	2	1	3
Develop & Test	2	2	2	1	1

Escriba-Esteve & Urra-Urbieta (2002)

Purpose

This is a conceptual framework, the purpose of which is to consider cooperative agreements or partnerships from a knowledge and learning perspective; it
is clearly stated in this respect. Discussion is clear and sets the context, and the
authors provide contrasting views of knowledge management from a robust
literature review, which is well reasoned to establish their own approach to
knowledge management. The main focus from a knowledge management
perspective is on learning and knowledge creation processes that take place in
inter-organisational partnerships or alliances. Reference is made to learning
theory, and there is no evidence of empirical work.

Knowledge Management Process

Learning and the knowledge creation process are explicitly and clearly discussed in the context of cooperative agreements. The knowledge creation
process includes creation, transfer, and integration of knowledge between
companies. The authors provide a reasoned argument for using cooperative
agreements to achieve superior performance, specifically by focussing on the
process of knowledge creation, rather than just the settlement of mutual gain.

Learning processes are discussed as to what actually occurs within the cooperative agreements and is divided into two perspectives:

- Learning to design and manage the cooperation as a strategic option.
- Learning as a means of acquiring know-how, skills, and competencies from another company to improve its own strategies and competitive advantage.

A distinction is made between individual, group, and organisational learning, and how individual learning relates to organisational or group learning. Factors that may facilitate or inhibit learning and the knowledge creation process are recognised and discussed, with reference to theory. There is no reference to empirical work to validate this approach.

Knowledge Management Activities

Knowledge management activities are not explicitly referred to.

Development and Testing

Development of the framework has been undertaken from a robust literature review, underpinned by theory. Discussion is clear, well reasoned, and balanced, incorporating different perspectives and why the authors have chosen a particular approach. There is no evidence of empirical work, and testing has not been undertaken; therefore, as explicitly stated by the authors, this is a conceptual framework.

Results and Conclusions

The authors conclude by highlighting the benefits of this framework and future research that would be useful to unravel additional issues in relation to cooperative agreements. The importance of the learning process is highlighted as this may facilitate or inhibit the knowledge creation process and competitive superiority.

Summary

The purpose, development, discussion, and reasoning in this framework are clear and are underpinned by theory and a robust literature review. There is no evidence of empirical work, therefore, the framework remains conceptual or aspirational. Knowledge management process is explicitly identified in relation to knowledge creation. Learning processes are discussed in relation to knowledge creation and the impact on cooperative agreements. Knowledge management activities are not referred to. This framework concentrates on the benefits and advantages that can be gained from mergers, which is useful from an evaluation perspective. This is also helpful to articulate the similar benefits that could be achieved from an internal merger of departments when evaluating restructure and an organisation's readiness to engage with knowledge management.

Score Key	1 = lowest possible score; 5 = highest possible score				
Total Score 60	Explicitness	Clarity	Reasoning	Theory	Empirical Work
Purpose	5	5	5	4	1
Process	5	5	5	4	1
Activities	1	1	1	1	1
Develop & Test	3	3	4	4	1

Lee & Kim (2001)

Purpose

This is an integrated framework intended to build organisational capabilities of knowledge management. The purpose is explicitly stated and discussion is undertaken with reasoning and clarity based on a sound review of knowledge management literature and theory. The authors consider resource-based theory and why this is becoming more important in knowledge-based organisations. In addition life cycle theory is related to the different stages of knowledge management which provides understanding about the overall framework. From this review the authors propose four key stages of the knowledge management process.

Knowledge Management Process

The knowledge management process is explicitly referred to as initiation, propagation, integration, and networking. These have been chosen based on resource-based theory and life cycle theory, and are described and reasoned as follows:

Initiation Stage—This is the stage whereby organisations begin to recognise the importance of organisational knowledge management and prepare for organisation-wide knowledge management efforts. To achieve this, the organisation requires, for example, commitment, voluntary involvement, and long-term planning.

Propagation Stage—This is when organisations begin to invest in their knowledge infrastructure to facilitate knowledge activities such as creating, sharing, and storing and utilising knowledge. At this stage a complete organisation wide-knowledge management process is identified including appropriate technology.

Integration Stage—At this stage organisational activities are institutionalised as daily activities. As more in the organisation become familiar with knowledge activities, the knowledge activities increase.

Networking Stage—This is an external integration stage where organisational knowledge is networked with suppliers, customers, research firms, and universities. At this stage the focus of organisational efforts becomes more specialist on core knowledge, and other required knowledge is outsourced.

The knowledge management process is well reasoned and theoretically under-pinned.

Knowledge Management Activities

The activities needed to achieve each stage in the process are clearly identified from a management perspective and labelled organisational actions. These are well structured and organised as follows:

- **Initiation**   Dissemination of the needs of knowledge management.

  Assess current problems of knowledge management

  Share visions and goals

  Compile long-term plan

  Conduct benchmarks pilot projects

- **Propagation**   Set up knowledge management process

  Build reward system

  Develop HRM programmes

  Develop knowledge typology

  Build knowledge management system

  Conduct events to activate knowledge activities

- **Integration**   Evaluate effectiveness of knowledge

  Scan changes in environment

  Monitor and control activities

  Define and focus on core knowledge areas

  Disseminate best practice

- **Networking**   Analyse internal and external environment

  Develop alliances with partners

  Share visions and goals with partners

  Link knowledge management with partners

  Facilitate inter-organisational knowledge sharing and collaborations.

The actions to achieve each activity are discussed with reasoning, and recognising that different organisations may approach this in a different way, the authors provide guidance rather than prescription.

Development and Testing

Development of this framework was undertaken through a literature review and tested through empirical research with 21 organisations—10 Korean and 11 international. The methodology to conduct this research and testing has been made explicit, and the authors recognise the level of subjectivity, which they attempted to reduce through triangulation using three external evaluators who are familiar with knowledge management.

Results and Conclusions

The authors conclude by reviewing what has been achieved in relation to this framework and recognise the limitations, such as subjectivity and their own personal biases; however, the methodology used has attempted to deal with this. The authors propose more solid empirical validations such as a cross-sectional survey and longitudinal case study.

Summary

Overall this is robust framework grounded in theory and empirical research. The theoretical base is a combination of resource-based theory and life cycle theory. Knowledge management processes are explicitly stated and reasoned. Knowledge management activities comprise actions that are required in an organisation to achieve the objectives of the process as well as specific knowledge activities. Development and testing has been undertaken using a clear methodology and critique. The main weakness in this framework is an assumption that individuals within an organisation will engage and commit to the concept of knowledge management. The authors do not consider the power and politics associated with knowledge sharing, but overall provide a well-structured framework that could contribute significantly to the development of an evaluative framework

Score Key	1 = lowest possible score; 5 = highest possible score				
Total Score 100	Explicitness	Clarity	Reasoning	Theory	Empirical Work
Purpose	5	5	5	5	5
Process	5	5	5	5	5
Activities	5	5	5	5	5
Develop & Test	5	5	5	5	5

Bower & Heminger (2002)

Purpose

This framework is intended to provide an overarching strategy to guide the identification and selection of knowledge management projects and as such is clearly stated. Although the purpose is clear, there is inadequate discussion and no evidence of theoretical underpinning. The framework has been subjected to a Delphi study, from which recommendations are presented to improve. However, although the criticisms of the framework are presented, the authors do not present improvements at this stage.

Knowledge Management Process

The knowledge management process is referred to as a six-step process to explore aspects of knowledge management and the selection of an appropriate knowledge management project. The six steps are:

- Analyse corporate strategic objectives using SWOT methodology.
- Identify potential knowledge opportunities and limitations.
- Identify and address potential knowledge management projects.

- Identify and address knowledge management project variables affecting project implementation and success.
- Identify and address factors for project variables affecting the successful implementation of knowledge management projects.
- Finalise knowledge management project selection.

Within each step, key tasks that need to be considered and decisions that should be made are highlighted. The knowledge management process is referred to generally, but it is not discussed in a structured manner with reasoning. The six-step approach referred to above appears to be more about project selection rather than a knowledge management process. There is no evidence of theoretical underpinning. Empirical work has been undertaken and is referred to in development and testing.

Knowledge Management Activities

Knowledge management activities are not explicitly referred to.

Development and Testing

The authors have referred to knowledge management literature in the development of this framework and indicate that empirical work has been undertaken through a Delphi assessment. They do not, however, appear to have taken action based on the results of the Delphi assessment in this case, but indicate their intention to do so.

Results and Conclusions

The authors conclude by recognising the feedback and results that were received from the Delphi assessment. The feedback suggests that it is a viable framework for identifying and selecting knowledge management projects. Criticisms include comments such as:

- Knowledge management is not a project.
- More attention should be given to organisational culture.

- Consideration should be given to preparing for support of a project, including financial and human resources.
- More attention to maintaining flexibility.
- Proposed customers of the project should be defined.
- A cost-benefit approach to the exercise should be introduced.

The authors finally state that the next stage is to review and empirically test the framework.

Summary

The purpose of this framework is clearly stated and based on a literature review. There is no theoretical underpinning for any aspect of the framework. The knowledge management process is referred to in a general manner, with the main focus on the process of project selection. Knowledge management activities are not included. Empirical work and constructive feedback in the development of the framework has been undertaken at this stage, and the authors identify areas for future improvement. The research undertaken in relation to the development of this framework provides a useful contribution to the development of an evaluation framework for an organisation's knowledge management readiness by highlighting associated issues of consideration gathered through feedback undertaken through a Delphi assessment.

Score Key	1 = lowest possible score; 5 = highest possible score				
Total Score **41**	**Explicitness**	**Clarity**	**Reasoning**	**Theory**	**Empirical Work**
Purpose	5	3	3	1	3
Process	3	3	3	1	3
Activities	1	1	1	1	1
Develop & **Test**	3	3	2	1	3

Zack (1999)

Purpose

The purpose of the framework is made explicit and intended to configure organisational and technical resources and capabilities to gain advantage from codified knowledge. The framework has been developed from a brief review of literature. Although the purpose of this proposed framework is clearly stated, subsequent discussion is not clear or well reasoned. The authors initially present the content of the framework, offer descriptive examples that do not reflect the benefit of the framework per se, and follow this by continuing discussion about managing knowledge processes in relation to organisational context and knowledge repositories. There is no theoretical underpinning and although empirical work is indicated, it remains ambiguous.

Knowledge Management Process

The knowledge management process is referred to within the scope of a knowledge management architecture, which has four elements:

- *Repository of explicit knowledge* contains knowledge as an object, defined as structure and content, and within which knowledge units exist. Knowledge units are linked by the knowledge object and are labelled, indexed, stored, retrieved, and manipulated.

- *Knowledge refinery* is the process for creating and distributing knowledge contained in the repository and includes a five-stage process: acquisition, refining, storage and retrieval, distribution, and presentation.

- *Knowledge management roles* are cross-organisational processes and include: educating the organisation, knowledge mapping, and integrating organisational and technical resources.

- *Information technologies* are concerned specifically with the flow of explicit knowledge, which has a five-stage process: capturing knowledge; defining, storing, categorising, indexing, and linking knowledge; searching relevant content; subscribing to relevant content; and presenting content in a flexible, meaningful, and applicable manner across various contexts of use.

The relationship between the overall five-stage process (architecture) and processes within are not explicitly drawn out in a clear and understandable way. The author then adds to this with another process referred to as integrative and interactive applications. Integrative applications relate to the sequential flow of explicit knowledge into and from the repository. Interactive applications focus on people and tacit knowledge. There is no reference to theory to underpin this approach, and although reference is made to empirical work, this remains ambiguous.

Knowledge Management Activities

Having identified the process(es), the author does not explicitly refer to activities. For example the foregoing identifies processes within processes, some of which could be defined as activities and have been addressed in the foregoing.

Development and Testing

The author uses literature in the development of this framework, however discussion and reasoning appear weak. There is no theoretical underpinning and no reference to methodology. The author states that research has been conducted in two case organisations cited which provide examples of managing explicit knowledge. The author, however, does not explicitly state that this research was undertaken in the development of the framework, and the cases do not reflect use of the framework.

Conclusions

The author concludes by specifically referring to the case organisations, stating that organisations that manage knowledge effectively understand strategic knowledge requirements and develop a knowledge strategy appropriate to the business strategy. Organisational and technical architecture is implemented and commitment to the knowledge cycle is evident. Little reference is made to the framework except to indicate that it provides a guide to managing knowledge.

Summary

Overall the purpose of the framework is explicitly stated, but discussion is disjointed and reasoning is weak. There is no theoretical underpinning, and empirical work is referred to but remains ambiguous. The knowledge management process is referred to, both as the overall process and processes within the process, which have been considered here as activities. Development has been undertaken through literature, and there is no evidence of testing. This provides another alternative example to consider in relation to the structure of a framework.

Score Key	1 = lowest possible score; 5 = highest possible score				
Total Score 42	Explicitness	Clarity	Reasoning	Theory	Empirical Work
Purpose	4	2	2	1	1
Process	5	3	2	1	2
Activities	3	2	2	1	1
Develop & Test	3	2	2	1	2

Joshi (2001)

Purpose

This is a framework for the systematic study of knowledge management behaviours during decision making. The purpose, methodology, and discussion are clear and well reasoned. The framework identifies and characterises the constructs for studying knowledge management behaviours that emerge during decision-making and the impact of the behaviour on process outcome. The author applies decision-making processes to knowledge management by reviewing knowledge resources and activities, and the type of decision-making processes that may be undertaken according to the circumstances and type of knowledge under consideration. The framework is underpinned by decision theory and a theoretical approach to knowledge management based on the author's own previous empirical research.

Knowledge Management Process

The knowledge management process is briefly referred to in the context of the learning that is achieved during the decision-making process and how the learning process alters an organisation's resources. No further reference in terms of the knowledge management process in relation to the structure of the framework is offered.

Knowledge Management Activities

Knowledge management activities are explicitly referred to as the activities required to meet knowledge needs. These include knowledge selection, acquisition, use, transfer, and internalisation. Each activity is described and used in the framework, which cross-references the activities with different knowledge management situations, sources, and factors that influence knowledge management.

Development and Testing

Development has been undertaken from literature review primarily in relation to decision-making and knowledge management. The framework's theoretical underpinning is derived from decision theory and the author's previous empirical research into knowledge management. Testing and empirical work, specifically in relation to the framework produced, has not been undertaken.

Results and Conclusions

The author concludes in a general way by highlighting that this framework defines and characterises knowledge management behaviours during decision-making, and provides a basis for further research.

Summary

The purpose, discussion, and reasoning about this framework are clear and well presented in a structured way. The knowledge management process is briefly referred to and knowledge management activities are discussed in more depth. There is clear evidence of theoretical underpinning and empirical work from the author's previous research in the development stage. Testing of this framework has not been undertaken. If considered in the context of evaluation, this framework contributes useful information relating to an organisation's readiness to engage with knowledge management specifically focussing on the decision-making process.

Score Key	1 = lowest possible score; 5 = highest possible score				
Total Score 76	Explicitness	Clarity	Reasoning	Theory	Empirical Work
Purpose	5	5	5	5	3
Process	3	3	3	3	3
Activities	5	5	5	5	3
Develop & Test	4	3	3	3	2

De Gooijer (2000)

Purpose

This is a model of knowledge management for measuring the performance of knowledge management strategies for a public sector agency. Within the model, there are two frameworks: The first is intended to measure knowledge management performance and is based on a balanced scorecard approach.

The second is a behaviour framework intended to identify the levels of practice demonstrated by individuals and is based on change management. The purpose is explicitly stated and discussion is presented with clarity and reason. The background and empirical work in relation to the development of the frameworks is based on a public sector organisation, and the main issues that needed to be addressed in this organisation are clearly presented. This provides context and understanding.

Knowledge Management Process

Three main approaches to the knowledge management process are referred to. These include:

- Knowledge management map.
- Tacit and explicit knowledge transfer processes.
- Sensemaking as a key element in ICT.

There is no further discussion in relation to these approaches, and the author's chosen approach is to use a knowledge management map, the elements of which the author deems appropriate to meet the requirements of the case being considered. The elements include strategy, infrastructure, products and services, relationships, culture and behaviour, processes, and content. There is an indication that this approach was chosen as a result of discussion and empirical research with the case organisation, but there is no methodology to demonstrate how this was achieved and no reference to theoretical underpinning.

Knowledge Management Activities

Knowledge management activities have not been included.

Development and Testing

Development of the model and frameworks has been undertaken through empirical work and issues raised in the case organisation in addition to a literature review. However although the discussion justifies the chosen approach, there is no discussion about alternative approaches that may have been considered and why they were rejected. The performance framework focuses mainly on the balanced scorecard, with knowledge management concepts broadly applied to provide a knowledge management approach. The behavioural framework has been developed around change management and the sequences of behaviour that individuals will go through during the change process. There has been no empirical work or testing of this model and the two frameworks. Theoretical underpinning is briefly considered in relation to the behavioural framework only.

Results and Conclusions

The author concludes by recognising that implementation is still at an early stage, but does not indicate what implementation has taken place. In addition there is a final assertion made that the design of the frameworks provides an approach for hard business measures to be linked to soft social measures, but there is no indication of how these could be measured.

Summary

The purpose and discussion about this framework is clear, however reasoning in some areas of discussion appears weak. For example, the frameworks are each underpinned by logical approaches to performance measurement using a balanced scorecard approach in the first framework, which has been well justified. The second framework in relation to management behaviour is underpinned by one theoretical approach in relation to change management. This choice has not been reasoned out. Development is specific to one public sector organisation and in this sense the frameworks are very focussed, particularly in relation to the approach taken. They have not been tested in the case organisation or beyond and therefore remain conceptual. This framework provides a useful contribution to evaluation through the knowledge management map and associated elements that comprise the process, i.e., strategy, infrastructure, products and services, relationships, culture and behaviour, process, and content.

Score Key	1 = lowest possible score; 5 = highest possible score				
Total Score **48**	**Explicitness**	**Clarity**	**Reasoning**	**Theory**	**Empirical Work**
Purpose	5	5	3	2	4
Process	3	3	2	2	2
Activities	1	1	1	2	2
Develop & **Test**	2	2	2	2	2

Kwang, Pervaiz, & Mohamed (1999)

Purpose

The purpose of this framework is twofold, firstly to measure knowledge management and to use the results for leveraging an organisation against its competitors, and secondly to improve customer satisfaction. The authors provide a brief example of knowledge management—distinguishing between tacit and explicit knowledge—and apply quality strategy to knowledge management, which is then connected with a cost model to produce the actual framework. There is no theoretical underpinning or empirical work. Discussion is weak, with many assertions made and inadequate attention to knowledge management literature.

Knowledge Management Process

The overall knowledge management process is not referred to, but the activities as indicated in the next section could be identified as the process, with further activities highlighted to meet the requirements of the process.

Knowledge Management Activities

Knowledge management activities or process are explicitly referred to and connected with a plan-do-check-act cycle associated with quality strategies as follows:

- Capturing or creating knowledge (plan)
- Sharing knowledge (do)
- Measuring the effects (check)
- Learning and improvement (act)

In each case additional activities are briefly described to achieve the main activities or process as listed. The main activities are then cross-referenced with a cost model to develop a matrix or framework. The cost model includes:

- *Customer*—specifically refers to the information and learning that can be derived from the customer base.
- *Organisation*—relates to the key skills of people and how skills are shared.
- *Suppliers*—explores the cost, quality, and delivery service from suppliers, however there is no mention of the opportunity to share or glean knowledge from suppliers.
- *Technology*—refers to how many PCs there are and whether they are linked and used effectively.

Overall there is inadequate discussion of the knowledge management activities and the rationale behind the interaction with the cost model. A surface-level description is offered and there is no reference to empirical work or theoretical underpinning.

Development and Testing

Development has been undertaken in a fairly superficial way, and although some reference to literature has been made, it is inadequate for reasoning and justification of the statements made. There is no indication that empirical work and testing has been undertaken.

Results and Conclusions

The author concludes by highlighting the benefits of considering knowledge management as a quality strategy to improve the customer experience, but the purpose of the framework does not indicate this as being the intention, but part of the process.

Summary

This is a fairly superficial presentation of a knowledge management framework with a clear purpose, but ambiguous outcome. Throughout, there is little discussion and limited evidence or reasoning to support any of the assertions made. Although some literature has been referred to, the extent of what is being proposed requires more in-depth discussion and reasoning for it to be in some way valid. Statements are unsupported by empirical work and theoretical underpinning. The contribution that this framework makes to the evaluation of an organisation's readiness to engage with knowledge management relates directly to the application of a quality process and potential quality audit.

Score Key	1 = lowest possible score; 5 = highest possible score				
Total Score **41**	**Explicitness**	**Clarity**	**Reasoning**	**Theory**	**Empirical Work**
Purpose	5	2	2	1	1
Process	4	3	2	1	1
Activities	5	4	3	1	1
Develop & **Test**	1	1	1	1	1

Kwan & Balasubramanian (2002)

Purpose

The authors present a knowledge management system, the purpose of which is explicitly stated. It is intended to provide an integrated workflow support capability that captures and retrieves knowledge within context and then organises the knowledge and context in a knowledge repository. A clear methodology and rationale for undertaking this approach is provided through discussion of secondary research and literature. There is no theoretical underpinning.

Knowledge Management Process

The knowledge management process is specifically discussed as one aspect of the overall proposed system (KnowledgeScope) and is a model for knowledge in context, which includes process designs, process instances, and knowledge resources that are captured, stored, and retrieved from a repository. Knowledge management is categorised into three types, and the authors propose that a knowledge management system should organise knowledge around organisational processes, and the processes are the scope of an application. Each application then contains the three types of knowledge—process knowledge, case knowledge, and knowledge resources. This is clearly discussed, and although a technical approach to knowledge management, the authors consider the human interface with technology.

Emphasis is placed on the process of knowledge capture, sharing, and utilisation. Through a review of knowledge management technology intended to underpin the process, the authors identify both the technical weaknesses and consider the failures that have been experienced in relation to human interface with the technology. The technology reviewed includes knowledge repositories, process memory systems, and organisational memory information systems. Discussion is presented in a balanced and understandable manner for non-technically minded users, which engenders understanding about the system being proposed.

The overall system is divided into four perspectives:

- *Functional perspective*—asks what tasks are performed and why.
- *Informational perspective*—describes the information used and produced by tasks in the process and relationships between them.
- *Organisational perspective*—answers who, where, and with what resources tasks are performed.
- *Behavioural perspective*—answers questions about when and how tasks are performed.

The development of the process has been undertaken through empirical work, but there is no evidence of theoretical underpinning.

Knowledge Management Activities

Knowledge management activities are not explicitly referred to, but the system concentrates on the overall process and sub-processes, which can also be activities.

Development and Testing

The system has been developed based on secondary research and literature to establish the rationale at every stage of the system development. Testing has been undertaken by applying the system to a case organisation and evaluating its performance. There is no explicit theoretical underpinning.

Conclusions

The authors conclude by highlighting the results of testing and recognising the weaknesses in the system, proposing further development work to improve. The weaknesses identified include the need for additional information in relation to specific context to be made available, for example, geographical locations, strategic intents, and customers. In addition the authors point out that provision of this system does not entirely address knowledge management in an organisation, as this requires culture change and a change in mental models where the workforce begin to think in terms of knowledge management.

Summary

The purpose, discussion, and reasoning about the development, implementation, and evaluation of this system are robust. During the development stage, specific applications of the system have been further discussed and benchmarked against current systems and technology available to justify the need for this particular approach. The knowledge management process is discussed in relation to business processes and what can be achieved within the scope of this model. Knowledge management activities are not explicitly referred to, but are easily derived from sub-processes. Empirical work has been undertaken by implementing and evaluating the system in a case organisation from which weaknesses were identified and proposals to improve presented. The attention to the technical interface and this system's four perspectives that comprise the process provide a useful contribution to evaluation.

Score Key	1 = lowest possible score; 5 = highest possible score				
Total Score 79	Explicitness	Clarity	Reasoning	Theory	Empirical Work
Purpose	5	5	5	1	5
Process	5	5	5	1	5
Activities	4	3	3	1	5
Develop & Test	5	5	5	1	5

Hatten & Rosenthal (2001)

Purpose

The purpose of this framework is clearly stated, the intention of which is to integrate knowledge into corporate strategy. The authors state that the production of the framework has arisen from previous research, which pointed to the need for practical frameworks to help corporate managers participate more effectively in strategy formulation and knowledge management processes. There is no referencing or evidence of this empirical work. However when describing how the framework could be implemented, a retrospective view on several case organisations is offered, but there is no methodology or indication as to whether these form part of the research referred to. There is no evidence of theoretical underpinning.

Knowledge Management Process

The framework contains seven key tools, which are intended to assist managers in implementing the overall knowledge process. These are:

- *An Action Alignment Model*—This focuses on the current strategy and associated operating activities, and is a process for assessing the organisation's effectiveness and business processes through targeted knowledge management.

- *A Do/Contract Decision Process*—This relates external contracting and partnerships with the acquisition of new skills and abilities achieved through partnership.

- *A 3C Test*—This is intended to test for strategic balance by assessing the feasibility of the current business strategy and in doing so considers the customer base, business process capabilities, and organisational competencies (hence 3C). Organisational competencies refer to the 'know-how' that already exists. Overall, the 3C test is intended to provide an overview allowing for an integrative approach to understand strategic capabilities and competencies, and identify any gaps.

- *A Strategic Stretch Test*—This relates to the future of the organisation and new business opportunities. In this case the 3C test is used to compare future requirements to what is currently available. It then extends this to consider competitive advantage and external and internal stakeholders, and potential constraints they may impose on the organisation. At this stage a strategic risk assessment is carried out, along with options for managing the decisions that may be taken.

- *A Review of Experimental Knowledge Gained*—This includes learning in action and gaining knowledge to support subsequent decisions about opportunities to pursue. At this stage of the process, the experimental knowledge from strategic business experiments is assessed.

- *Performance Metrics*—These relate to the choice of performance measures and systems to support this, for example setting performance targets.

- *The Knowledge Ignition Process*—This relates culture and knowledge-based behaviour to cycles of learning in action and essentially the establishment of a learning culture.

None of the foregoing processes are underpinned by theory, nor is there explicit evidence of empirical work.

Knowledge Management Activities

Knowledge management activities are referred to as specific actions that should be taken to meet the requirements of the seven-stage process. These are too numerous to repeat here, but suffice to say they comprise a list of practical actions that are clearly stated and offer an effective guide for practitioners.

One activity that has been clearly presented and differs from the standard knowledge/business process relates to the assessment of risk. The authors propose that once a new strategy has been provisionally decided upon, a risk assessment should be undertaken. The model to undertake this includes knowledge content according to the seven-stage process assessed against key aspects of an organisation, for example customers, competencies, country and currency, and the Chief Executive Officer. Guidance is offered as to how to implement this model.

There is no evidence of empirical work or theoretical underpinning.

Development and Testing

There is no methodology to indicate how the framework was developed. Having established the framework, the authors apply specific stages of it retrospectively to several case organisations to justify how it could be beneficial. There is no indication that actual empirical work has been undertaken.

Results and Conclusions

There is no overall conclusion, but at the close of each chapter relating to aspects of the framework, the authors tend to conclude by emphasising the benefits of the framework.

Summary

The purpose of this framework is clearly stated, and discussion is clear; however, reasoning lacks robustness. Assertions are made throughout, with poor referencing, weak use of literature, no clear empirical work to test the framework, and no theoretical underpinning. The knowledge management process and activities are explicitly referred to in a clear way, and guidance is offered about implementation. Generally, this framework provides a comprehensive and practical approach, which could contribute to the development of a framework intended to evaluate an organisation's knowledge management readiness.

Score Key	1 = lowest possible score; 5 = highest possible score				
Total Score **52**	**Explicitness**	**Clarity**	**Reasoning**	**Theory**	**Empirical Work**
Purpose	5	5	2	1	1
Process	5	5	3	1	1
Activities	5	5	3	1	1
Develop & **Test**	2	2	2	1	1

Knight & Howes (2003)

Purpose

Overall the purpose of this framework is clear: to assist in consultancy and investigation into knowledge management in organisations. The framework comprises a tool set to structure thinking and is intended by the authors to provide a holistic approach to knowledge management at a strategic level. As discussion unfolds, however, the approach becomes ambiguous, partly because although the authors emphasise the importance of addressing knowledge management at a strategic level, they tend to place equal emphasis on individual projects and the process of project management. The background and introduction to the framework contains reference to previous literature and theory, but this does not appear to have been directly applied to the framework.

Knowledge Management Process

The knowledge management process has been clearly identified as a five-stage process, which comprises:

- A definition of pressures on organisations and assessment of the potential for leveraging knowledge to deliver corporate objectives.
- Development of strategy by assessing the current state of knowledge and defining the knowledge vision and benefits.
- Design of the new order of the organisation, which includes leadership, people issues, process, technology, and information.
- Leadership includes responsibility for the delivery of a knowledge management programme.
- People include consideration for behaviours, communication and knowledge sharing, skills, and cultural issues.
- Processes involve analysis of business process to improve knowledge identification, use, creation, sharing, and recording.
- Technology is the IT tools that support knowledge management.
- Information refers to the relevance, availability, context, and quality of information and IT to support this.

- Implementation and planning for change, including budgets and priorities. At this stage the authors argue that it is unlikely for a strategy to be solely top-down and reach across the organisation. It is more likely to build from the bottom or middle of the organisation.

- An assurance that the expected benefits are realised and relevant resources are committed to identifying future opportunities.

The authors emphasise project management, benefit management, and change management, and explicitly state that the framework is a model for knowledge management programmes. In addition links are made between workgroup level and overall organisational strategy level. Discussion is clear and well presented. There is no evidence of theoretical underpinning. The authors indicate that empirical work has been conducted through use of the framework in organisations from which adjustments have been made periodically when required.

Knowledge Management Activities

Knowledge management activities are not explicitly highlighted but can be deduced from the guidance offered about the process. For example, at each stage of the process, the authors both propose and provide, where relevant, activities such as surveys, self-assessment tools, training, and other analytical tools that will draw out the activities necessary to meet the process.

Development and Testing

Initial development of the framework has been undertaken based on a literature review. The literature review, however, does not appear to have been explicitly and directly applied to the stages of the framework. Testing of the framework has been undertaken based on the authors' experiences of using the framework in organisations, of which specific examples are provided. The authors provide a methodology of how the framework was used and what developments or adjustments were made from inception to the current state. There is no indication of theoretical underpinning.

Results and Conclusions

In conclusion the authors review and summarise the stages of the framework again and follow this up with general discussion about knowledge management in the current business world and the potential difficulties organisations might face, which knowledge management could address.

Summary

The purpose of the framework has been clearly stated, providing a framework comprising a set of tools to structure thinking and implementation of knowledge management in an organisation at a strategic level. Although the intended purpose relates to organisational strategy, subsequent discussion focuses more on knowledge projects within an organisation, with comment about linking these to strategy. At this point discussion becomes disjointed. The knowledge management process is explicitly referred to and clearly discussed and justified in a practical sense, but contains no reference to theory. Knowledge management activities are not explicitly referred to but can be deduced from the guidance offered to underpin the process; these include surveys, self-assessment tools, training, and other analytical tools.

Empirical work throughout, including development and testing, is based specifically on the authors' own experiences, and descriptions of case studies are offered.

Score Key	1 = lowest possible score; 5 = highest possible score				
Total Score 75	Explicitness	Clarity	Reasoning	Theory	Empirical Work
Purpose	5	4	4	2	5
Process	5	5	5	1	5
Activities	4	3	2	1	5
Develop & Test	5	4	4	1	5

There is no clear conclusion and the authors purport to present the lessons learned; however, a summary and review of the stages of the framework is presented with a reaffirmation of the frameworks benefits. This is followed by a general discussion about knowledge management in the current business world. This framework significantly contributes to the concept of evaluating an organisation's knowledge management readiness. The tools and guidance provided offer a practical approach that could be adapted.

5.4 Discussion

To recap, the approach to this review has been structured carefully by establishing the criteria up front involving a three-stage process:

1. The establishment of a set of keywords to conduct the initial search from which over 3,000 papers were found. From these, 267 articles were identified as having potential relevance to this research; however, 107 of these focussed solely on technology and technical aspects of information, and were not, therefore, considered suitable.

2. An initial review of knowledge management frameworks and a process of elimination using keywords from which 35 papers were regarded as having frameworks that were worth serious assessment.

3. A systematic review of the remaining and most appropriate frameworks with the help of an evaluation grid that has been developed as part of this work

The two key objectives of the evaluation were to show that, firstly, there is no single existing framework that addresses KMR, highlighting gaps in concepts and practice, and secondly to identify useful elements and concepts that ought to be in the framework being developed. The first objective was achieved showing that a new framework for the evaluation of an organisation's potential to engage in knowledge management will contribute to knowledge; the shortfall is clearly demonstrated in Table 5.3.

Table 5.2: Total and Average Scores of Frameworks

Score Key	1 = lowest possible score; 5 = highest possible score				
Total Scores 1,943/3,500	Explicitness	Clarity	Reasoning	Theory	Empirical Work
Purpose	159(4.54)	139(3.97)	118(3.37)	64(1.82)	64(1.82)
Process	139(3.97)	120(3.42)	108(3.08)	59(1.68)	68(1.94)
Activities	107(3.05)	91(2.6)	82(2.34)	56(1.6)	63(1.8)
Develop & Test	82(2.34)	74(2.11)	73(2.08)	53(1.51)	67(1.91)

Table 5.2 identifies overall and average scores for each cell of the evaluation grid. The total score of all frameworks is 1,943 of a potential 3,500. The figures in parentheses represent average scores, and the overall average score per framework is 55.5 out of a possible 100. The highest scoring aspects of the frameworks relate to explicitness of purpose and knowledge management process. The lowest scores relate to theory and empirical work, and development and testing. The difference in scores within cells are nominal, and to some extent reflect the close association between approaches and content of the frameworks reviewed. The basis for judgement in distinguishing between the frameworks has been derived from the discussion provided and is, in essence, a qualitative decision according to the main focus of this research.

The overall results suggest that for managers wishing to introduce knowledge management into their organisations, there is little to offer that is soundly based and accessible. Papers tend to be over simplistic or too theoretical. Many fail to offer a reasonable set of coherent activities in a connected form that could be described as a holistic framework. Many frameworks tend to focus on one particular aspect of knowledge management such as intellectual capital or knowledge sharing. It is difficult to find a holistic framework that managers could use to assess their own organisation's potential to feasibly consider or introduce knowledge management to their organisations.

The second objective, the identification of useful elements and concepts that ought to be in the proposed framework being developed, has been achieved by identifying elements of best practice within the reviewed frameworks, and as such Table 5.3 shows a further breakdown of scores, from which the highest scoring aspects can be drawn out.

Table 5.3: Individual Scores per Framework

	20 = lowest score 100 = highest score	**Purpose**	**Process**	**Activities**	**Develop & Test**	**Theory**	**Empirical**
Abou-Zeid (2002)	66	17	17	17	15	4	6
Achterbergh & Vriens (2002)	82	23	20	22	17	17	12
Arora (2002)	39	15	8	11	5	4	4
Balasubramanian, Kumar, Henderson, & Kwan (1999)	50	13	14	13	10	4	11
Bhatt (2002)	41	17	11	8	5	4	4
Binny (2001)	39	17	12	5	5	4	7
Bolloju, Khalifa, & Turban (2002)	38	14	10	5	9	10	4
Bower & Heminger (2002)	45	15	13	5	12	4	10
Carneiro (2001)	51	17	12	5	8	4	4
Connell, Klein, Loebbecke, & Powell (2001)	48	18	18	10	5	7	4
DeGooijer (2000)	48	19	12	7	10	8	10
Duru Ahanotu (1998)	50	16	13	16	5	11	4
Escriba-Esteve & Urra-Urbieta (2002)	60	20	20	5	15	13	4
Firestone (1999)	60	7	14	14	5	4	4

Table 5.3: Individual Scores per Framework (continued)

	20 = lowest score 100 = highest score	Purpose	Process	Activities	Develop & Test	Theory	Empirical
Gao, Li, & Nakamori (2002)	43	13	13	12	5	10	4
Goh (2002)	37	16	11	5	5	6	4
Hatten & Rosenthal (2001)	52	14	15	15	8	4	4
Hlupic, Pouloudi, & Rzevski (2002)	46	18	18	5	5	6	4
Holsapple & Joshi (2002)	92	21	22	24	25	12	20
Hylton (2002)	33	11	11	6	5	4	6
Joshi (2001)	76	23	15	23	15	16	11
Kamara, Chimay, & Carrillo (2002)	54	18	14	12	10	4	10
Knight & Howes (2003)	75	20	21	15	19	5	20
Kwan & Balasubramanian (2002)	79	21	21	16	21	4	20
Kwang, Pervaiz, & Mohamed (1999)	41	11	11	14	5	4	4
Lee & Kim (2001)	100	25	25	25	25	25	25
McAdam & Reid (2001)	47	15	12	5	15	4	4
Merali (2000)	47	13	15	5	14	7	9
Mullich (2001)	20	5	5	5	5	4	4
Newman & Conrad (2000)	44	15	9	15	5	4	4
Pérez Pérez, Sanchéz, Carnicer, & Jiménez (2002)	56	16	19	12	8	4	9
Pervaiz, Kwang , & Mohamed (1999)	34	10	9	10	5	4	4

Table 5.3: Individual Scores per Framework (continued)

	20 = lowest score 100 = highest score	Purpose	Process	Activities	Develop & Test	Theory	Empirical
Robertson (2002)	30	8	6	8	8	4	7
Snowden (1998)	50	15	15	15	5	4	4
Zack (1999)	42	10	13	9	10	4	6

The highest scoring frameworks provide specific areas of interest, for example, Achterbergh and Vriens (2002) use Beer's (1979) Viable System Model (VSM) to support the diagnosis, design, and implementation of knowledge processes, to establish what kind of knowledge an organisation needs to remain viable and how to manage knowledge to achieve this. This is a logical systems approach to knowledge management and reflects the complexity of organising and defining activities to establish a system of managing knowledge. The five functions of the VSM and associated activities demonstrate that a systems approach provides a robust underpinning to knowledge management. Holsapple and Joshi (2002) offer a sound methodology based on the Delphi process which provides validation and adds to the credibility of their framework, which relates to the process and activities that should be considered to implement knowledge flow and manipulation. Knight and Howes (2003) introduce a practical framework comprising a set of tools to structure thinking and implementation of knowledge management in an organisation, but containing no reference to theory. Kwan and Balasubramanian (2002) provide a robust system of knowledge management, paying particular attention to the technical interface. Lee and Kim (2001) use a combination of resource-based theory and life cycle theory to underpin knowledge management and provide a well-reasoned, empirically tested framework.

Overall, the papers present aspirational frameworks for implementing knowledge management, but few consider the readiness and ability of organisations to engage or make assumptions about an organisation's ability and willingness.

As a consequence the frameworks do not adequately consider all aspects to effectively implement knowledge management in a sustainable way. As has been established in this research, knowledge management is still an emerging field, and until recently the main focus of development has been in the technical domain, retaining the emphasis on speedier information exchange, data storage, and explicit knowledge sharing. Tacit knowledge sharing is now gaining greater recognition as practitioners are beginning to experience the limitations of technology and the driving forces to engage with knowledge management relate to people, management, and the culture of the organisation.

It has become clear from this chapter that there is no unified approach to knowledge management, but the author is not advocating that there should be one prescriptive approach for the management of knowledge in different organisations. The challenge is to establish a generic framework with an appropriate theoretical underpinning that is understandable and provides guidance for managers to consider successful engagement, implementation, and ultimately a sustainable approach.

Such a framework would be strengthened if it were based both in theory and practice, and considered the management and human capability as a significant element in the knowledge management process. The kind of framework proposed here should be at a strategic level if it is to work properly, therefore strategy is one area that could offer theoretical underpinning. Systems literature, however, has a lot of strength and potential to offer strategic knowledge management a theoretical basis and critical systems thinking links to learning and knowledge, providing a means to consider whether the right kinds of issues are being addressed. For example, are technological issues and hard processes being debated when the real area of concern is highly cultural? Soft Systems Methodology provides a useful means to undertake action research, and evaluating an organisation's knowledge management readiness would involve action research, which also provides appropriate empirical work, development, and testing—areas that have been identified as significantly weak in this review. Soft Systems Methodology is discussed in more detail in Chapter 7.

Chapter VI

A Framework for Knowledge Management

6.1 Introduction

Previous chapters have discussed the importance of systems and knowledge management. This is especially important with the shifts from traditional, highly structured organisations, to more fluid businesses in areas as diverse as manufacturing, healthcare, entertainment, and education.

However, it would be idealistic and naïve to assume that knowledge management can somehow provide gain without pain. If knowledge management is to be considered seriously then the possible costs must be recognised. These may include the following.

- Suitable server and client hardware and upgrades of staff machines.

- Suitable system software to support a knowledge management application.

- Knowledge management software.

- Time.
- Training.
- Staff appointments.
- Consultancy.
- Other professional advice—legal, IS security, financial.
- Staff unrest (e.g., new ways, why share knowledge, what we know is best, why change?).
- Initial slowdown in activities whilst staff adjust to a new system, with possible initial customer dissatisfaction.
- Development of incentives systems.
- Development of a system of measures of achievements.
- Costs associated with the implementation of rewards (e.g., profit sharing).
- Ongoing dialogues with staff.
- The financial costs of all of the above, including loans and interest.

Considering all of the above and the trade-offs against, any gains to be made for knowledge management will take time, effort, and commitment. The investigation alone will require a shift in strategic thinking. It should therefore be clear that knowledge management does not provide a quick fix. Organisations that are serious about competing in the twenty-first century should consider KM as a long-term, ongoing strategy, with an initial implementation time scale of between three to five years. Organisations should be aware that the 80:20 rule seems often to be interpreted as 20% feasibility study and 80% technical implementation. This often results in "quick fix" failures. An 80:20 split in favour of finding out what is fit for purpose, what is feasible, and what is desirable would place greater emphasis on the finding out stages and would result in a far higher success rate of implementation and actual business usage of computer-based systems.

One of the most prominent knowledge management initiatives is the establishment of some type of corporate knowledge base or memory. This normally takes the form of a process of structuring existing reports, etc., and eliciting further information such as lessons learned, and making that available electronically. Some estimates suggest that 80-90% of information is unstructured and poorly represented on conventional structured databases. To develop a corporate knowledge base, information needs to be extracted from all relevant parts of the organisation to make it available.

The experiences of knowledge management initiatives highlight the central role of organisational culture in determining the way that knowledge sharing is managed. The ways people relate in organisations, particularly in groups and teams, are important in knowledge processes. Trust is a part of culture that is considered one of the basic elements of effective teamwork, and lack of trust generates suspicion that people will misuse the information, distort it, or deprive one of deserved recognition. Table 6.1 highlights some issues relating to trust.

Knowledge management requires that the strategic process be centred on the recognition of knowledge as the key to the success of the corporation. In particular, knowledge management moves beyond the customer as someone to be serviced and whose needs are to be met, to a partner in understanding the business and how business can be developed to expand its market and enhance its appeal.

A well-thought-out strategy that is supported from the highest level is key to the introduction of knowledge management, and this may incorporate a number of factors. Wherever knowledge is seen to be power, the message of knowledge

Table 6.1: Trust

Friction	Possible Solution
Lack of trust	Build relationships and trust through face-to-face meetings
Different cultures, vocabularies, frames of reference	Create common ground through education, discussion, publications, teaming, job rotation
Lack of time and meeting places; narrow idea of productive work	Establish times and places for knowledge transfers: fairs, talk rooms, conference reports
Status and rewards go to knowledge owners	Evaluate performance and provide incentives based on sharing
Lack of absorptive capacity in recipients	Educate employees for flexibility; provide time for learning; hire for openness to ideas
Belief that knowledge is prerogative of particular groups, not-invented-here syndrome	Encourage non-hierarchical approach to knowledge; quality of ideas more important than status of source
Intolerance for mistakes or need for help	Accept and reward creative errors and collaboration; no loss of status from not knowing everything

sharing, and its benefits to the sharer, must be given clearly and persuasively. The shift to 'sharing knowledge gives corporate power', rather than 'knowledge is power', is cultural rather than technical, although technology may be used to support change. But how is this to be introduced in an organisation? This is discussed next.

6.2 A KM Framework

Table 6.2 and Figure 6.1 show a set of themed activities which together address suggested stages in a knowledge management initiative. Individual organisations may approach such an initiative in a variety of ways, but at least some of the phases of this general framework are likely to be relevant to most organisations.

The arrows that link the phases and the activities within the phases shown in Figure 6.1 indicate uncertain logical dependency, and suggest that the foregoing activities or phases are probably necessary, but are not necessarily sufficient for the current activity to commence. That is, all the preceding activities may have occurred, so that the next activity may commence, but it may not do so. The logical dependencies relate to both technical and cultural aspects of the initiative. A good example of this is in Phase 4, where the concepts and technology must have been introduced for conceptual modelling to commence, but unless there is agreement on measures and incentives, the outcome may be dubious.

The concepts may be new to many organisations, and senior managers may be just as resistant to change as those below them. If senior managers are persuaded that they should find out more, it will be necessary to establish feasibility within an organisation, and key stakeholders should be identified and invited to participate in the development.

Prior to addressing each phase, it is worth mentioning here that the monitoring, test, and control activity is essential, and it is there to provide feedback controls to help the project keep on track. Monitoring picks up information from all other activities, and from external sources, and it is important that measures of progress are made explicit so that when information is received, appropriate control actions can be taken.

The framework moves from strategies to methodologies to techniques. It recognises the important mix needed in organisations of decision-making, dialogue, and application. It begins with a two-phase feasibility study. The trade-off is desirability versus feasibility. The existing and potential capability of a business to engage in knowledge management is assessed in terms of the support (or not) from senior management. The cultural feasibility (or not) of change is also assessed. The results of the feasibility study determine if proceeding to the latter stages would be beneficial to the organisation (and if they would be feasible). Do they want it? Can they do it?

If appropriate, the organisation then works through development and implementation, including incentives, performance measures, training, and cultural and technical implementation. Why is it different? There are frameworks around, but they suffer from one or more of the following major faults. They are geared specifically to vendor products (usually software). Such frameworks tend to point the organisation in the direction of the products, and these (pre-existing) products are suggested to provide the solutions needed. They are too

Table 6.2: Phases for Introducing Knowledge Management

Phase 1 (feasibility - senior) (knowledge management survey)
A	Identify and select knowledge areas of major importance and low current effectiveness.
B	Make an initial assessment of risks.
C	Agree on working objectives and timescales.

Phase 2 (feasibility - cultural) (knowledge mapping)
A	Assess the cultural feasibility and systemic desirability of introducing knowledge management practices and technology.
B	Identify key knowledge workers, knowledge groups, and lines of communication.

Phase 3 (development) (champion)
A	Appoint a senior knowledge officer, who is part of, or who reports directly to, the highest level.
B	Explain the potential benefits to staff.
C	Create task force—employ/train.
D	Evaluate and select appropriate technology.
E	Formulate a detailed project plan.
F	Develop, test, assess, and publicise pilot application (e.g., department).

Phase 4 (incentives and measures, learning and training) (balanced scorecard)
A	Introduce the concepts and technology (e.g., by using appropriate training modules).
C	Formulate transparent and workable incentives.
D	Formulate transparent and workable measures of achievements.
D	Install technology.
E	Begin conceptual modelling of organisation

Phase 5 (implementation)
A	Decide security procedures, access levels, protocols.
B	Build full-scale organisation domain model on computer, enter data, and ensure retrieval links are working.
C	Implement practices and technology.

---

general and provide wonderful overviews but no detail as to how to actually do anything. They are too detailed. There are no links from strategy to detail. Typically, these frameworks would be at the technique level, and typically they are geared towards technical solutions.

As the project progresses, and in the light of new information, the objectives may be reviewed and adjusted. The zig-zag arrows, emanating from the monitoring, test, and control activity, represent lightning—able to strike anywhere with power and speed. The ownership of this activity must be cascaded for the initiative to succeed. In the first instance, ownership will rest with the consultant and senior managers. As progress is made, it will be taken up by the knowledge officer, the task force, and the rest of the staff. This cascading is not relinquishing, as senior staff must retain their own monitoring and control mechanisms. Only the consultant will expect to hand over responsibility entirely.

It is assumed that iterations will occur between activities within phases, and it is suggested that such iterations are important in helping reduce problems that may be more costly if they are recognised later rather than sooner. Some iterations are likely to arise between phases, but these are not envisaged as complete return loops, so that phases are repeated. Rather, they are considered as revisions or qualifiers to previous phase decisions that may arise through discussions based on learning that occurs within a phase. In other words, a decision taken in an earlier phase be revised in the light of new information obtained in this phase. Such information is likely to have resulted from learning, from undertaking activities in the current phase, and would not have been available previously.

Given the above, this framework is doubly systemic in the tradition of Checkland (1981) and Soft Systems Methodology. It provides a basis for assessing and implementing what is culturally feasible and systemically desirable, and it is also a system for learning. The latter point is important, as knowledge management is based upon the concept of a learning organisation. Such an organisation learns and advances by assessing its own strengths and weaknesses, and by encouraging critical reflection.

Figure 6.1: A Framework for Introducing Knowledge Management Concepts and Technology

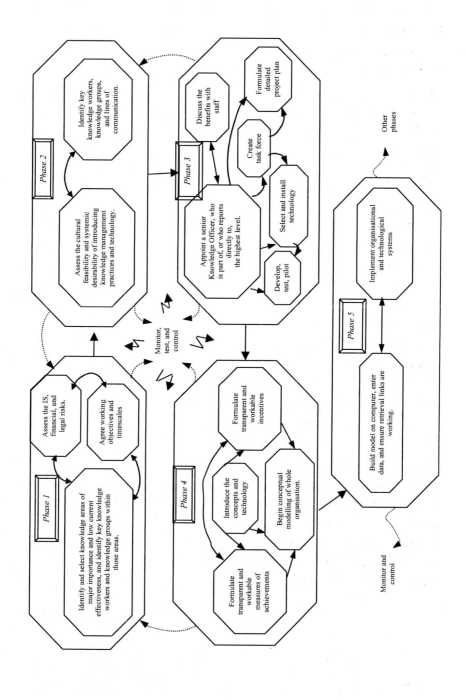

Chapter VII

Conclusions

Three areas (staff, structures, and technology) interact in knowledge manage-ment. Knowledge processes are about the creation, retention, sharing, identi-fication, acquisition, utilisation, and measurement of information and new ideas, in order to achieve strategic aims, such as improved competitiveness or improved performance. Knowledge types are about the ability to know-that, know-who, know-how, know-where, know-why, know-where. These are all key to gaining and retaining competitive edge in the dynamic environment of the new economy. The shift in culture has to be from 'individual knowledge is individual power' to 'organisational knowledge is organisational power'.

Knowledge management has become more relevant as the nature of western economies has shifted from manufacturing to services. In a service-oriented economy, knowledge, rather than physical assets, is at a premium. Companies engaging in successful knowledge management gain an important edge in the market. Organisational knowledge is too valuable to be left to chance or ad hoc approaches. If firms are to gain and retain competitive edge, organisational knowledge must be managed, just as any other major asset would be managed. However, for it to succeed, knowledge management should not be viewed as just "another project" or fad. It is key to its success that knowledge management is seen as an important aspect of business strategy. Knowledge management is neither a strategic objective nor a goal, as there is no end state. It must be viewed as an integral part of organisational culture.

For businesses to succeed in a competitive climate, they have always needed to get the right information, in the right place, and in good time. Now they must also turn that information into new, viable ideas to improve effectiveness and efficiency. They must be creative, and they must retain their hard-earned knowledge. Ten years ago it was difficult to obtain information, let alone obtain information at the desktop. Today, information overload is experienced at the desktop, and intelligent tools are needed to help limit the time spent searching, filtering, and selecting. If such tools are not available at reasonable cost, the time spent dealing with customers and producing better quality products and services will decline, and an organisation will be less competitive.

Thus, technology plays a vital role in knowledge management. Technology changes what we can do, how we think, and how we work (think of email, attachments, Internet, Web folders). However, from a business perspective, the point is not technology, it is technology to achieve an organisational purpose. It is people who determine purposes, not technology (which either assists or constrains). People issues are therefore fundamental, as are organisational processes. However, an organisation without the technology that people need to undertake and improve organisational processes will not compete effectively with organisations that do have it. Many exponents place great emphasis on technological change, and some articles may give the impression that knowledge management is solely about technology. However, major gains can be made by changing organisational culture to create, share, and retain organisational knowledge by:

- using existing technology more effectively;
- improving business processes;
- staff development.

This book offers a framework for the introduction of knowledge management that is broader than others and that is based on sound principles and concepts. We wish our readers every success in their knowledge management initiatives.

References

Abou-Zeid, E.S. (2002). A knowledge management reference model. *Journal of Knowledge Management, 6*(5), 486-499.

Achterbergh, J., & Vriens, D. (2002). Managing viable knowledge. *Systems Research and Behavioural Science, 19*(3), 223-241.

Ackoff, R.L. (1991). Ackoff's fables. *Ackoff's best: His classic writings on management.* New York: John Wiley & Sons.

Alavi, M. (1997). Knowledge management and knowledge management systems. *Proceedings of 18th International Conference on Information Systems,* Atlanta Georgia, December 14-17.

Alavi, M., & Leidner, D.E. (2001). Review: Knowledge management and knowledge management systems: Conceptual foundations and research issues. *MIS Quarterly, 25*(1), 107-136.

Allee, V. (1997). *The knowledge evolution. Expanding organisational intelligence.* Boston, MA: Butterworth-Heinemann.

Allee, V. (2000). The value evolution—addressing larger implications of an intellectual capital and intangibles perspective. *Journal of Intellectual Capital, 1*(1), 17-32.

APQC. (1996). *Knowledge management: Consortium benchmarking study final report.* Available online at: http://www.store.apqc.org/reports/Summary/know-mng.pdf.

Arora, R. (2002). Implementing knowledge management—a balanced scorecard approach. *Journal of Knowledge Management, 6*(3), 240-249.

Audi, R. (1998). *Epistemology: A contemporary introduction to the theory of knowledge.* London: Routledge.

Balasubramanian, P., Kumar, N., Henderson, J.C., & Kwan, M.M. (1999). Managing process knowledge for decision support. *Decision Support Systems, 27*(1/2), 145-162.

Beekun, R.I. (1989). Assessing the effectiveness of sociotechnical interventions: Antidote or fad? *Human Relations, 4*(10), 877-897.

Beer, S. (1979). *The heart of enterprise.* Chichester: John Wiley & Sons.

Bhatt, G. (1998). Managing knowledge through people: Knowledge and process. *Management Journal of Business Transformation, 5*(3), 165-71.

Bhatt, G. (2002). Management strategies for individual knowledge and organisational knowledge. *Journal of Knowledge Management, 6*(1), 31-39.

Binny, D. (2001). The knowledge management spectrum—understanding the KM landscape. *Journal of Knowledge Management, 5*(1), 33-42.

Boje, D.M, Gephart, R.P., & Thatchenkerry, T.J. (1996). *Postmodern management and organisation theory.* Thousand Oaks, CA: Sage Publications.

Bolloju, N., Khalifa, M., & Turban, E. (2002). Integrating knowledge management into enterprise environments for the next generation decision support. *Decision Support Systems, 33*(2), 163-176.

Bower, W.D., & Heminger, A.R. (2002). Development of a strategic decision framework for identifying and selecting knowledge management projects. *Proceedings of the 35th Hawaii International Conference on Systems Sciences (HICSS-3502).*

Bradburn, A., Coakes, E., DSilva, A., & Sugden, G. (2002a). Getting the knowledge habit (part 1). *Knowledge Management,* (April), 32-33.

Bradburn, A., Coakes, E., DSilva, A., & Sugden, G. (2002b). Getting the knowledge habit (part 2). *Knowledge Management,* (May), 18-19.

Brelade & Harman (2001). How human resources can influence knowledge management. *Strategic HR Review, 1*(1), 30-33.

Bressand, A., & Distler, C. (1995). *La planete relationelle*. Paris: Flammarion.

Breu, K., Grimshaw, D., & Myers, A. (2000). *Releasing the value of knowledge: A survey of UK industry 2000*. Cranfield University School of Management.

Britton, G.A., & McCallion, H. (1994). An overview of the Singer/Churchman/Ackoff school of thought. *Systems Practice, 7*(5), 487-522.

Brocklesby, J. (1995). Intervening in the cultural constitution of systems—methodological complementarism and other visions for systems research. *Journal of the Operational Research Society, 46*(11), 1285-1298.

Brown, J.S., & Diguid, P. (1991). Organisational learning and communities of practice: Towards a unified view of working, learning and organisation. *Organisation Science, 2*(1), S40-57.

Brown, J.S., & Diguid, P. (2000). *The social life of information*. Boston, MA: Harvard Business School Press.

Burrell, G., & Morgan, G. (1979). *Sociological paradigms and organisational analysis*. London: Heinemann.

Carneiro, A. (2001). The role of intelligent resources in knowledge management. *Journal of Knowledge Management, 5*(4), 358-367.

Checkland, P. (1981). *Systems thinking, systems practice*. Chichester: John Wiley & Sons.

Cherns, A. (1976). The principles of sociotechnical design. *Human Relations, 29*(8), 783-792.

Cherns, A. (1987). The principles of sociotechnical design revisited. *Human Relations, 40*(3), 153-162.

Churchman, C.W. (1968). *The systems approach*. New York: Dell.

Clarke, S.A. (2000). From socio-technical to critical complementarist: A new direction for information systems development. In E. Coakes, R. Lloyd-Jones, & D. Willis (Eds.), *The new SocioTech: Graffiti on the long wall* (pp. 61-72). London, Springer.

Clarke, S.A., & Lehaney, B. (1999). Organisational intervention and the problems of coercion. *Systemist, 21*(December), 40-52.

Clarke, S.A., & Lehaney, B. (2000). Mixing methodologies for information systems development and strategy: A higher education case study. *Journal of the Operational Research Society, 51*(5), 542-556.

Clarke, S.A., & Lehaney, B. (2002). Human-centred methods in information systems: Boundary setting and methodological choice. In E. Szewczak & C. Snodgrass (Eds.), *Human factors in information systems* (pp. 20-30). Hershey, PA: IRM Press.

Clarke, S.A., Lehaney, B. et al. (1998). A theoretical framework for facilitating methodological choice. *Systemic Practice and Action Research, 11*(3), 295-318.

Coakes, E. (2002). Knowledge management: A sociotechnical perspective. In E. Coakes, D. Willis, & S. Clarke (Eds.), *Knowledge management in the sociotechnical world: The graffiti continues* (pp. 4-14). London: Springer-Verlag.

Coakes, E., Bradburn, A., & Sugden, G. (2003). Managing and leveraging knowledge for organisational advantage. In J. Edwards (Ed.), *KMAC03* (pp. 54-65). Birmingham: Aston University.

Coakes, E., Willis, D., & Clarke, S.A. (2001). *Knowledge management in the sociotechnical world: The graffiti continues.* London: Springer-Verlag.

Cohen, S.G., Ledford, G.E., & Spreitzer, G.M. (1996). A predictive model of self-managing work team effectiveness. *Human Relations, 49*(5), 643-676.

Cohen, W.M., & Levinthal, D.A. (1990). Absorptive capacity: A new perspective on learning and innovation. *Administrative Science Quarterly,* (March), 128-152.

Cole, R.E. (1985). The macropolitics of organisational change: A comparative analysis of the spread of small group activities. *Administration Science Quarterly, 30,* 560-585.

Connell, C., Klein, J.H., Loebbecke, C., & Powell, P. (2001). Towards a knowledge management consultation system. *Knowledge and Process Management, 8*(1), 48-54.

Cummings, N. (2000). The intractability of tacit knowledge. *OR Newsletter,* (September), 12-13.

DeBono, E. (1977). *Lateral thinking.* Aylesbury, UK: Pelican Books, Hazell Watson & Viney Ltd.

Decrop, A. (1999). Triangulation in qualitative tourism research. *Tourism Management, 20,* 157-161.

DeGooijer, J. (2000). Designing a knowledge management performance framework. *Journal of Knowledge Management, 4*(4), 303-310.

Demarest, M. (1997). Understanding knowledge management. *Journal of Long Range Planning, 30*(3), 374-384.

Dixon, N. (2000). The insight track. *People Management, 17* (February), 34-39.

Duru Ahanotu, N. (1998). A conceptual framework for modelling the conflict between product creation and knowledge development amongst production workers. *Journal of Systemic Knowledge Management,* (July).

Earl, M. (2001). Knowledge management strategies: Toward a taxonomy. *Journal of Management Information Systems, 18*(1), 215-233.

Escriba-Esteve, A., & Urra-Urbieta, J.A. (2002). An analysis of co-operative agreements from a knowledge based perspective: An integrative conceptual framework. *Journal of Knowledge Management, 6*(4), 330-346.

Fayol, H. (1949). *General and industrial management.* London: Pitman.

Firestone, J.M. (1999). *Enterprise knowledge management modelling and distributed knowledge management systems.* Accessed January 2003 from: http://www.dkms.com/EKMDKMS.html.

Flood, R.L. (1995). Total systems intervention (TSI): A reconstitution. *Journal of the Operational Research Society, 46*, 174-191.

Flood, R.L., & Jackson, M.C. (1991). *Creative problem solving: Total systems intervention.* Chichester: John Wiley & Sons.

Flood, R.L., & Romm, N.R.A. (1996). *Diversity management: Triple loop learning.* Chichester: John Wiley & Sons.

Frahmann, initial. (1999). Transformation through knowledge sharing. *Strategic Communication Management, 3*(4), 16-19.

Gao, F., Li, M., & Nakamori, Y. (2002). Systems thinking on knowledge and its management—systems methodology for knowledge management. *Journal of Knowledge Management, 6*(1), 7-17.

Gerth, H.H., & Mills, C.W. (1970). *From Max Weber.* London: Routledge & Kegan Paul.

Gilligan, C. (1982). *In a different voice.* Boston, MA: Harvard University Press.

Goh, S.C. (2002). Managing effective knowledge transfer: An integrative framework and some practice implications. *Journal of Knowledge Management, 6*(1), 23-30.

Grant, R.M. (1991). The resource-based theory of competitive advantage: Implications for strategy formulation. *California Management Review, 34,* 114-135.

Habermas, J. (1971). *Knowledge and human interests.* Boston, MA: Beacon Press.

Habermas, J. (1976). On systematically distorted communication. *Inquiry, 13,* 205-218.

Habermas, J. (1987). *Lifeworld and system: A critique of functionalist reason.* Boston, MA: Beacon Press.

Harrison, S., & Sullivan, P. (2000). Profiting from intellectual capital. Learning from leading companies. *Journal of Intellectual Capital, 1*(1), 33-46.

Hill, P. (1971). *Towards a new philosophy of management.* City: Gower.

Hirschheim, R., & Klein, H.K. (1989). Four paradigms of information systems development. *Communications of the ACM, 32*(10), 1199-1216.

Hirschheim, R.A. (1986). Understanding the office: A social-analytic perspective. *ACM, 4*(4), 331-344.

Hlupic, V., Pouloudi, A., & Rzevski, G. (2002). Towards an integrated approach to knowledge management—hard, soft and abstract issues. *Journal of Knowledge and Process Management, 9*(2), 90-102.

Hoerr, J., Pollock, MA., & Whiteside D.E. (1986). Management discovers the human side of automation. *Business Week,* (September 29), 60-65.

Holsapple, C.W., & Joshi, K.D. (2002). Knowledge manipulation activities: Results of a Delphi study. *Journal of Information and Management, 39*(6), 477-490.

Hylton, A. (2002). *Measuring and assessing knowledge. Value and the pivotal role of the knowledge audit.* City: CEO Hylton Associates.

Jackson, M.C. (1982). The nature of soft systems thinking: The work of Churchman, Ackoff and Checkland. *Applied Systems Analysis, 9,* 17-28.

Jackson, M.C. (1985). Social systems theory and practice: The need for a critical approach. *International Journal of General Systems, 10,* 135-151.

Jackson, M.C. (1990). Beyond a system of systems methodologies. *Journal of the Operational Research Society, 41*(8), 657-668.

Jackson, M.C. (1993). Social theory and operational research practice. *Journal of the Operational Research Society, 44*(6), 563-577.

Jackson, M.C. (1995). Beyond the fads: Systems thinking for managers. *Systems Research, 12*(1), 25-42.

Jackson, M.C. (1999). Towards coherent pluralism in management science. *Journal of the Operational Research Society, 50*(1), 12-22.

Jackson, M.C. (2000). *Systems approaches to management.* New York: Kluwer/Plenum.

Jackson, M.C., & Keys, P. (1984). Towards a system of systems methodologies. *Journal of the Operational Research Society, 35*(6), 473-486.

Joshi, K.D. (2001). A framework to study knowledge management behaviours during decision making. *Proceedings of the 34th Hawaii International Conference on System Sciences 2001.*

Kamara, J.M., Chimay, J.A., & Carrillo, P.M. (2002). A CLEVER approach to selecting a knowledge management strategy. *International Journal of Project Management, 20*(3), 205-211.

Kant, I. (1787). *Critique of pure reason.* Basingstoke, Hampshire (2003), Palgrave Macmillan.

Katz, D., & Kahn, R.L. (1978). The social psychology of organisations. New York: John Wiley & Sons.

Kling, R., & Courtright, C. (2003). Group behaviour and learning in electronic forums: A sociotechnical approach. *Information Society, 19*(3), 221-235.

Knight, T., & Howes, T. (2003). *Knowledge management: A blueprint for delivery.* Oxford: Butterworth Heinemann.

Kogut, B., & Zander, U. (1992). Knowledge of the firm, combinative capabilities, and the replication of technology. *Organization Science, 3,* 383-397.

KPMG. (1999). *The power of knowledge. A business guide to knowledge management.* London: KPMG Consulting.

KPMG. (2000). *Knowledge management report.* Available online at: http://www.kpmg.co.uk.

Kwan, M., & Balasubramanian, initial. (2002). KnowledgeScope: Managing knowledge in context. *Decision Support Systems, 35*(4), 467-487.

Kwang, K.L., Pervaiz, K.A., & Mohamed, Z. (1999). Managing for quality through knowledge management. *Total Quality Management, 10*(4/5), 615-621.

Land, F.F. (2000). *Evaluation in a socio-technical context.* LSE working paper, London.

Land, F.F., Detjearuwat, N., & Smith, C. (1983). Factors affecting social control. *Systems Objectives Solutions, 3*(5), 155-164 and *3*(6), 207-226.

Lawrence, P.R., & Lorsch, J.W. (1969). *Developing organisations: Diagnosis and action.* Reading, MA: Addison-Wesley.

Leavitt, H.J. (1965). Applied organisational change in industry: Structural, technological, and humanistic approaches. In J. March (Ed.), *Handbook of organisations* (pp. 1144-1170). Chicago, IL: Rand McNally.

Lee, J.H., & Kim, Y.G. (2001). A stage model of organisational knowledge management: A latent content analysis. *Expert Systems with Applications, 20*(4), 299-311.

Liebowitz, J., & Suen, C.Y. (2000). Developing knowledge management metrics for measuring intellectual capital. *Journal of Intellectual Capital, 1*(1), 4-67.

Liikanen, E. (1999). Report on workshop—intellectual capital/intangible investments. European Commission Information Society technologies. *Proceedings of the IST Conference,* Helsinki, November 22.

Lincoln, Y.S., & Guba, E. (1985). *Naturalistic enquiry.* Beverly Hills, CA: Sage Publications.

Lyytinen, K., & Hirschheim, R. (1989). Information systems and emancipation: Promise or threat? In H.K. Klein & K. Kumar (Eds.), *Systems development for human progress* (pp. 115-139). Amsterdam: North Holland.

Majchrzak, A., & Wang, Q. (1996). Breaking the functional mind-set in process organisations. *Harvard Business Review,* (September-October), 93-99.

McAdam, R., & Reid, R. (2001). SME and large organisation perceptions of knowledge management: Comparisons and contrasts. *Journal of Knowledge Management, 5*(3), 231-241.

McDermott, R. (1999). Why information technology inspired but cannot deliver knowledge management. *California Management Review, 41*(4), 103-117.

McDermott, R. (2001). *Building and sustaining communities of practice.* City: APQC.

McKenna, S. (1999). Storytelling and real management competence. *Journal of Workplace Learning, 11*(3), 95-104.

McKinlay, A. (2002). The limits of knowledge management. *New Technology, Work and Employment, 17*(2), 76-88.

Merali, Y. (2000). Individual and collective congruence in the knowledge management process. *Journal of Strategic Information Systems, 9*(2/3), 213-234.

Meriluoto, J. (2003). *Knowledge Management and Information Systems— Finding a Sociotechnical Golden Mean ROCKET Workshop ICE (9th International Conference on Concurrent Enterprising) (Information Society Technologies),* Helsinki, Finland, June 18. Accessed July 2003 from: http://rocket.vub.ac.be/KM_IS_ROCKET.pdf.

Midgley, G. (1992). The sacred and profane in critical systems thinking. *Systems Practice, 5*(1), 5-16.

Midgley, G. (1996). The ideal of unity and the practice of pluralism in systems science. In R.L. Flood & N.R.A. Romm (Eds.), *Critical Systems Thinking: Current Research and Practice* (pp. 25-36). New York, Plenum.

Midgley, G. (1997a). Dealing with coercion: Critical systems heuristics and beyond. *Systems Practice, 10*(1), 37-57.

Midgley, G. (1997b). Developing the methodology of TSI: From the oblique use of methods to their creative design. *Systems Practice, 10*(3), 305-319.

Mingers, J., & Gill, A. (Eds.). (1997). *Multi methodology.* Chichester: John Wiley & Sons.

Mullich, J. (2001). growing a knowledge management system. *Knowledge Management, 4*(3), 54.

Mumford, E. (1996a). *Systems design: Ethical tools for ethical change.* Basingstoke: Macmillan.

Mumford, E. (1996b). Designing for freedom in a technical world. Chapter 25 in W. Orlikowski, G. Walsham, M.R. Jones, & J.I. DeGross (Eds.), *IT and changes on organisational work* (pp. 425-441). London: Chapman & Hall.

Mumford, E. (1997). The reality of participative design: Contributing to stability in a rocking boat. *Proceedings of the UKAIS 2nd Conference.* Southampton: University of Southampton.

Mumford, E., & Henshall, D. (1979). *A participative approach to computer systems design.* London: Associated Business Press.

Mumford, E., & MacDonald, B. (1989). EXEL's progress: The continuing journey of an expert system. New York: John Wiley & Sons.

Murray, P., & Myers, A. (1997). The facts about knowledge. *Information Strategy,* (September), 31-3.

Newman, B., & Conrad, K.W. (2000). *A framework for characterising knowledge management methods and technologies.* Available via email: Theorypapers@km-forum.org.

Nonaka, I. (1994). A dynamic theory of organisational knowledge creation. *Organisation Science, 5*(1), 14-37.

Nonaka, I., & Takeuchi, H. (1995). *The knowledge-creating company: How Japanese companies create the dynamics of innovation.* Oxford: Oxford University Press.

Nurminen, M.I. (1987). In R. Whitaker (Ed.), *Historical background to CSCW and groupware: Attention to team-level work organisation (the socio-technical tradition).* Accessed 13 May 2000, from: http://www.informatik.umu.se/%7erwhit/SocioTechnical.html.

Okunoye, A. (2002). Towards a framework for sustainable knowledge management in organisations in developing countries. In K. Brunnstein & J. Berleur (Eds.), *Human choice and computers: Issues of choice and quality of life in the information society* (pp. 225-237). IFIP World Computer Congress, August 25-30. Toronto: Kluwer.

Okunoye, A. (2003). *Knowledge management and global diversity: A framework to support organisations in developing countries.* Unpublished PhD Thesis, University of Turku, Finland, May.

Oliga, J.C. (1991). Methodological foundations of systems methodologies. In R.L. Flood & M.C. Jackson (Eds.), *Critical systems thinking: Directed readings* (pp. 159-184). Chichester: John Wiley & Sons.

Orlikowki, W., Walsham, G., & Jones, M.R. (1996). Information technology and changes in organisational work: Images and reflections. In W. Orlikowski, G. Walsham, M.R. Jones, & J.I. DeGross (Eds.), *IT and changes on organisational work* (pp. 1-10). London: Chapman & Hall.

Owen, H. (1997). *Open space technology.* San Francisco: Berrett-Koehler.

Pan, S.L., & Leidner, D.E. (2003). Bridging communities of practice with information technology in pursuit of global knowledge sharing. *Journal of Strategic Information Systems, 12,* 71-88.

Pan, S.L., & Scarbrough, H. (1998). A socio-technical view of knowledge sharing at Buckman Laboratories. *Journal of Knowledge Management, 2*(1), 55-66.

Pan, S.L., & Scarbrough, H. (1999). Knowledge management in practice: An exploratory case study. *Technology Analysis & Strategic Management, 11*(3), 359-374.

Pasmore, W.A., & Sherwood, J.J. (1978). *Socio-technical systems: A sourcebook.* San Diego: University Associates.

Pervaiz, K., Kwang, K.L., & Mohamed, Z. (1999). Measurement practice for knowledge management. *Journal of Workplace Learning: Employee Counselling Today, 11*(8), 304-311.

Peters, T., & Waterman, R. (1988). *In search of excellent companies.* London: Harper & Row.

Prusak, L. (1997). Knowledge in organizations. Oxford: Butterworth-Heinemann.

Quinn, J.B, Anderson, P., & Finkelstein, S. (1996). Managing professional intellect. *Harvard Business Review,* (March-April), 71-83.

Quinn, J.B., Anderson, P., & Finkelstein, S. (2000). Managing professional intellect. *Harvard Business Review,* (March-April), 71-83.

Rice, A. (1958). *Productivity and social organisation: The Ahmedabad experiment.* London: Tavistock Publications.

Robertson, S. (2002). A tale of two knowledge sharing systems. *Journal of Knowledge Management, 6*(3), 295-308.

Ruggles, R., & Holtshouse, D. (1999). *The knowledge advantage: 14 visionaries define marketplace success in the new economy capstone.* Publication information needed.

Sapsed, J., Bessant, J., Partington, D., Tranfield, D., & Young, M. (2002). Teamworking and knowledge management: A review of converging themes. *International Journal of Management Reviews, 4*(1), 71-85.

Scarbrough, H. (1995). Blackboxes, hostages and prisoners. *Organizational Studies, 16*(6), 991-1019.

Scarbrough, H. (2003). Why your employees don't share what they know. *KMReview, 6*(2), 16-19.

Selznick, P. (1948). Foundations of the theory of organisations. *American Sociological Review, 13*, 25-35.

Sena, J., & Shani, A. (1999). Intellectual capital and knowledge creation: Towards an alternative framework. In J. Liebwitz (Ed.), *Knowledge management handbook*. Boca Raton, FL: CRC Press.

Senge, P.M. (1992). *The fifth discipline. The art and practice of the learning organisation*. London: Doubleday.

Silverman, S., Ellul, I.R., Yarus, J.M., & Zamora, D.H. (2000). Reaping the rewards. *Oil & Gas Investor*, (Knowledge Management Edition), 13-15.

Snowden, D. (1998). A framework for creating a sustainable programme. In S. Rock (Ed.), *Knowledge management, a real business guide*. City: Caspian Publishing.

Snowden, D. (2000). The codification of tacit and explicit knowledge in IBM. *Proceedings of the KM Annual Conference,* The Hague, The Netherlands.

Spender, J.C. (1992). *Knowledge management: Putting your technology strategy on track*. Management of Technology III, Institute of Industrial Engineers.

Starbuck, W. (1992). Learning by intensive firms. *Journal of Management Studies, 29*(6), 713-740.

Stebbins, M.W., & Shani, A.B. (1998). Organisation design and the knowledge worker. *The Journal of Systemic Knowledge Management*, (February). Available online at: http://www.tlainc.com/.

Stewart, T.A. (1997). *Intellectual capital the new wealth of organizations*. London: Nicholas Brealey.

Storck, J., & Hill, P.A. (2000). Knowledge diffusion through strategic communities. *Sloan Management Review, 14*(2), 63-74.

Sutton, D.C. (2001). What is knowledge and can it be managed? *European Journal of Information Systems, 10,* 80-88.

Sveiby, K. (1999). What is knowledge management? Accessed 30 November 2000, from: http://203.32.10.69/ KnowledgeManagement.html.

Taket, A., & White, L. (1996). Pragmatic pluralism: An explication. *Systems Practice, 9*(6), 571-586.

Taylor, D. (1998). Knowledge management: Hot button or hot air? *Computer Weekly, 2*(July), 26.

Taylor, F.W. (1947). *The principles of scientific management.* New York: Harper and Row.

Teram, E. (1991). Interdisciplinary teams and the control of clients: A sociotechnical perspective. *Human Relations, 44*(4), 343-356.

Tobin, D.R. (1996). *Transformational learning. Renewing your company through knowledge and skills.* Chichester: John Wiley & Sons.

Trist, E.L., & Bamforth, K.W. (1951). Some social and psychological consequences of the Longwall method of coal-getting. *Human Relations, 4,* 3-38.

Ulrich, W. (1983). *Critical heuristics of social planning: A new approach to practical philosophy.* Berne: Haupt.

Ulrich, W. (1996). A primer to critical systems heuristics for action researchers. *Forum One: Action Research and Critical Systems Thinking,* Hull, UK, University of Hull, Centre for Systems Studies.

Ulrich, W. (2003). Beyond methodology choice: Critical systems thinking as critically systemic discourse. *Journal of the Operational Research Society, 54*(4), 325-342.

Vestal, W. (2003). Ten traits for a successful community of practice. *KM Review, 5*(6), 6.

Von Bertalanffy, L. (1950). The theory of open systems in physics and biology. *Science, 111,* 23-9.

Wall, T., Kemp, N., Jackson, P., & Clegg, C. (1986). Outcome of autonomous workgroups: A long-term field experiment. *Academy of Management Journal, 29,* 280-304.

Williams, T.M., & Wilson, J.M. (Eds.). (2003). *Journal of the Operational Research Society,* (Special Issue: Knowledge Management and Intellectual Capital). Birmingham, England: Palgrave.

Xerox. www.xerox.xom.

Zack, M.H. (1999). Managing codified knowledge. *Sloan Management Review, 40*(4), 45-88.

About the Authors

Brian Lehaney is Head of Statistics and Operational Research and Professor of Systems Management at Coventry University's School of Mathematical and Information Sciences (UK). He is an experienced, active researcher, and was recently Project Leader on an EC-funded project on knowledge management. He has published in many international refereed journals, and he has also worked as a referee and editor for such journals. He has examined PhDs for other universities, and has had his own students complete PhDs successfully. His focus is on theory into practice in the knowledge management domain. His current PhD students are working on knowledge culture and knowledge sharing. He has been a reviewer of large-sum projects for various funding bodies. He has given keynote and plenary papers at major international conferences on the theme of culture, process, and outcomes. He is a Fellow of the Operational Research society and a member of the Committee of Professors in Operational Research. Brian is joint editor of *OR Insight*.

Steve Clarke received a BSc in Economics from The University of Kingston Upon Hull, an MBA from the Putteridge Bury Management Centre, The University of Luton, and a PhD in Human Centred Approaches to Information Systems Development from Brunel University all in the United Kingdom. He is Professor of Information Systems at the University of Hull (UK). He has extensive experience in management systems and information systems consultancy and research, focusing primarily on the identification and satisfaction of user needs and issues connected with knowledge management. His research interests include: social theory and information systems practice;

strategic planning; and the impact of user involvement in the development of management systems. Major current research is focused on approaches informed by critical social theory. Steve is joint editor of *OR Insight*.

Elayne Coakes is Senior Lecturer in Business Information Management at the Westminster Business School, University of Westminster (UK), teaching Strategies for Information Management and Knowledge Management as well as e-Business Strategies. Her research interests relate to the sociotechnical aspects of information systems especially knowledge management systems and at Westminster she is the co-ordinator of a research cluster, looking at Information and Knowledge Management. She is a member of the British Computer Society's Sociotechnical Specialist Group and active in promoting this view of information systems strategy and development. She has co-edited a number of books in this, and in the knowledge management field, as well as writing conference papers, articles in journals and several chapters in books. Elayne is also an Associate Editor of *OR Insight* with special responsibility for knowledge management and recently edited a special edition of the journal *JORS* on knowledge management and intellectual capital. Her PhD (Brunel Univesrity, UK) relates to a sociotechnical view of the insufficiencies of boundaries and stakeholders in the strategic planning of information systems.

Gillian Jack is the Head of Student Services at the University of Glamorgan (UK), with responsibility for the strategic development and implementation of support to some 18,000 students. Her research interest is in knowledge management and the development of frameworks to assess an organisations readiness to engage with the concept. Her interest in knowledge management is both at the conceptual side and at the implementation side. As a professional manger with responsibility for managing important resources and liaising at the highest level, she is very interested in the practical implications of knowledge management and in finding useful and sensible ways for organisations to engage with it. She is an associate editor of *OR Insight* with special responsibility for change management. She has written and presented conference papers at regional and international conferences and contributes to the 'Learning Community' in South Wales. More recent interests include e-mentoring and e-student support.

Index

U

V

W

X

Z

NEW from Idea Group Publishing

- **The Enterprise Resource Planning Decade: Lessons Learned and Issues for the Future**, Frederic Adam and David Sammon/ ISBN:1-59140-188-7; eISBN 1-59140-189-5, © 2004
- **Electronic Commerce in Small to Medium-Sized Enterprises**, Nabeel A. Y. Al-Qirim/ ISBN: 1-59140-146-1; eISBN 1-59140-147-X, © 2004
- **e-Business, e-Government & Small and Medium-Size Enterprises: Opportunities & Challenges**, Brian J. Corbitt & Nabeel A. Y. Al-Qirim/ ISBN: 1-59140-202-6; eISBN 1-59140-203-4, © 2004
- **Multimedia Systems and Content-Based Image Retrieval**, Sagarmay Deb ISBN: 1-59140-156-9; eISBN 1-59140-157-7, © 2004
- **Computer Graphics and Multimedia: Applications, Problems and Solutions**, John DiMarco/ ISBN: 1-59140-196-86; eISBN 1-59140-197-6, © 2004
- **Social and Economic Transformation in the Digital Era**, Georgios Doukidis, Nikolaos Mylonopoulos & Nancy Pouloudi/ ISBN: 1-59140-158-5; eISBN 1-59140-159-3, © 2004
- **Information Security Policies and Actions in Modern Integrated Systems**, Mariagrazia Fugini & Carlo Bellettini/ ISBN: 1-59140-186-0; eISBN 1-59140-187-9, © 2004
- **Digital Government: Principles and Best Practices**, Alexei Pavlichev & G. David Garson/ISBN: 1-59140-122-4; eISBN 1-59140-123-2, © 2004
- **Virtual and Collaborative Teams: Process, Technologies and Practice**, Susan H. Godar & Sharmila Pixy Ferris/ ISBN: 1-59140-204-2; eISBN 1-59140-205-0, © 2004
- **Intelligent Enterprises of the 21st Century**, Jatinder Gupta & Sushil Sharma/ ISBN: 1-59140-160-7; eISBN 1-59140-161-5, © 2004
- **Creating Knowledge Based Organizations**, Jatinder Gupta & Sushil Sharma/ ISBN: 1-59140-162-3; eISBN 1-59140-163-1, © 2004
- **Knowledge Networks: Innovation through Communities of Practice**, Paul Hildreth & Chris Kimble/ISBN: 1-59140-200-X; eISBN 1-59140-201-8, © 2004
- **Going Virtual: Distributed Communities of Practice**, Paul Hildreth/ISBN: 1-59140-164-X; eISBN 1-59140-165-8, © 2004
- **Trust in Knowledge Management and Systems in Organizations**, Maija-Leena Huotari & Mirja Iivonen/ ISBN: 1-59140-126-7; eISBN 1-59140-127-5, © 2004
- **Strategies for Managing IS/IT Personnel**, Magid Igbaria & Conrad Shayo/ISBN: 1-59140-128-3; eISBN 1-59140-129-1, © 2004
- **Information Technology and Customer Relationship Management Strategies**, Vince Kellen, Andy Drefahl & Susy Chan/ ISBN: 1-59140-170-4; eISBN 1-59140-171-2, © 2004
- **Beyond Knowledge Management**, Brian Lehaney, Steve Clarke, Elayne Coakes & Gillian Jack/ ISBN: 1-59140-180-1; eISBN 1-59140-181-X, © 2004
- **eTransformation in Governance: New Directions in Government and Politics**, Matti Mälkiä, Ari Veikko Anttiroiko & Reijo Savolainen/ISBN: 1-59140-130-5; eISBN 1-59140-131-3, © 2004
- **Intelligent Agents for Data Mining and Information Retrieval**, Masoud Mohammadian/ISBN: 1-59140-194-1; eISBN 1-59140-195-X, © 2004
- **Using Community Informatics to Transform Regions**, Stewart Marshall, Wal Taylor & Xinghuo Yu/ISBN: 1-59140-132-1; eISBN 1-59140-133-X, © 2004
- **Wireless Communications and Mobile Commerce**, Nan Si Shi/ ISBN: 1-59140-184-4; eISBN 1-59140-185-2, © 2004
- **Organizational Data Mining: Leveraging Enterprise Data Resources for Optimal Performance**, Hamid R. Nemati & Christopher D. Barko/ ISBN: 1-59140-134-8; eISBN 1-59140-135-6, © 2004
- **Virtual Teams: Projects, Protocols and Processes**, David J. Pauleen/ISBN: 1-59140-166-6; eISBN 1-59140-167-4, © 2004
- **Business Intelligence in the Digital Economy: Opportunities, Limitations and Risks**, Mahesh Raisinghani/ ISBN: 1-59140-206-9; eISBN 1-59140-207-7, © 2004
- **E-Business Innovation and Change Management**, Mohini Singh & Di Waddell/ISBN: 1-59140-138-0; eISBN 1-59140-139-9, © 2004
- **Responsible Management of Information Systems**, Bernd Stahl/ISBN: 1-59140-172-0; eISBN 1-59140-173-9, © 2004
- **Web Information Systems**, David Taniar/ISBN: 1-59140-208-5; eISBN 1-59140-209-3, © 2004
- **Strategies for Information Technology Governance**, Wim van Grembergen/ISBN: 1-59140-140-2; eISBN 1-59140-141-0, © 2004
- **Information and Communication Technology for Competitive Intelligence**, Dirk Vriens/ISBN: 1-59140-142-9; eISBN 1-59140-143-7, © 2004
- **The Handbook of Information Systems Research**, Michael E. Whitman & Amy B. Woszczynski/ISBN: 1-59140-144-5; eISBN 1-59140-145-3, © 2004
- **Neural Networks in Business Forecasting**, G. Peter Zhang/ISBN: 1-59140-176-3; eISBN 1-59140-177-1, © 2004

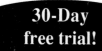
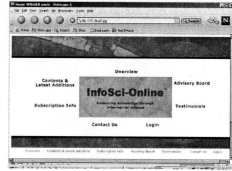

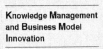

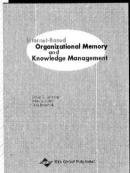

Coventry University